Irony/Humor

Candace D. Lang

Irony/Humor

Critical Paradigms

The Johns Hopkins University Press
Baltimore and London

This book has been brought to publication with the generous assistance of the Andrew W. Mellon Foundation.

The Johns Hopkins University Press
701 West 40th Street
Baltimore, Maryland 21211
The Johns Hopkins Press Ltd., London

The paper used in this publication meets the minimum requirements of American National Standard for Information Sciences—Permanence of Paper for Printed Library Materials, ANSI Z39.48-1984. ∞

Library of Congress Cataloging-in-Publication Data

Lang, Candace D., 1950–
  Irony/humor.

  Bibliography:p.
  Includes index.
  1. French literature—19th century—History and criticism. 2. Irony in literature. 3. French wit and humor—History and criticism. 4. French literature—20th century—History and criticism. I. Title.
PQ282.L26 1988   840'.91   87-45483
ISBN 0-8018-3528-3 (alk. paper)

The most profound philosophers . . . by the force of intense reflection, which discloses to them that what exists is unintelligible and has no reason for existing . . . and since their moral and religious prejudices do not allow them to say that to be irrational and unintelligible is the character proper to existence . . . are driven to the alternative of saying that existence is illusion and that the only reality is something beneath or above existence. That real existence could be radically comic never occurs to these solemn sages; they are without one ray of humour and are persuaded that the universe must too be without one.

—George Santayana

Contents

Acknowledgments

I wish to thank Josué Harari for his invaluable help in reading and rereading this manuscript at each of its several stages, always offering the most perceptive and incisive criticism. I would also like to express my profoundest gratitude to Al Baum, for frequently solicited advice and counsel and for many long hours devoted to helping me with the tedious and frustrating tasks of typing, editing, and coaxing print-outs out of a recalcitrant computer. To both of the above, and to Wilda Anderson and numerous other friends and colleagues at Johns Hopkins and at Tulane, my deepest appreciation for their patience and encouragement in my darker moments. Finally, a word of thanks to my copyeditor, Marie J. Blanchard, for anglicizing my frequently Gallic (and sometimes totally idiosyncratic) spelling, for normalizing my eccentric punctuation, and for proposing a variety of other stylistic improvements.

I am most grateful to the American Council of Learned Societies for a 1983 grant-in-aid supporting my work on the Proust chapter of this book, and to the Tulane University Committee on Research for a 1984 Summer Faculty Fellowship enabling me to complete extensive rewriting on several chapters.

An earlier version of the Stendhal chapter was published in *MLN* 94, no. 5 (1979), as "Stendhal: Une autobiographie en dérive"; an earlier version of the Barthes chapter appeared in *Neophilologus* 65, no. 2 (1981), under its present title, "Barthes: Ecrire le corps." A small portion of the Proust essay has also been published as "Jean est un autre / Je n'est personne," in the University of South Carolina *French Literature Series* 12 (1985), and part of the argument of Chapter Two was developed in "Irony/Humor: Assessing French and American Critical Trends," *Boundary 2* 10, no. 3 (1982).

Author's Note

Where not otherwise indicated, English translations of French texts are my own. For Baudelaire's *Fleurs du mal,* I have found my own rather literal prose translations more suitable to the type of reading I am doing here than more poetic renderings in verse. When I have quoted existing translations of French texts, specifics are given in the endnotes, in the first reference to each work cited. Subsequent references appear in abbreviated form in the body of the text. Whenever two numbers are given, separated by a slash, the first refers to the French edition and the second to the English translation. I have made occasional silent modifications in the translations when it seemed necessary.

Abbreviations

BF   Leo Bersani, *Baudelaire and Freud* (Berkeley and Los Angeles: University of California Press, 1977).

CI   Søren Kierkegaard, *The Concept of Irony, with Constant Reference to Socrates*, trans. Lee M. Capel (Bloomington: Indiana University Press, 1971).

CSB Marcel Proust, *Contre Sainte-Beuve* (Paris: Gallimard, 1954).

DLP Barbara Johnson, *Défigurations du langage poétique: La seconde révolution baudelairienne* (Paris: Flammarion, 1979).

HA   Alan Wilde, *Horizons of Assent: Modernism, Postmodernism, and the Ironic Imagination* (Baltimore: Johns Hopkins University Press, 1981).

HB   Stendhal, *Vie de Henry Brulard* (Paris: Garnier, 1961).

IEN Gary J. Handwerk, *Irony and Ethics in Narrative: From Schlegel to Lacan* (New London: Yale University Press, 1985).

JS   Marcel Proust, *Jean Santeuil*, précédé de *Les Plaisirs et les jours* (Paris: Pléiade, 1971).

LS   Gilles Deleuze, *Logique du sens* (Paris: Minuit, 1969).

OC   Charles Baudelaire, *Oeuvres Complètes* (Paris: Pléiade, 1961).

PJ   Marcel Proust, *Les Plaisirs et les jours*, in *Jean Santeuil* (Paris: Pléiade, 1971).

PT   Roland Barthes, *Le Plaisir du texte* (Paris: Seuil, 1973).

RB   Roland Barthes, *Roland Barthes* (Paris: Seuil, 1975).

RI   Wayne C. Booth, *A Rhetoric of Irony* (Chicago: University of Chicago Press, 1974).

RT   Paul de Man, "The Rhetoric of Temporality," in *Interpretation: Theory and Practice*, ed. Charles S. Singleton (Baltimore: Johns Hopkins University Press, 1969), 173–209.

S   Jean-Paul Sartre, *Baudelaire* (Paris: Gallimard, 1963).

SM   Gilles Deleuze, *Présentation de Sacher-Masoch: Le froid et le cruel* (Paris: Minuit, 1967).

SZ   Roland Barthes, *S/Z* (Paris: Seuil, 1970).

References to Marcel Proust, *A la recherche du temps perdu* (Paris: Pléiade, 1954), are indicated simply by volume and page number.

Irony/Humor

Introduction

This book grew out of a reading of Kierkegaard's *Concept of Irony, with Constant Reference to Socrates*, however far it may lead from this point of departure. What could a master's thesis written in 1841 by a Danish theology student have to do with the work of Roland Barthes? *The Concept of Irony* is, after all, a religious-political polemic leveled at the impious egotism of certain German romantics and the complacent authority of contemporary Hegelians. It is a search for the true Socrates in view of establishing his role as prototype and harbinger of Christ, thereby making Socratic irony an instrument of Truth—and romantic irony a perversion of it. Yet that is precisely why *The Concept of Irony* is eminently "relevant" to contemporary critical theory. Kierkegaard's approach to the problem of irony, his presuppositions regarding the nature of language, his conception of truth, and the religious fervor with which he condemns sustained irony as a sin against Truth, all characterize a long tradition of commentaries on irony, a tradition that is carried on today by a number of critics, particularly Anglo-American, who persist in condemning postmodern literature and contemporary continental criticism as extravagant, perverse, or even depraved new manifestations of irony.

Indeed, all of the categories that inform my discussion of contemporary critical approaches to irony in Chapter Two are developed from my reading of Kierkegaard in Chapter One, so that this chapter is as essential to my own intellectual itinerary in attempting to understand the concept of irony as I feel *The Concept of Irony* should be to any reader interested in tackling the problematic. For Kierkegaard's work has the merit of rendering explicit much of what is only implicit in other texts dealing with irony, or those that evoke it in passing, ignorant or insouciant of its philosophical implications. Founding his entire analysis on the difference between essence and phenomenon, Kierkegaard clarifies the relationship between irony as a figure of speech (in which the phenomenon, or word, does not correspond to the essence, or meaning) and irony as a mode of existence (in which the ironist's appearance or behavior does not correspond to his true, that is, internal and eternal, self). In so doing, he makes quite evident the fundamental similarity of all those manifestations of irony—linguistic, existential, dramatic, Socratic, romantic, "irony of fate," etc.—of which so many critics have lamented the confusing diversity. Furthermore, through his "constant reference" to Socrates (and hence to Plato), he clearly establishes the roots of his own philosophy, and that of the romantics, in Platonic thought: in the Kierkegaardian universe, as in the Platonic one, man is condemned to struggle incessantly and vainly to attain an abstract and eternal truth that is forever hidden or distorted by the veil of mere appearance. Language is one form taken by this phenomenal veil—and for the romantics, champions of the individual, it will be the most significant, since it is what impedes, even while making possible, communication between human beings, frustrating our longing for self-knowledge or for sincere self-expression. With the romantics, then, the private individual becomes the primary object of the search for truth, though the eternal validity of that truth is of course still guaranteed by God.

The same preoccupations animate a major current of literary criticism today, which posits as its primary object the disclosure of the meaning of literary texts; and meaning being defined as the author's intention, the critic's ultimate object is the revelation of the true character or self of the author, conceived of as an autonomous *cogito*. Like the romantics, critics of this persuasion regard language with some distrust, as an inadequate, yet indispensable, vehicle for thought; also like the romantics, they pursue a truth which constitutes a fraction of a universal design, that is, which presupposes the existence of a primary and originary Intention. Moreover, this man-behind-the-work—or, as I shall call it, *ironic*—criticism is firmly rooted in an economic conception of language which is also developed in Kierkegaard and goes back at least to Plato: meaning, or truth, is equated with gold (an absolute standard of value), whereas language functions as a kind of paper currency or other medium of exchange, false or insincere language naturally being regarded as bogus or counterfeit money.

Perhaps the most remarkable aspect of Kierkegaard's thesis, in the context of the present discussion, is that, along with the classic essence/phenomenon (or "vertical," because the meaning is said to be concealed *under* the language) conception of irony, he develops simultaneously, and in opposition to the preceding, another ("horizontal") conception of irony (and of language), which eludes the traditional Platonic categories because it is not definable in terms of a disparity between a hidden, valid content and a deceptive appearance. He does so in the course of an argument intended to demonstrate that Plato's depiction of Socrates is inaccurate in that it presents Socratic irony as a mere façade of ignorance concealing a superior wisdom (metaphorically expressed as "golden images"), whereas the real Socrates was "all surface," so to speak: his irony was by no means the product of a malicious or even simply playful intent to mystify while holding back the knowledge which motivated his behavior. Socratic irony, insists Kierkegaard, concealed *no positive content;* an incessant questioning, a perpetual *remise-en-cause,* a nondialectical negation of existing modes of thought, it would yield no concrete result, and could not be considered a phase in mankind's progressive acquisition of truth. Socratic irony is therefore not subject to interpretation, in the traditional sense, since there is no underlying message.

Clearly, then, Kierkegaard is here positing a form of irony that differs radically from that which he defines as a disparity between form and content: another notion of irony, which demands that one conceptualize discourse in other terms than that of a present signifier (word) referring to an absent signified (meaning)—for Socrates' discourse, although "all signifier," is far from meaningless. Kierkegaard therefore suggests, without thoroughly elaborating, a theory of reading, an approach to texts not predicated on the notion that the word itself is but an envelope for the idea—that is, an approach oriented toward the signifier rather than the signified, and which defines meaning as the product of the interrelationships among signifiers. Add to this the fact that he is particularly fond of linguistic metaphors, so that in his analysis not only literature but persons and the world are to be read as texts, and Kierkegaard takes on all the appearances of a structuralist or even a poststructuralist critic.

This surprisingly postmodernist aspect of *The Concept of Irony* is, however, eclipsed by the more traditional conception of language and of communication represented by the essence-versus-phenomenon definition of irony, in that Kierkegaard nonetheless ends up conceding to Socratic irony a positive role in the development of world history (of Absolute Spirit). He can scarcely do otherwise, given his theological convictions, for to accept all the consequences of irony conceived as an irreducible text would be to renounce his belief in a transcendent signified and ultimately in Transcendence itself (or Himself). He must retreat to a more conservative position in order to condemn the romantic ironists in the name of a Truth that they perpetually dissimulate or defer, because their actions do not correspond to their intimate being, and their works are not a true expression of that being. In fact, Kierkegaard consistently describes romantic irony as a disgusting self-titillation, an unnatural activity intended to compensate for the subject's frustrating failure to relate "naturally" (directly) to the Other, a theme he develops in his *Diary of a Seducer.*

Many contemporary readers will recognize that irony so defined has precisely the status of the chain of "dangerous supplements" (of which

masturbation and writing are the prime examples) whose logic Jacques
Derrida analyzes in his reading of Rousseau, in *De la grammatologie.*[1]
I elaborate on the relationship between irony and writing in Chapter
Two, in which I concentrate on the fate of the concept of irony in contemporary discourse, arguing, as I have already suggested, that the two
notions of irony defined by Kierkegaard and the world views implied
by them constitute the two poles of contemporary critical approaches
to irony. To anticipate my discussion in those pages, I might say simply
that it appears to me that *irony* has become a, if not *the*, privileged
term for supplementarity or symbolic deferral/mediation in critical
texts of the past decade or so. It has, in fact, become virtually synonymous with the now-(in)famous *écriture*, or writing, in the Derridean
sense. In the mouths of signified-oriented critics, it has a variety of
negative connotations (frivolity, bad faith, onanism, etc., i.e., deviation
or perversity), while on the tongues of those with poststructuralist
sympathies it often takes on the positive overtones of liberation (with
play, self-referentiality, etc., considered as healthy manifestations of a
naïve good faith). Not surprisingly, this has been the cause of considerable confusion, since the two uses of the term reveal far more than
two different attitudes toward the same phenomenon; they imply
radically divergent critical paradigms, that is, totally irreconcilable
conceptions of language, of meaning, and of subjectivity. Hence my
contention that critics would do better to designate the two "ironies"
by two distinct terms, as some critics, for example, Gilles Deleuze,
Jean-François Lyotard, and Louis Marin, already do. My own conceptions of the two "types" of irony are largely borrowed from these
French critics, as is the term *humor*, by which I designate the "postmodern," "other" irony.

This much said, I must add that I rather doubt if my proposal for
a less misleading terminology will have the slightest effect on general
usage; I only hope to convince those readers or critics who have a spe-
cial interest in irony that that term is in fact often extended to include
a concept and practice of writing, as well as an entire philosophy (or
antiphilosophy), which are essentially different from, and therefore incommensurable with, the notion of ironic discourse that tradition has
inculcated in us. If I could further persuade students of irony to take
those differences into account before attempting any classifications of
ironies, before expounding any theories on the extremely "ironic" nature of recent literature and theory, and especially before seeking to
interpret the "ironies" of postmodern fiction or poststructuralist critical texts, then I would consider that the theoretical portion of this
work—Chapters One and Two—had more than fulfilled one of its
primary purposes.

Let me then summarize as briefly as possible the distinguishing characteristics of the ironic and the humorous, as I shall be using those terms throughout this book. The ironic text is primarily "expressive," by which I mean that it is intended to transmit a message, communicate an idea, or express a thought or sentiment. It is no different from the nonironic, "sincere" (for want of a better word) text, insofar as it is based on the same notion of language considered as a medium, a form, a supplement whose sole function is to represent a preexistent idea or concept. If the ironist chooses to transmit his message in a less direct way than the "straightforward" expository writer (the reasons for this—rhetorical, personal, political—while important, do not fall within the scope of this study), his work is nonetheless potentially interpretable, and generally contains indications as to how it is to be read. As Kierkegaard himself remarks, some irony is meant to mystify, and is therefore difficult or even impossible (except perhaps, for a small circle of initiates) to interpret; even then, however—even when language is used to frustrate understanding—writing is still perceived of as an act of representation, albeit in this case a misrepresentation.

When I speak of the "ironic" critic, I am referring, not to the critic whose own work is rich in verbal ironies (though I am not excluding such), but rather to one who shares those assumptions about the nature and function of language which are implicit in the definition of irony outlined above, and who therefore defines the critic's task as the discovery or revelation of meaning (i.e., authorial intent). The ironic critic assumes that language is by nature subservient to conceptualization, and considers any text in which this hierarchy is reversed or put into question to be at best frivolous, at worst aberrant or perverse.[2] Needless to say, the ironic critic strives to write "normally," that is, in transparent, unequivocal, and univocal (even if ironic) prose.

It is scarcely necessary to point out that some of the distinguishing characteristics of modern and postmodern literature, as well as of recent French or French-inspired critical texts, have been an increasing exploitation of linguistic ambiguity and polyvalence, the foregrounding of language in the production of narrative or in the process of reasoning, and a preference for inconclusive or aporetic closure. It is apparently because of the "unreadability" of such works that it has become common practice to pronounce them "ironic," with irony being taken in the classical sense, as a disparity between essence and appearance, or meaning and expression. Thus critics frequently imply that the works of a Beckett, a Robbe-Grillet, a Barthes, or a Derrida constitute but so many obscurantist attempts to mystify the hapless reader. Applying a traditional model of irony to such texts generally leads the critic to one of two unsatisfactory conclusions: either (1) there

is a message darkly concealed under these layers of ironies—a message
that usually turns out to be a cry of despair over the human condition,
especially the inadequacy of language for self-expression, or (2) there
isn't any message, just gratuitous wordplay; hence the work is meaningless and therefore worthless—but then this can also easily be read as
an expression of despair, as well, so that (2) is finally the same as (1).
Such readings, while defensible at a certain level, do suffer from one
major, and to my mind, crippling fault: they leave an immense residue
of text unaccounted for. My judgment is based on the assumption that
a good reading should take into account as many aspects of a work (or
at least of whatever facet of a work one has chosen to examine) as possible, *even* (or perhaps *especially*) those that resist decipherment or
present obstacles to the critical approach one has adopted.

To write off any text that does not lend itself to the traditional inter-
pretative process as an example of extreme irony is to ignore the spirit
as well as the letter of the postmodern practice of writing. Inasmuch
as the major thrust of recent literature and theory has been to rethink
the notion of representation, rejecting the idea of a simple correspondence between word and concept, and particularly the belief in the
ontological priority of the signified over the signifier, it is futile to
analyze or criticize such works on the basis of axioms that it is their
primary function to refute. It is those authors who do not subscribe to
the essentially Platonic notion of language as a mere representation of
ideas, or of writing as a necessary but potentially dangerous supplement to conceptualization, and who work out the consequences of
their antimetaphysical presuppositions in their texts, whom I call
"humorists." The humorist writes with the conviction that language is
always an essential determinant of thought (not only accidentally or
when used perversely), and that its semantic ambiguities and connotative resonances are to be explored and actualized rather than limited or
suppressed. Thus the ironist's perpetual source of distress, the inadequacy of language for self-expression, is a false issue for the humorist,
since he or she accords a priori to language a constitutive role in
thought and therefore in the ego. If the fundamental problem raised
(implicitly or explicitly) by the ironic work is the expression of meaning, it is for the humorous text the production of meaning. The
humorous text, then, does not express meaning in the traditional, etymological sense of exteriorizing what was interior to the authorial
psyche (for Barthes, the verb *exprimer* evoked nothing so much as
squeezing juice out of a lemon);[3] it organizes a number of linguistic
elements into systems offering a variety of potential meanings to be
actualized by the reader. The humorist critic focuses on the functioning of the text—any text, however traditional—at the level of the

signifer, rather than seeking to somehow "see through" the language to its referent or authorial source. Moreover, the humorist conceives of that author as a product rather than as a producer of his text.

The practice of *écriture* is, as I have said, increasingly called irony, both by its detractors and by its proponents, the former equating it with the "old," romantic irony, the latter describing it much as I have humor. It should be added that these, the "humorous" critics, have as great a penchant for rereading traditional texts from within their own critical paradigm as do "ironic" critics for attacking postmodern texts with a Platonic bias—at times with equally questionable results. The "humorous" reader who, having demonstrated that a text heretofore considered quite readable is in fact unreadable (contains unresolvable ambiguities or paradoxes, or ends in aporia), then attributes the text's unreadability to a secret authorial intent to subvert his own announced intentions is barely distinguishable from his ironic counterpart. Humor is a textual phenomenon, and need not be intended, whereas irony implies an intender. Irony is to be interpreted or translated; humor can only be commented or rewritten.

This is not to say that a critic should, or even *can*, change paradigms according to the text being read. Once one has adopted a theoretical model of literary meaning, one must assume that model to be valid for all texts. I have perhaps inadvertently created the impression that for certain, classical ironic (or nonironic, for that matter) works, the traditional form/content conception of language, according to which idea precedes and determines expression (i.e., the signifier is the mere representative of an independent, preexistent signified) is perfectly adequate, whereas another model that overturns the signifier/signified hierarchy is needed for contemporary or "humorous" literature only. But the poststructuralist, "horizontal" conception of meaning has, for its proponents, superseded the old "vertical" conception precisely because the latter was found to be inadequate for all *texts*.

When I say that there are classical "ironic" works (e.g., those of Voltaire or Swift), I am not suggesting that to read these texts we must reinstate the essence/phenomenon, meaning/expression model, whose exponents I have dubbed the "ironic" critics. I mean only that these works imply the assumption of such a model on the part of the author, and are written in a manner consistent with it, so that the "play" or plurality of meaning is minimized, and that they lend themselves quite well to interpretation in the sense of the extraction of a message or the revelation of an authorial intent. The "humorous" critic might well agree with his "ironic" counterpart as to what the author's intent probably was, though he would not define that intent in terms of an idea that preexisted in its expression in language; nor would that idea be the primary focus of his reading. The "ironic" critic, on the other hand, will have great difficulty in dealing with the "humorous" text, because his theory of meaning does not allow for ambiguity or contradiction.

I hope it is clear that despite my preference for the humorous critical paradigm, I am not denying the existence of (conscious) intentions, ironic or humorous; nor would I deny the reader any access to those intentions. Moreover, I doubt if any reader ever renounces all curiosity regarding authorial intent, or all claims to having divined that intent. The ironic and the humorous critic differ primarily regarding the status they accord the notion. For the former, authorial intent is sacrosanct; it dominates every aspect of the literary work, and the revelation and explication thereof is the critic's sole ultimate goal; inasmuch as the critic feels morally bound to respect that intent, it serves a screening function, enabling him to distinguish the pertinent elements of the text (all those that support the author's putative intentions) from irrelevant ones (those that contradict or undermine the dominant authorial voice). The latter, however, while he may make assumptions about authorial intent, recognizes that these, no matter how well reasoned-out, well-founded in historical-biographical research, etc., can only be assumptions, and that a text always says more, or less, or simply something *other* than what its author may have intended. The humorous critic therefore feels no moral compulsion to produce a reading consistent with the writer's presumed intentions; furthermore, he values the criterion of exhaustivity (a reading must take into consideration as many elements of a text as possible) above that of univocity.

Thus I do make assumptions about the intentions of authors I read, based on their texts (but not by extrapolation from biographical information, e.g.: "X was a devout Catholic; therefore he couldn't have intended to blaspheme . . ."). I assume, for instance, that writers such as Robbe-Grillet or Sollers or Barthes, whose works foreground the signifier or maximize the polyvalence of language, intend such effects— that is, that they intentionally produce "humorous" texts. Likewise, I assume that the relative univocity of Voltaire's works is intentional. Moreover, I lend some credence to writers' theoretical works, and approach their other writings accordingly. All things considered, then, I show a great deal of respect for the authorial voice. Indeed, it is quite often by naïvely posing the question of intent ("what is X trying to say?") that I stumble upon the traces of that humor which I believe to affect nearly every text to some degree.

A text is humorous to the extent that it implicitly or explicitly casts doubt upon the supposed priority of the signified and, consequently, the priority of the *cogito* itself. There is a fairly widespread tendency among contemporary critics with poststructuralist leanings to claim that all texts do so at least implicitly (or to deny those that do not the status of "text"), and while I have some sympathy for this view, I have chosen to deal, in the "practical" chapters of this book, with works in which language in general and writing in particular are thematized, and in which problems of language are quite obviously linked to questions of self-identity. These problems and questions may be raised and interrelated in a variety of ways, and they are, by the authors I will be discussing. Each, I like to think, is somehow exemplary of a certain unstable, transitional moment in literary history (though history is probably composed only of transitional moments). Stendhal is a curious hybrid of rationalism and naïve romanticism; Baudelaire's decadent romanticism is tinged with a cynical realism; an early, Baudelairean Proust goes on to flirt with surrealism, only to transcend it in the direction of postmodernity; and Barthes is one of the most eloquent voices of structuralism's soul-searching attempts to inaugurate a poststructuralist era.

Stendhal's *Vie de Henry Brulard* was written in the early 1830s at the height of French romanticism, when individuality, self-knowledge, and self-expression (i.e., sentiment) were supreme values among literati. Upon initiating his quest for self-knowledge, Stendhal recognizes, somewhat begrudgingly, Rousseau and Chateaubriand as his predecessors in the genre. But Stendhal is not a lyrical writer. *His* confessions will not be a mere outpouring of emotions; they will be an objective analysis of the author's life, observed from without. Hence his recourse to scientific metaphor, his claims to classify the major events of his life, even his love affairs, like a collection of plants; hence as well, his efforts to distance himself, via pseudonym, from the protagonist of his autobiography. Although he does not use the term *irony* in *Brulard,* Stendhal has thus formulated the quintessential ironic project: to split oneself in two, to be at once oneself and another, to know oneself through dispassionate, impassive observation. Language is the tool by means of which he will record his observations. Early on, he sets up (implicitly) a series of equivalent dichotomies: truth is to falsehood as immediate perception (seeing) is to representation (writing or painting) or any form of mediate perception (i.e., hearsay), as autobiography is to novel, as self is to other. Therefore, he surmises, he must report only observed events of his past, in as transparent a prose as possible; indeed, he intersperses his text with sketches in order to *present* scenes from his past without recourse to the medium of language. Nonetheless, he soon discovers that, perversely, language calls up images of doubtful authenticity, that immediate experience melds disconcertingly with hearsay, and that his attempt at autobiography is constantly threatened by the temptation to "novelize." In short, his dichotomies break down, as the distinctions between reality and representation, signified and signifier, truth and fiction, self and other blur. In other words, the ironic position he has adopted proves to be untenable, but his assumptions regarding the nature of the self do not permit him to conceive of autobiographical writing as anything other than a continuous, coherent, and above all, referential narrative, so that he interrupts *Brulard* abruptly, reiterating his refusal to "faire du roman" and leaving his protagonist with the French troops in Milan, precisely where he will pick up the story of Lieutenant Robert in *La Chartreuse de Parme* a few years later. Stendhal fails, then, to write the autobiography he ostensibly set out to write, for want, one might say, of a sense of humor about the self. That is, rather than relinquish his belief in the identity and autonomy of the self, he abandons his autobiographical project. In this respect he remains very much a romantic in naïve good faith, nourishing a nostalgic belief in the recuperability of the past. Not until the mid-twentieth century will the notion that the ego itself is a fiction be widely accepted, giving rise to a radically different, "humorous" notion of autobiography—as in the case of Barthes's *Roland Barthes*. In retrospect, however, *Brulard* can be (and currently is) read as a commentary on the problems inherent in the traditional concept of autobiography. Better yet, I find, it is a novel about autobiography, a theoretical fiction about the self, its longing to reconstitute its identity through a return to the maternal, Edenic space of one's origins, and about writing as a compensatory activity destined to deny the impossibility of that return.

In Baudelaire, irony, self-detachment, and a dogged, darkly narcissistic obsession with self-observation are prominent themes. In his poems, the sunny nostalgia that characterized the Stendhalian text is generally overshadowed by a gloomy, bitter regret for an irrecuperable paradisiacal (prelapsarian and prelinguistic) origin. The subject of most of Baudelaire's poetry and much of his prose and journals is the divided subject, morbidly self-conscious, torn between self-hatred and self-adulation. It is easy, then, to read his works as the confessions of an ironist; every trait of Kierkegaard's hedonistic ironic aesthete or his arrogant yet despairing seducer is already present in the cynical narrators of *Les Fleurs du mal* or the *Petits poèmes en prose* and the artists and dandies of the essays and *Journaux intimes*. The quintessential disillusioned romantic seems to speak from these pages, the alienated self alternately lamenting and glorifying the bitter solitude of a self-imposed exile. This is Sartre's Baudelaire, the perverse, self-pitying and self-vindicating narcissist living in defiant bad faith, frozen before his own reflection in a perpetual and vain effort to capture the image of his *moi*. However, to speak about irony is not necessarily to speak ironically—and if Baudelaire is speaking ironically about irony, the reader is confronted with something like the paradox of the liar. The situation is further complicated by the fact that one can discern other voices in Baudelaire's works than that of the sterile, embittered romantic deploring the irreparable loss of the golden age of innocence and purity. There are also traces of a humoristic conception of the self and of language: texts that celebrate the fragmentation of the self and the polyvalence of the linguistic sign, texts in which a modern metaphorics of economic exchange supersedes the idealist vocabulary of stable values and eternal essences that dominates much of Baudelaire's work. This conflict of languages reflects the changing social and economic climate of the poet's time, that is, the rise of bourgeois capitalist society, which was to destroy traditional notions of value and romantic myths of the artist and of art as guardians of those values. It is difficult, given the complexities and ambiguities of the Baudelairean text, to define with any certitude the position of Baudelaire, though many have claimed to do so. Traditionally, critics have sought to choose between the two Baudelaires or to reconcile them via some sort of dialectical synthetic reading. The tendency among contemporary readers under the influence of poststructuralist theory is to focus on the text rather than the subject, respecting the contradictions of his work. My reading falls, predictably, into the latter category, because such an approach brings out the elements of play—or of humor—in the Baudelairean text. Nevertheless, I do conclude that the dominant voice in Baudelaire is that of a modern, an ironist who praises appearances but worships essences, who revels in duplicity but mourns unity.

I have taken Proust's works as exemplary of the transition from modern to postmodern mentality, a transition primarily characterized by the gradual disappearance of that nostalgia (or desire to "go home") so apparent in Stendhal and Baudelaire. Like Stendhal and unlike Baudelaire, Proust does not thematize irony; he does, however, particularly in *Contre Sainte-Beuve* and *A la recherche du temps perdu*, thematize writing, in an ongoing reflection on the relationship of sign to referent in the work of art, the relationship of the artist to his work, and the function of writing in the constitution of the self. Furthermore, the different stages of the theory of art that gradually unfolds across the pages of the *Recherche* are illustrated, in retrospect, as it were, in the evolution of Proust's style in his preceding works. In moving from the early to the late Proust, one observes a progressive shift away from an ironic conception of language as representation of an objective reality or expression of an ego, to a humoristic theory of the text as the creation of a new, subjective reality, and hence an ongoing production of the subject through language. Moreover, he will propose what is in essence a "reader response" theory of criticism, insisting that each reader does and should read a literary work through a different "lens."

My reading of Proust is unabashedly chronological, sketching the evolution of his writing from *Les Plaisirs et les jours* to *Jean Santeuil* and, finally, via the essays collected in *Contre Sainte-Beuve*, to *A la recherche du temps perdu*. This evolution can be described in terms of thematics, narrative technique, and style. The short stories, vignettes, and poems of *Les Plaisirs* are populated with lonely, remorseful figures, lamenting the loss of a paradise most often identified with maternal affection; the narrative technique is ironic in the sense that the nearly exclusive use of the third person establishes a theoretical distance between personage and narrator, and, *a fortiori*, between personage and author. Indeed, the narrator's commentaries on the characters' behavior are often bitingly ironic—all of which, paradoxically, only serves to heighten the sense that these characters are but thinly disguised projections of the author. Finally, the style of *Les Plaisirs* is both lyrical and banally referential: expressive and descriptive, and rich in romantic clichés.

In *Jean Santeuil*, Proust's early novel and prototype of the *Recherche*, an ironic distance is maintained between narrator and protagonist, through the use of the third person, yet once again, the reader who knows anything of Proust can scarcely resist concluding that the hero is an idealized projection of the author's ego, an attempt to create and capture a self-image. This desire to ratify his existence is symbolized with discomfiting transparency in a scene in which Jean effectively assumes his father's role vis-à-vis his mother, thereby returning "home" to a maternal paradise and constituting himself as a subject in the eyes of the Other. The style of *Jean Santeuil* is consistent with the notion of literature implied here, the conviction that the object of writing is to capture an exterior, objective referent.

Nonetheless, Proust is already beginning to question such a conception of art, and in the *Recherche*, he will finally develop a practice of writing that corresponds to the theory elaborated therein. As the protagonist Marcel gradually comes to the realization that literature is not *about* anything (that art is not a reproduction of a preexistent reality), the Proustian text increasingly flaunts its nonreferentiality via the celebrated "metaphors" that are determined least of all by the nature of the objects "described." Finally, Marcel realizes that the only continuity of experience, and therefore of the self, is that created through writing, so that if he is to be a writer, he must first of all *forget* things past, just as he must renounce his earlier belief that it is his duty to somehow recapture exterior reality in his work. In terms of narrative technique, that relinquishment of the desire to produce a stable self-representation manifests itself in the *Recherche* through the shift from the third-person Jean to the content-less pronoun "I." The narrator/protagonist of the *Recherche* is omnipresent, yet virtually invisible. Here again, the protagonist's relationship to the "objective" world as well as his own concept of self is bound up with his relationship to his mother. In the *Recherche,* the narrator recognizes that the affirmation of her absence is prerequisite to his becoming a writer. Thus *A la recherche du temps perdu,* though it is a novel about nostalgia, is not a nostalgic novel. We are on the verge, in Proust, of a humorous conception of textuality and of the subject, though it will be nearly half a century before the problematic will be formulated in such terms.

The final text that I have chosen to discuss in these pages is the autobiography of Roland Barthes, who not coincidentally, owed much to Proust. Barthes's *Roland Barthes* constitutes an attempt to write a "humoristic" autobiography—that is, to write about a self that cannot be written "about," since, as he remarks, "I" has no referent. As I have suggested earlier, then, Barthes's *Barthes* presupposes what Stendhal seems to dimly realize upon abandoning *Brulard.* The Barthesian subject is a discontinuous, fragmented self, which the author explicitly opposes to the Baudelairean divided self. The fundamental problem of the postmodern autobiographer, Barthes demonstrates, is how to *avoid* irony: how to escape the illusion that the ego is a fixed, autonomous entity, and how to avoid in one's writing the temptation to project a stable self-image—or even more importantly, the danger of being reduced to one by the Other. Just as he had earlier eschewed irony in critical writing, as an attempt to step outside the text and to pronounce the last word by reducing it to one coherent meaning, he seeks here to respect and preserve the multiplicity of beings that constitute the writing subject Barthes, by refusing to effect the self-reflective, ironic splitting of the self into observed and observer. In this respect, Barthes's autobiography is but a continuation of his earlier critical work, an extension of his theory of the text as the locus of the author's *disappearance,* into the very genre where the author is supposedly most in evidence. Here, as throughout his work, generic boundaries are effaced; criticism merges with fiction and with autobiography, and the man-behind-the-work becomes a multifaceted textual corpus. Or so, at least, is Barthes's autobiographical project: to dispense with the ego, not with a sigh, but with laughter, not with irony, but with humor.

In choosing texts by Stendhal, Baudelaire, Proust, and Barthes, I have opted for a sort of chronological survey (or at least, a spot-check) of irony/humor from the romantic period to the present. Conveniently,

I have been able to detect an evolution away from a more ironic world view and style of writing in the earlier authors, toward the humor of contemporary literature and critical theory as exemplified in Barthes. Indeed, it will become apparent to the reader that, at times, *ironic* and *modern* are used almost synonymously, as are *humorous* and *postmodern*. I do not wish to equate these pairs of terms, but rather to relate them closely: irony is a salient characteristic of the modern world view, and humor is a necessary and perhaps sufficient condition for the postmodern mentality. Labels such as "modern" and "postmodern" are much criticized for their vagueness or artificiality, as conventional mental categories projected on reality; but the same may be said of all signifiers, so I shall continue to avail myself of these, though not without an attempt at definition.

The "modern" period, according to the dictionary, is the post–Middle Ages, that is, covers the Renaissance to the present. This obviously leaves little room for postmodernism. Is there such a phenomenon? While the term certainly owes its existence in part to theoreticians' eagerness to declare the end of things as we know them and the dawn of a new age, I am assuming here that it does reflect some fundamental change in the zeitgeist, and am following contemporary thinkers (Foucault perhaps foremost among them) in defining that change in terms of the history of the subject. In these terms, the advent of modernism is marked by the emergence of the concept of the individual (favored by both socioeconomic and technological developments: the decline of the feudal system and concomitant increase in capitalist endeavor) and the invention of the printing press, which would enhance the notion of authorship by saving the text from the relative anonymity of oral tradition. The notion of the author reached maturity under the aegis of capitalism, with the institution of the copyright, by which the writer acquired sole authority over and responsibility for his works. Historically, that development coincided with the rise of romanticism, which glorified the unique and ineffable self.

Paradoxically, the very capitalism that had fostered the triumph of individualism would soon be decried for suppressing the individual, as well as authentic artistic expression, as the work of art became a mass-produced commodity. Thus the romanticism of the mid- and late nineteenth century is characterized by a somewhat mournful preoccupation with the self and a gloomy nostalgia for a lost golden age of individuality and unmediated self-expression, that combination of sentiment and cynicism which constitutes romantic irony. Insofar as the concept of a unified and autonomous self is prerequisite to irony, then, I consider all of the modern period to be the age of irony, but in the present study, limited almost exclusively to the nineteenth and twentieth centuries, my references to "modernist mentality" generally designate more specifically the nostalgic self-consciousness of the romantic period, which was in fact an era of decadent modernism. Modernism is by no means extinct, for it is carefully tended by the defenders of the Cartesian *cogito*—so in a sense there is no postmodern period—but the zeitgeist is elsewhere. Psychoanalysis, phenomenology, and structural linguistics prepared the now-famous "decentering of the subject," and if "postmodernism" corresponds to any historical reality, it is to this process and the literary and critical texts that celebrate it. (Those that mourn it remain essentially modern.) The assumption and affirmation of the discontinuity and inherent otherness of the self is humor; the denial of it, irony.

As for my use of the terms *structuralism* and *poststructuralism*, I admit that I have not sought to define them precisely, nor will I here, for to do so would require at least an additional chapter, so diverse are their applications. Suffice it to say that by *structuralism* I am referring primarily to the literary critical movement of the fifties and sixties that shifted attention away from the specific contents of works—and of consciousness—to seek the processes governing the production of texts. (But I also have constantly in mind the roots of the movement in Marxist, Freudian, and Saussurean thought.) Structuralism belongs to postmodernism insofar as it emptied out the full subject of modernism. Yet its most astute critics (generally, structuralists themselves) were to find that it remained too faithful to the old canons of subjectivity by retaining a center, albeit a hollow one; hence a variety of attempts to divest theory of that last vestige of the *ancien régime*, which of course acquired the label poststructuralism. Thus I have used the term *poststructuralism* to refer to structuralism's ongoing moment of self-critique.

It should be evident from the foregoing if not from the title that the main focus of this work is not irony as a rhetorical device. The trope irony interests me only as a paradigm or model for irony in a larger sense, that is, for the kind of ironic universe implied by the critical practice of explaining everything—texts, behavior, life, the world—in terms of reality-versus-appearance. Just as the classic definition of the ironic figure of speech calls for a speaker who knows his own thought while couching it in potentially misleading language, the ironic world view presupposes a Knower whose infinite wisdom is communicated only obscurely through the phenomenal world. The tendency to see irony (disguised intentions) everywhere reflects much more than a simple theory about how to interpret texts; it is symptomatic of a weltanschauung, or paradigm, in the sense given that word by Thomas S. Kuhn in *The Structure of Scientific Revolutions*. Similarly, the critical practice of treating meaning either as an effect of language or as the product of the reader's interpretive activity (or some combination of the two) is one manifestation of a paradigm whose determinate feature is the presupposition of a universe without Transcendence. In the two theoretical chapters that follow, I seek to characterize what I call the ironic and humorous critical paradigms and their relationship to each other by giving some of their historical background, particularly that of irony, and by briefly discussing the positions of some of their contemporary proponents. In the subsequent chapters, my readings of specific French authors focus on the manner in which their works seem to imply—and lend themselves to analysis through—an ironic or a humorous critical paradigm.

Having thus defined my terms, set forth my presuppositions, and outlined the general theoretical framework of my study in what I hope is a clear exposition, I shall proceed to the customary disclaimers. The principal drawback of clarification is that it inevitably entails simplification, which, in an argument with any pretensions to subtlety or sophistication, may naturally be taxed with *over*simplification. Nonetheless, categorizations such as I have attempted above (and to which I refer throughout this book) are to some extent necessary if one is to enter the "interaction of intellectual communication" by "mak[ing] oneself intelligible," as Barthes has said,[4] and if I have not found the narrow and elusive path between obscure complexity and clear (over-) simplicity, I have preferred to err on the side of the latter. I have nevertheless tried to suggest, and now reiterate, that the opposition between irony and humor is a far from simple one. To call once more on Barthes as an "authority," I might say that the dichotomy between irony and humor is as unstable as his dichotomies, pleasure versus bliss, and work versus text; that is, the members of each opposition can only be defined in terms of an absolute or extreme that no text ever in fact realizes. To my mind, such an opposition—like all theoretical abstractions—is useful only as a heuristic device, that is, insofar as it furnishes the critic with a set of questions with which to approach a text, and a terminology with which to analyze it; in short, with some kind of theoretical grid through which to read. And to anyone who objects that such a grid "distorts" our perception of a work, I can only reply that we may consciously or unconsciously adopt a theoretical grid, but that we never read without one. What has come to be called "critical theory" is in large part simply the practice of consciously assuming a set of "prejudices" and testing the results. Such a conscious operation in no way assures the "objectivity" or even "lucidity" of any reading; there will always be another, subliminal set of presuppositions at work, an "imaginary" (about which, see Chapter Six) whose distortive effects will escape the reader in any case. They will in turn fuel the commentaries of other readers. If the dichotomy irony/ humor seems to me to be a particularly useful heuristic device at this point in literary critical history, it is because the term *irony* has recently acquired immense popularity among critics of all ilks, becoming a pivotal concept in recent critical controversies, and therefore offers one important key to the understanding of those controversies. As I hope will be evident from what follows, if it is not from what precedes, this book is as much about the connotations of the terms *irony* and *humor* for those who use them as about whatever textual phenomena they might denote.

The diachronic dimension I give the irony/humor opposition should be regarded with even greater suspicion than the synchronic one. Although I do perceive a general trend away from irony and toward humor in the authors I shall be reading here (and this is partly the reason I chose them), I certainly do not wish to imply that irony is limited to the "modern" period, and humor to the "postmodern," only that they are salient characteristics of the literature of these periods. Nothing is to prevent an author from striving to be a contemporary Voltaire or Swift (though, as Borges's Pierre Menard would attest, were his works identical to theirs, they would be read differently), and humor appears whenever a text (Rabelais comes to mind) puts into question, explicitly or implicitly, the subordination of signifier to signified, of language to reality. And then, of course, there are the master humorists of antiquity: the Sophists, the Stoics, and by some accounts, Socrates. But we shall never know whose Socrates is the "real one."

In the coming chapters, then, I shall rely on my readers' perspicacity to supply the necessary nuances whenever, in what I deem to be the interest of clarity, I may be guilty of summary or sweeping statements.

1 : Kierkegaard
The Concept of Irony

If there is anything for which one must praise modern philosophic endeavor with its splendid progress, its grand appearance and manner, it is certainly for the genial strength with which it grasps and holds fast to the phenomenon. Now if it is fitting for the latter, which as such is always *foeminini generis,* to surrender itself to the stronger because of its feminine nature, then one may fairly demand of the philosophical knight the courteous demeanour, the deep enthusiasm, instead of which one too often hears the jangling of spurs and the master's voice. The observer should be an eroticist, no feature, no moment should be indifferent to him; on the other hand, he should also feel his own preponderance, but only use it to assist the phenomenon to its complete manifestation. Even though the observer brings the concept with him, therefore, it is essential that the phenomenon remain inviolate and that the concept be seen coming into existence through the phenomenon.[1]

In the opening paragraph of *The Concept of Irony,* as in a musical prelude, the attuned ear will detect themes and phrases which, recurring, will give form to the entire opus—and whose reverberations will be heard throughout later works. *The Concept* develops simultaneously a number of overlapping motifs: biographical, aesthetic, ethical, philosophical, and theological. The aesthetic finds its expression in the erotic relationship that the romantic ironist maintains with reality (see "The Diary of a Seducer" in *Either/Or*), as well as in the more authentic pleasure of the ethical existence that has transcended the ironic (this is the "Or"); both have their literary counterparts, as in the romanticism of Schlegel's *Lucinde* or the personified doubt of Goethe's *Faust.* There is a prescience here of Kierkegaard's imminent decision to break his engagement with Regine Olsen and of the many pseudonymous works that would be born of that decision, among them the abovementioned *Either/Or,* and *Fear and Trembling,* a speculation on the paradox of Abraham, who, in giving up his most dearly beloved, yet still hoping, by virtue of the absurd, to regain him, exemplifies the "knight of faith"—of whom the philosophical knight (also in search of eternal truth) can be but an ironic parody. For *The Concept of Irony* is essentially a religious work, its first thesis being the similarity/dissimilarity of Socrates and Christ, later to be elaborated in conjunction with the concept of sin, in *The Sickness unto Death*. It is in the name of a Christian world view that Kierkegaard will denounce (with Hegel) romantic irony, to propose (against Hegel) a philosophy that reinstates the dignity of the individual through his relationship to God.

Indeed, this pro- and anti-Hegelian project is what structures *The Concept of Irony*. The work is divided into two parts, the first of which ("The Standpoint of Socrates Conceived as Irony") is devoted to a close examination of the extant Greek texts depicting Socrates, in order to demonstrate that his standpoint was in fact irony, a point denied by Hegel. Part 2 ("The Concept of Irony") deals with contemporary (to Kierkegaard) notions of irony, moving rapidly on to German romantic irony, which he judges wholly unwarranted, as opposed to the historically justified Socratic version. A few concluding pages on the mastery of irony through faith provide a somewhat cryptic culmination to the series of biblical allusions which punctuate the essay.

The initial remarks of Kierkegaard's thesis serve equally as a justification for his method of securing a "dependable and authentic conception of the historical-actual, phenomenological existence of Socrates" (*CI*, 47)—who, having left no written legacy, is for us "silence . . . in relation to world history" (49). Kierkegaard's chief reproach against Hegel is that the latter violated, rather than seduced, the phenomenon: that, insensitive to the nuances variegating our record of the past, he imposed his own concept of Socrates upon world history. While it is true that history is "mere appearance," as opposed to "essential truth," philosophy, in seeking that truth, "relates to history as a confessor to the penitent, and, like a confessor . . . ought to have a subtle and searching ear for the penitent's secrets" (48).

Even while maintaining the fundamental metaphysical distinction between essence and appearance, Kierkegaard's approach presages a post-Freudian conception of meaning: the truth is not *behind* the phenomenon, but negatively present within it; the figure of Socrates is not to be unveiled and perceived directly, but may only be conceived of "through an integral calculation" (*CI*, 50) based on the interrelationship of the various texts claiming to represent him. Socrates is not a hidden identity, but an ineffable difference, for "the system is infinitely eloquent, irony infinitely silent" (63). Thus *loquere ut videam te* ("speak that I may see you") serves as Kierkegaard's motto for the quest after the invisible Socrates. But to be heard, irony demands "an ear for the infinitely reverberating, backward echo of the reply in personality (for otherwise a reply merely transmits thought forward in sound)" (56); and lest one expect the ironist's words to project a positive image of him, Kierkegaard proposes the following analogy:

There is an engraving that portrays the grave of Napoleon. Two
large trees overshadow the grave. There is nothing else to be seen in
the picture, and the immediate spectator will see no more. Between
these two trees, however, is an empty space, and as the eye traces out
its contour Napoleon himself suddenly appears out of the nothingness, and now it is impossible to make him disappear. The eye that
has once seen him now always sees him with anxious necessity. It is
the same with Socrates' replies. As one sees the trees, so one hears his
discourse; as the trees are trees, so his words mean exactly what they
sound like. There is not a single syllable to give any hint of another
interpretation, just as there is not a single brush stroke to suggest
Napoleon. Yet it is this empty space, this nothingness, that conceals
what is most important. (56–57)

Here, as elsewhere in *The Concept of Irony,* one senses a certain conflict between a "vertical" and a "horizontal" notion of meaning; while
the "psychoanalytic" method Kierkegaard advocates suggests that sense
is produced by a play of differences, his theological allegiance is to a
"vertical" conceptualization that situates true reality in the superior
realm of the intelligible, concealed by the inferior domain of the sensible. This ambivalence will be reflected in the conflicting assessments
of Socratic irony advanced in the two parts of the thesis.

Xenophon, Plato, and Aristophanes undergo Kierkegaardian analysis
in Part 1. Xenophon is rather summarily dismissed for his tin ear: insensitive to Socratic irony, he has made of the master a Sophist, preoccupied
not with the ideal good but with its parodic empirical counterpart, the
useful. The Platonic conception of Socrates will, in turn, be judged too
ideal, yet only in the course of a lengthy demonstration that there are
in Plato two modes of questioning, two types of irony, and two forms
of dialectic: in short, two Socrates. Kierkegaard's discussion of Plato's
"duplicities" (*CI,* 77) constitutes a crucial moment in his critique of
Hegel. His analysis of the Socratic maieutic is essential to the comparison of Platonism and Hegelianism, paganism and Christianity, which is
one of Kierkegaard's major preoccupations. The Platonic dialectic,
based on question asking, advances by means of a "hobbling" alternation of terms (75), and can therefore never attain a truly speculative
mode of thought culminating in a higher unity. The Hegelian dialectic,
because it incorporates negativity as a necessary moment of the thought
process (rather than bringing it to thought from without, in the form of
a question), effects the unification of opposites, thus moving both forward and upward toward the higher unity of Absolute Spirit.[2]

However, Kierkegaard also draws a distinction between two methods of questioning, as a criterion for discerning the authentically
Socratic in the Platonic dialogues: the speculative method consists in

asking a question "for the purpose of obtaining an answer containing the desired content," while the ironic aims solely to "suck out the apparent content with a question and leave only an emptiness remaining" (*CI*, 73). Socrates practiced the latter, with the result that the essentially Socratic dialogues move from the concrete to the totally abstract and end in aporia—in irony. A case in point is the *Symposium*, in which Socrates, having heard his interlocutors' various concrete determinations of love, proceeds by means of his "blood-sucking questions" (82) to empty each of the preceding discourses of all content in order to arrive at an utterly abstract and negative determination of love as pure desire and longing. Kierkegaard's choice of illustration is scarcely an arbitrary one, for he takes the occasion to contrast this unrequited longing for an unknown, inaccessible ideal, with the "fullness" of Christian love for an "infinitely self-communicating" God (82).

The more Platonic dialogues, on the other hand, seek to rescue the Idea from evanescing into the nothingness of pure abstraction through the conscious assimilation into the dialectic of the mythical-as-image: that is, the mythical presented, not naïvely as the Idea itself, but as the reflection of the Idea (*CI*, 134). Thus the later Platonic dialogues, initiating a movement toward the reconciliation of the ideal and the concrete, arrive at the threshold of speculation. In these dialogues, argues Kierkegaard, Plato strays from the faithful portrayal of Socratic "irony in its total striving, and dialectic in its negative, emancipating activity," and, unable to "refrain from any admixture of positive content," reduces irony to "a negative power in the service of a positive Idea" (152–53). Hence the necessity, if one is to accurately determine Socrates' standpoint, of discriminating between the two species of irony in the Platonic text, an undialecticizable negativity that serves as "a goad for thought" (151), and a dialecticized, teleological negativity that "sets itself up whenever possible as lord and master" (122), as well as between the two corresponding species of dialectic:

> There is a dialectic which, in constant movement, is always watching to see that the problem does not become ensnared in an accidental conception, a dialectic which, never fatigued, is always ready to set the problem afloat should it ever go aground; in short, a dialectic which always knows how to keep the problem hovering. . . . There is another dialectic which, since it begins with the most abstract Ideas, seeks to allow these to unfold themselves in more concrete determinations; a dialectic which seeks to construct actuality by means of the Idea. (151)

In the latter, the historical-actual Socrates has "return[ed] transfigured from the grave" (68)—"transfigured" (*forklarede*) (361, n. 7) having both the religious sense of *exalted* and the intellectual sense of *explained*. "Plato has attempted to fill in the mysterious nothingness which constituted the essential point in Socrates' life by giving him the Idea" (181).

"Irony oscillates between the ideal and the empirical self; [Plato] would make of Socrates a philosopher, [Xenophon] a Sophist" (*CI,* 158). Aristophanes' representation of Socrates, however, is "comically correct" (180): incarnating neither the ideal nor the empirical, nor effecting a synthesis of the two, the Aristophanic Socrates *hovers,* suspended in a basket between earth and the heavens; the clouds, with their ability to assume any form at will, "describe perfectly the completely directionless movement of thought" in its "infinite possibility" (163)—that "desultory dialectic" (179) of Socratic irony, originating anywhere, concluding nowhere. Kierkegaard maintains that Socrates was not the Platonic philosopher, "far removed from the clamour of the world" (205); indeed, he was "in a certain sense . . . the greatest of the Sophists" (168), and may best be conceived of in relation to them.

The Sophists, according to Kierkegaard, were one incarnation of "the arbitrary freedom of finite subjectivity," that "evil principle" responsible for the decay of the Greek state. Sophistry "is the troll which haunts the landscape of reflection and its name is legion" (*CI,* 224–25; Mark 5:9).[3] "Everything is true" was the Sophistic motto; it remained for Socrates to effect the passage from that moment into the next, "nothing is true" (228), as the Socratic maieutic little by little hollowed out the multifarious positivity of Sophistic knowledge of the particular, leaving only the "negative infinity" of an abstract universal (231). For such a task Socrates was "perfectly endowed" (233) with total ignorance (for Kierkegaard insists repeatedly that this was not a feigned ignorance concealing knowledge): for each of the Sophists' answers, he had a question; by his silence—that is, his refusal to advance any positive assertion—he drew them out, brought them to reveal themselves. Playing upon the Sophistic discourse, he exposed its inner mechanism, yet Socrates himself never constructed a systematic philosophy, nor did he intend to (see *CI,* 199). In this sense he was an eroticist, his acute ear sensitive to every feature and moment of the phenomenon, all the while remaining himself in retreat. He seduced his students in a like manner, inciting them to reflection yet offering them no content for thought; analogous to the pagan deities, he failed to "communicate, fill, enrich" (213).[4]

Although in many respects Socrates is symbolic of the spirit and the religion of his time, he is fundamentally opposed to them in that he awakened reflection among the Greek citizens,[5] for which, Kierkegaard acknowledges, the state was justified in condemning him to death. In a society in which the individual has no existence beyond his membership in the state, the Socratic exhortation to "know thyself"—interpreted by Kierkegaard as "separate yourself from the 'other'" (*CI*, 202, 204)—is profoundly subversive. For the "other" consisted, to be sure, of other individuals, but only insofar as they embodied the laws and religious beliefs of the state. Singling himself out from the other, Socrates marked the inception of subjectivity in the world, though his was yet an abstract, egotistical subjectivity, wanting an "empirical self" (177). Once again, the dialectic lacks a third moment, a return-to-the-world: "Socrates appears as one who stands poised ready to leap into something, yet at every moment instead of leaping into this 'other,' he leaps aside and back into himself . . . in ironic satisfaction" (192). Therefore, Hegel's insistence that "for irony nothing is serious" (254) is ratified in the person of Socrates, for whom virtue—despite his preoccupation with it—is a mere abstraction. Since Hellenic actuality had lost its validity for him, the various virtues which some (e.g., Hegel) have said him to possess were for Socrates but abstract possibilities whose value for him could only be qualified as "experimental": "they still lack that deep seriousness which every virtue only acquires by being assimilated into a totality" (249–50; 254). "Indifferentism" (*apragmosyne*) (217) is the single term that best characterizes Socratic detachment, for he neither served the system nor opposed it.[6]

Socratic irony, then, created a clearing in the concrete actuality of Hellenism, the clearing in which would flower a new mentality of ideality. It is Socrates who first arrived at the abstract notion of the good, indeed, the very notion of the abstract itself: "[He] also arrived at the true, i.e. the true in and for itself, the beautiful, i.e. the beautiful in and for itself, and in general at being-in-and-for-itself as being-in-and-for-itself for thought. . . . [He] caused being-in-and-for-itself to become visible out of the determinateness of the manifold" (254).

He did not, however, move beyond that to the manifestation of the abstract in the concrete, and this is the point on which Kierkegaard differs—ever so slightly—from Hegel. Nevertheless, as the translator of *The Concept* aptly remarks, it is upon Kierkegaard's "slight modification" of Hegel—just as with Socrates' "slight modifications" of his adversaries' arguments—that everything turns (*CI*, 403–4, n. 31). The negativity of Socratic irony, in the Kierkegaardian conception, is utter and absolute, as opposed to that Hegelian negativity which already bears within it the germ of the positive to which it will give way. Hence Kierkegaard denies Hegel's contention that Socrates at points works from the abstract toward the concrete, claiming that the "commanding general in world history" confounds Socratic and Platonic irony because he has not concerned himself with such "trifles" as the phenomenal aspect of Socrates' existence (243–44). Hegel succeeds

Plato in the penitent's role—or on the analyst's couch; the world-his-torical stage is set for Part 2: "The Concept of Irony."

With the appearance of the romantic ironists, object of Hegel's loathing, we discover what has so grievously misled him in his concep-tion of Socrates: "On every occasion Hegel seizes the opportunity to talk about these ironists, and always discusses them in the most sarcas-tic fashion; indeed, he looks down with intense scorn and superiority on these 'superior persons,' as he often calls them. But the fact that Hegel has become infatuated with the form of irony nearest him has naturally distorted his conception of the concept" (*CI*, 282). Socratic and romantic irony are, in Kierkegaard's view, conceptually identical: their difference is essentially historical. With Socrates, irony—and hence subjectivity—first appeared in the world, thereby fundamentally altering the course of history.

Irony's second coming, in the person of the German romantic, took place in a world in which subjectivity was already given; it therefore manifested itself as a self-conscious irony, "a subjectivity raised to the second power, a subjectivity of subjectivity, corresponding to reflec-tion on reflection" (*CI*, 260). Whereas the original irony has been proven valid by world history, the later version did not correspond to the Idea and was thus not world historically justified. Here Kierke-gaard once again finds himself in agreement with Hegel, in justifying Socrates and condemning the romantics—or does he? For if it is clear that Kierkegaard did not believe romanticism to be in the service of the Idea, it is not so clear that his Idea corresponded to Hegel's. Kierke-gaard reminds the reader too often of the "jangling of spurs" with which the Hegelian dialectic has stridden through history, for irony not to be apparent in his praise of Hegel's dismissal of the romantics: "Finally, irony here met its master in Hegel. Whereas the first form of irony was not combated but pacified in that subjectivity received its due, the second form of irony was both combated and destroyed, for since it was unjustified it could only receive its due by being abro-gated" (260). The ambivalence of the passage becomes even more evi-dent when one considers that *abrogate* is the term used to translate *ophaeve*, the Danish equivalent of Hegel's *aufheben*. But the question of Kierkegaard's ironic relationship to the Hegelian text will receive fuller treatment later, as will the intimately associated question of the real significance of the distinction he draws between Socratic and romantic irony—for in effect, the second part of Kierkegaard's thesis dialectically abrogates the Socratic negativity that he has gone to such great pains to prove undialecticizable. These issues are best held in abeyance, however, pending the exposition of the theoretical strategy at work in Part 2.

A definition of the ironic figure of speech (whose importance Kierkegaard has minimized throughout "The Standpoint of Socrates"; see *CI*, 82, 101) serves as the point of departure for the entire argumentation of "The Concept of Irony." This treatment of the topic is consistent with that of Part 1, in its continued emphasis on the fact that irony is fundamentally a linguistic phenomenon, although the direction of the analysis is reversed: originally, Socratic irony was presented as a pervasive phenomenon of textual interplay, illegitimately reduced to a pregnant moment by overzealous idealists; here a simple figure of speech will be expanded to "accommodate" even Socratic irony.[7]

In the ironic figure of speech, the thought, or essence, is the opposite of the word, or phenomenon. This non-coincidence of essence and phenomenon is characteristic of all forms of irony, as is a second determination, the "negative freedom" of the subject:

> If I am conscious when I speak that what I say is my meaning, and that what is said is an adequate expression for my meaning, and I assume that the person with whom I am speaking comprehends perfectly the meaning in what is said, then I am bound by what is said, that is, I am here positively free. . . . If, on the other hand, what is said is not my meaning, or the opposite of my meaning, then I am free both in relation to others and in relation to myself. (*CI*, 264–65)

Since "truth demands identity [between essence and phenomenon]" (264), irony is always potentially a form of falsehood or duplicity, though in most cases the figure of speech is correctly interpreted by the hearer, and thus "cancels itself" (265). Nevertheless, because irony is not immediately and directly understood by everyone, "it travels in an exclusive incognito, as it were, and looks down from its exalted station with compassion on ordinary pedestrian speech" (265). The ironist may elevate himself to a position of intellectual superiority by mystifying his audience—though, ironically, he then requires a coterie of initiates to recognize his superiority. Such irony has a polemic purpose as well, that of inducing the mystified other to reveal himself. To this end, Kierkegaard writes, in one of numerous self-reflexive passages of *The Concept*, the ironist employs two tactics: "Either . . . [he] identifies himself with the nuisance he wishes to attack, or he enters into a relation of opposition to it, but in such a way, of course, that he is always conscious that his appearance is the opposite of what he himself ascribes to, and that he experiences a satisfaction in this disparity" (266).

All irony is not motivated by external objectives, however; it also assumes an acute, intensified, yet abstract form in which the ironist merely "seeks to lead the outside world astray respecting himself"

(*CI*, 268). This is "irony in the eminent sense" (271), irony as an end in itself, by which the subject seeks to wrench himself free from the bonds of finitude imposed upon him by the actuality of a given time and situation. It is the movement of subjectivity asserting itself, the awakening sense of a "certain inward infinity" (269) incommensurable with empirical reality. Suddenly all actuality has become meaningless for the ironist; his irony is not a mask donned to project a false (but positive) image, it is pure subjective freedom: "It is not this or that phenomenon but the totality of existence which it considers *sub specie ironiae*. To this extent one sees the propriety of the Hegelian character-ization of irony as infinite absolute negativity" (271). Kierkegaard has again arrived at the conception of irony as a standpoint, as it were, from the opposite direction. It is no longer solely a question of mysti-fying phrases (at least in the narrow linguistic sense); the whole of the ironist's empirical existence has become a text that does not corre-spond to its meaning, as will be evident in the passages on the roman-tic "poetization" of actuality.[8]

First, however, Socrates must be called back onto the scene, to act as a foil to romantic irony. In a brief chapter entitled "The World Histor-ical Validity of Irony: The Irony of Socrates," Kierkegaard reiterates his objections to Hegel's attribution of a certain positivity to Socratic irony, insisting that it is indeed "infinite absolute negativity. It is nega-tivity because it only negates; it is infinite because it negates not this or that phenomenon; and it is absolute because it negates by virtue of a higher which it is not" (*CI*, 178). It will nevertheless be necessary, some ten pages later, to relativize the absolute: "However, it was not actuality altogether that he negated, but the given actuality of a certain age, of substantiality as embodied in Hellas; and what his irony de-manded was the actuality of subjectivity, of ideality" (287–88). Enter the romantics.

Appropriating the Fichtean principle that subjectivity, conceived as the abstract eternal ego, has constitutive validity, Schlegel and Tieck displaced it from the metaphysical to the historical realm, with the consequence that "all historical actuality was negated to make room for a self-created actuality" (*CI*, 191). The omnipotent, "eccentric sub-jectivity" thus born was romantic irony, the parodic counterpart of Socratic subjectivity. Like its predecessor, this irony had a critical func-tion, but it criticized the whole of actuality, rather than particular phenomena. All existence, present and past, became but a vast domain of possibility for the romantic, who related to it only experimentally, endowing now this, now that phenomenon with validity, according to his pleasure. The ironist freed himself from the weight of the past by regarding all history as "myth, poetry, saga, fairy-tale" (294), in which his imagination could wander at will. Hellenism and the Middle Ages held a particular charm for the romantic, not as world historical moments, but as poetic moments, hypothetical pasts to be adopted tentatively and subsequently annulled. The same is true for ideas; religions, philosophies were tried on, then discarded without ever receiving the validation of commitment. Thus for the "poetic arbitrariness" of the ironist, "all existence becomes mere sport" (317), yet his playfulness is a form of despair[9] over the incommensurability of actuality to the Idea: "Irony knows the phenomenon is not the essence" (296). Romantic irony is a despondent idealism, an infinite longing for the Idea which fails to recognize that historical actuality is "the becoming concrete of the Idea," and that its various segments have relative validity as moments in that process (296).

Translated into the practical dimension, the theoretical duality Idea/actuality becomes possibility/actuality. Like the Aristophanic Socrates, the romantic "hovers" in a realm of sheer possibility: "As irony enjoys a critical satisfaction in theoretical concerns, so in practical affairs it relishes a similar divine freedom acknowledging no bonds, no chains" (*CI,* 296). The ironist's great concern is to "poetically create himself." The "self" he is to create, however, must be free of all concrete determinations. Whereas the serious individual conceives his task as one of self-actualization—to become *für sich* what he is *an sich*—the ironist, who will have no *an sich,* "has most often traversed a multitude of determinations in the form of possibility, poetically lived through them, before he ends in nothingness" (298). As opposed to the Christian who "allows himself to be poetically produced," that is, accommodates himself to a given context, the ironist is "a word without meaning for having been divested of connections and context"—for his only actuality is a mere poetic "pretext" of his own creation (299–300). It is no accident if the linguistic metaphor recalls the Socratic clouds, those emblems of infinite possibility, whose myriad shapes "are merely like so many predicates asserted in such a way that they are all coordinated without being connected to each other, without inner coherence and without constituting anything, in short, like so many predicates merely reeled off" (166).[10]

Although Kierkegaard contrasts the ironist with the Christian, he points out that the former cannot be called immoral in a strict sense,[11] for he lives on a much more abstract plane than that on which ethics and morals obtain. Indeed, the romanticist exists at one remove from actuality; to borrow from the Sartrian vocabulary that the Kierkegaardian text so strikingly anticipates, irony is sheer consciousness of consciousness. The ironist experiences himself as another:

Life is for him a drama, and what engrosses him is the ingenious unfolding of this drama. He is himself a spectator even when performing some act. . . . He is inspired by the virtues of self-sacrifice as a
spectator is inspired by them in a theater, and he is a severe critic
who well knows when such virtues become insipid and false. He
even feels remorse, but aesthetically not morally. At the moment of
remorse he is aesthetically above his remorse examining whether it
be poetically correct, whether it might be a suitable reply in the
mouth of some poetic character. (*CI*, 300)

The irony of the ironist's situation is that while his entire existence is
a strategy calculated to free him from the constraints of the phenomenon—actuality—he is in fact utterly bound by it, since he must perpetually fend it off. Dwelling in a self-imposed exile, frenetically
poetizing each moment into an aesthetically pleasing experience, he
knows no continuity but "boredom: this eternity void of content, this
bliss without enjoyment, this superficial profundity, this hungry
satiety" (302).[12]

Friedrich Schlegel's fiction and Ludwig Tieck's poetry are regarded
by Kierkegaard as the principal literary manifestations of this reprehensible form of irony. Their works are "immoral" and "unpoetical
. . . because they are irreligious" (*CI*, 312)—that is, because they attempt
to assuage the subject's infinite longing by positing a higher, more perfect, poetic actuality, rather than seeking, as does Christianity, to
reconcile the individual with the imperfect existing actuality.[13] Schlegel
and Tieck lack the "deep seriousness" with which an author should relate to his work; just as for Socrates, the virtues remained abstract and
hypothetical, for the romantic ironist literary productions are mere
playthings, poetic possibilities, rather than attempts at self-knowledge,
moments in a process of self-realization. The solipsistic detachment of
the romantic is a self-conscious version of the Socratic "intellectual
pederasty"; his irony is a "sickly longing" for an "impotent ideal," an
"effeminate ruse for sneaking oneself out of the world" (322, 341).

Only when each poetic production is regarded by its author as a
moment in his development does the truth of irony appear. Now the
subjective hypothesis represented by each work is no longer merely
one of an indefinite number of ironic experiments in an arbitrarily
ordered collection; each creation has taken its place within a harmoni-
ous totality and exhibits itself as precisely that which it is: an ironic
moment. Through a negation of the ironic negation, essence coincides
with phenomenon, and the positive truth manifests itself. For Kierkegaard, Goethe is exemplary as a poet for whom irony is a "mastered
moment."[14]

There can be no doubt but that Kierkegaard aspires to this mastery and that *The Concept of Irony* is to be an essential moment in his own development. In the pages censuring *Lucinde*, we have heard his pleading affirmation: "For to live poetically cannot mean to remain obscure to oneself, to work oneself up into a disgusting suggestiveness, but to become clear and transparent to oneself, not in finite and egotistical satisfaction, but in one's absolute and eternal validity. And if this be not possible for every human being then life is madness. . . . Either to be a human being is absolute, or the whole of life is nonsense" (314). The ironic standpoint is egotistical and self-sufficient. Maintained indefinitely, irony is an aesthetic category, and morally reprehensible; mastered, irony is an ethical category, a stage prerequisite to the religious. As there can be no philosophy without doubt, so "no authentic human life is possible without irony. . . . He who . . . has no ear for its whisperings lacks *eo ipso* what might be called the absolute beginnings of the personal life" (338–39).[15] If the authentic personal life is rendered possible by irony, it will remain mere possibility as long as the individual has not taken the leap of faith. In the realm of faith, irony is superseded by its religious counterpart, "humour," a concept that Kierkegaard introduces in the final paragraph of his thesis, without elaboration.[16] Nonetheless, he has earlier given us to understand what "humour" entails—a self-abnegation, a relinquishment of the ego, which irony has freed from the finite other: "[When] the devout mind perceives that all is vanity, it makes no exception regarding its own person . . . this, too, must be thrust aside so the divine will not be impeded by its resistance, but pour itself out in the mind made receptive by religious devotion. . . . The pious mind regards its own finite personality as the most wretched of all" (275).

Irony is to Kierkegaardian "humour" what Socrates is to Christ. The paradoxical analogy between the two figures, a central theme of *The Concept*, is expressed in the first of Kierkegaard's fifteen Latin theses as: "The similarity between Christ and Socrates consists essentially in dissimilarity" (*similitudo Christum inter et Socratem in dissimilitudine praecipue est posita*) (*CI*, 348–49). Kierkegaard admits their similarity in that both had validity as personalities, but insists upon their "absolute dissimilarity": "In Christ dwelt the immediate fullness of the godhead, and his relationship to the world is an absolutely real relationship" (242), whereas Socrates, as has been sufficiently demonstrated, brought nothing positive to humanity. Hence another recurrent analogy in the essay relating Socrates to John the Baptist. The latter destroyed the actuality of Judaism as embodied in the Law, though he had no knowledge of what should come (280); through a "cleansing baptism of irony" (339), he prepared his followers to receive grace, though he brought it not himself: "Irony is like the negative way, not the truth but the way" (340).[17]

The Concept of Irony abounds with biblical allusions too numerous to attend to here; the theological argument they support has been made sufficiently clear for our purposes. It is of greater interest, considering the literary-critical context of the present study, to remark on the onto-theological implications of Kierkegaard's own language. Earlier in this chapter, I mentioned in passing an apparent hesitation on Kierkegaard's part between a "vertical" and a "horizontal" conception of meaning. It would doubtless be more accurate to say that the latter notion asserts itself *despite* the prevalence of the former, revealing itself as the unspeakable. Kierkegaard's theoretical lexicon presupposes a metaphysics that simply does not admit of any conception of language other than that founded upon the disparity between the intelligible (the essence) and the sensible (the phenomenon)—a disparity with tragic implications, since the finite, imperfect phenomenon is but a deceptive simulacrum of the infinite, eternal essence. The Platonic dichotomy repeats itself at every level of Kierkegaard's argument, which posits the anteriority of idea to expression (of meaning to language), the superiority of spirit over body, and the absolute truth of the ideal world as opposed to the illusion of actuality. At the heart of Kierkegaardian theory is a Platonic melancholy ("There is, or at least . . . there ought to be, in every human being a longing for a higher and more perfect" [*CI*, 341]); Kierkegaard's metaphysics is fundamentally identical to the romantics', his condemnation of them notwithstanding, for the dialectical "reconciliation" of idea and actuality in no way alters the metaphysical hierarchy it presupposes. Hegelianism—and Christianity—aspire to the redemption of the phenomenal world, not the devaluation of the ideal.

The notion of redemption, it should be noted, is fundamentally an economic one. To redeem signifies—both etymologically and in current practice—"to buy back" and refers, among other things, to the conversion of paper (symbolic) money to gold or silver ("real" money). Both speculative philosophy and Christian doctrine are economic systems, the ultimate goal of which is to effect the exchange of finite words and deeds for infinite knowledge, eternal life. Metaphysics has christened that eternity "truth." Even the most insensitive ear can perceive the economic leitmotif which in *The Concept* associates irony with an unredeemable currency. Whereas speculative dialectic *unites*, Kierkegaard claims, the "negative [Socratic] dialectic, since it renounces the Idea, is a broker always negotiating in a lower sphere, that is, it separates" (*CI*, 179). The Idea represents "an enormous capital" that

Socrates possesses in the abstract, but "he is nevertheless bankrupt since he is unable to bring it to fruition" (96). Another such passage is of particular interest, since it bears upon Socrates' relation to the Sophists: "That there is in the ironist, to recall it once more, an *Urgrund*, a hard currency, is indisputable; yet the coin he mints does not itself bear the real value but is a nothingness like paper money; and yet all the ironist's transactions with the world are carried on with this kind of currency" (88).

The Sophists, with their empty, superficial oratory,[18] are "like bogus money" (*CI*, 226). The unbacked currency of Socratic irony is dangerously close to the fraudulent tender of sophistry; Kierkegaard has already qualified the Socratic maieutic as a "sophistic dialectic" (96) and has averred that Socrates was in a sense "the greatest of the Sophists" (168). He both is and is not a sophist. He both possesses and does not possess a wealth of knowledge. Kierkegaard is trapped in the inevitable paradox generated by his theoretical axioms: either a discourse (phenomenon) corresponds to a unified, coherent truth (essence), and then it is meaningful and valid, or it does not, and is meaningless and deceitful. There is no place for Socrates in this Platonic system. Thus Kierkegaard, like Plato, will ultimately find himself obliged to accord a positivity—a value—to Socrates, by assigning him a place within the system. If, in Part 1, Socrates' "irony is not an instrument that he employed in the service of the Idea" (236), in Part 2, irony's "emancipation of subjectivity takes place in the service of the Idea" (280); what was "infinite absolute negativity" now "correspond[s] to the negative in the [Hegelian] system" (279). Within a metaphysics that pits essence against phenomenon, Socrates must either be condemned or "transfigured." In Plato and in Hegel, Kierkegaard detects the traces of this transfiguration; to his own text, he is deaf.

Moreover, Socrates' metamorphosis in the Platonic text entails a surreptitious reevaluation of the term *irony*. That shift in meaning, which Kierkegaard apparently ignores, is crucial, I think, to our understanding of the curious ambivalence of the term in *The Concept*, as well as its fate in contemporary critical theory.

Εἰρωνεία and its verbal, adjectival, and adverbial forms appear but a dozen times in the Platonic dialogues. The majority of these cases are found in the earlier, more "Socratic" dialogues (the *Symposium*, the *Gorgias*, the *Republic* and the *Apology*); in all but two of these instances, the term is applied to Socrates, and conveys the sense of feigned ignorance or naïveté, playful mockery, or sarcasm.[19] However, in the later *Sophist*, a dialogue in which Socrates plays a minimal role, a surprising reversal occurs. In an exchange aimed at defining the Sophist, Theaetetus and the Eleatic Stranger eventually arrive at a distinction between two sorts of mimics [μιμητής]: those who imitate on the basis of knowledge and those who do so on the basis of mere opinion. A further distinction is then drawn between two types of opinion-imitators, the simple-minded mimic, who believes he has real knowledge, and the "insincere" mimic [εἰρωνικὸς μιμητής] (*Soph.*, 268a),[20] who strongly suspects that his apparent knowledge is really ignorance. Imitators of the second type appear in two guises as well: "one . . . can keep up his dissimulation publicly in long speeches [εἰρωνεύεσθαι] to a large assembly. The other uses short arguments in private and forces others to contradict themselves in conversation" (*Soph.*, 268b). Although the activity of the second mimic seems to be precisely that of Socrates, the definition is meant for his principal adversary, the Sophist: "Stranger: The art of contradiction making, descended from an insincere [εἰρωνικοῦ] kind of conceited mimicry, of the semblance-making breed, derived from image making, distinguished as a portion, not divine but human, of production, that presents a shadow-play of words—such are the blood and lineage which can, with perfect truth, be assigned to the authentic Sophist" (268c).

The ironist could not be more explicitly identified with the Sophist: the maker of contradictions, the creator of empty phrases, for whom truth is mere appearance.[21] As the Platonic dialogues take on a greater positivity, as Socrates himself fades from the Platonic text, irony is transformed from candid ignorance to willful deceit. Finally, in the *Laws,* alone marked by Socrates' absence, Plato will condemn the ironist (in Sophist's clothing) as a menace to the system. His crime is malicious impiety:

> [This type of atheist] furnishes our swarms of diviners and fanatics for all kinds of imposture; on occasion also it produces dictators, demagogues, generals, contrivers of private mysteries, and the arts and tricks of the so-called Sophist. Thus there are numerous types of these atheists, but two which legislation must take into account, the hypocritical [εἰρωνικόν], whose crimes deserve more than one death, or even two, and the others, who call for the combination of admonition with confinement. (*Laws,* 10: 908e)

Thus it is that, after the fact, Plato casts his own vote for the conviction of Socrates—and the death penalty. But this is already the *second* death of the master. Kierkegaard has born witness to the first: annihilation by assimilation, negation of negation to produce a higher, positive unity—the dialectical death and rebirth which redeem Socratic irony. A comical passage from the *Symposium* depicts this redemption in the most literal of terms, though here it is another student of Socrates, the love-lorn Alcibiades, who assures us of his mentor's true worth, declaring that even if Socrates "spends his whole life playing his little game of irony [εἰρωνευόμενος]," his playful exterior conceals a treasure: "I don't know whether anybody else has ever opened him up when he's been being serious, and seen the little images inside, but I saw them once, and they looked so godlike, so golden" (*Sym.*, 216e–217a).

Ironically, this is the Socrates, the Silenus full of golden images, whose mystifying, contradiction-laden surface conceals true wisdom (i.e., true value), that posterity has taken "seriously." For surface without depth, text without meaning, phenomenon without essence is unthinkable in the post-Platonic Western world. It is unthinkable because it is irreligious, a fact to which *The Concept of Irony* abundantly attests by its recuperation of Socratic negativity. If Kierkegaard must finally cast his vote with Plato and with Hegel, despite his efforts to prove Socrates' negativity was absolute—despite his denial that even the "golden images" passage just cited attributes a positivity to Socratic irony[22]—it is because he has conceived of a monster: pure negativity, which exceeds the limits of conceptual thought, as its very condition of possibility.

Thinking from within the Platonic-Hegelian system, Kierkegaard has sought to glimpse that which the entire system has been constructed to occult: pure difference, absence as such, death. If Socratic irony can only be thought, expressed, as a historical moment, it is because it is emblematic of a transition that cannot be pinpointed—a shift from a "positivistic" mentality that did not distinguish between word and thing, meaning and expression, abstract Being (*l'être*) and being-so (*l'étant*), to a mode of thought—conceptual thought—that has "always already" incorporated absence, negativity, as the *distance* separating the ideal from the empirical, the *disparity* between essence and phenomenon.[23] From the moment negativity dawned upon human consciousness, it could only be thought as an aberrance from positivity; absence could only be conceived of as a lack of presence. Part 1 of *The Concept* attempts to reverse this process, to say the unspeakable: that the circumscribed negativity of idealism is born of the suppression of an absolute negativity, in other words, that the postulation of a lost or concealed Idea is but philosophy's refusal (or inability) to recognize its own absence of ground. Consequently, the attribution of a hidden truth to Socratic irony constituted the denial of a conception of language as wordplay or production of meaning in favor of the reassuring belief that meaning preexists language.

But the implications of Part 1 are inadmissible in Kierkegaard's theology; there must be an essence behind the phenomenon, an ideal unity underlying the diversity of the empirical world (or else "the whole of life is nonsense"). Concealed or revealed, the truth exists; its appearance may be postponed—irony is just such a postponement—but its existence is never questioned. Through a strategic reversal in Kierkegaard's argument, Part 2 sets matters aright. Irony is first and foremost a figure of speech in which the word does not accurately represent the thought, or the phenomenon conceals the essence. All other forms of irony exhibit the same structure, even Socratic irony, even romantic irony;[24] for infinite absolute negativity has become a mere aberration, an unwarranted suspension of history's relentless dialectical movement toward the realization of absolute truth. Once pressed into the service of that truth, Socrates has inevitably taken on a Messianic aura ("In relation to Socrates . . . the Sophists [were] false Messiahs" [*CI*, 225]), an aura which, as will become apparent in the following chapter, continues to surround him in those literary critical circles which define the critic's task as the revelation of a text's true meaning. Redeemed by an ever-prevalent Platonic world view, the ironic Socrates has become the model of the serious critic, for as (ironically) Kierkegaard himself remarks, "it will always remain extremely difficult for a Plato wholly to comprehend Socrates" (155–56).[25]

Kierkegaard's ultimate Platonization of Socratic irony notwithstanding, *The Concept of Irony* elaborates what, from a philosophical point of view, must be regarded as two radically different concepts, and one of the difficulties of reading this text arises from the fact that the unqualified term *irony* is used interchangeably for both. The invisible, ineffable irony which Kierkegaard takes such pains to grasp and which he claims to be "authentically Socratic" is anathema to the System (political or metaphysical), for it refuses to take a position. It "opposes" the System as "lack-of-system," not as negation-by-the-opposite, lays bare the fissures and flaws in the System without displacing it by another. It is unnamable and undefinable, that is, "meaningless," because it has no center or unifying *telos*. The second irony, ratified by metaphysics, has become "visible for those with eyes to see, audible for those with ears to hear" (*CI*, 234; cf. Matthew 11:15, Mark 8:18). It is "meaningful" because it is teleological, its position sharply defined in opposition to the System, and readily assimilable as an antithetical moment. More precisely, this irony is already implicit in the System, whose theoretical presuppositions it shares, and it becomes "meaningful" at the moment it is recognized as an opposing term. Such is the case with romantic irony, which remains faithful to the essence-versus-phenomenon doctrine of metaphysics even though, as the assertion of an aberrant subjectivity, it would suspend the progress of the world historical dialectic. Insofar as it resists mediation, romanticism is subject to condemnation for its vacuity, or meaninglessness; yet that very condemnation constitutes a recognition and definition of romantic irony, which thereby situates it and assigns it a value (albeit negative) in world history.

Kierkegaard's use of the term *irony* to designate both a pre- and a post-metaphysical concept of negativity facilitates and camouflages his transformation of the former into the latter. Whether through theoretical confusion or by polemical prestidigitation, recent literary critics writing on irony foster the same conflation of two fundamentally different textual phenomena with dismaying regularity. Because the distinction between the "two ironies" is a crucial one for contemporary criticism, I have adopted (for reasons to be considered in the following chapter) the term *humor* to refer to that irony which eludes dialectization, retaining *irony* in its traditional sense of phenomenon-opposed-to-essence, expression-opposed-to-meaning. I hasten to discourage any assimilation of the humor in question to Kierkegaardian religious "humour." Although Kierkegaard insists that his "humour" differs essentially from irony in that it demands the relinquishment of the ego, whereas irony is a form of egotistical self-sufficiency (and we shall see that humor entails a renunciation of the ego as well) in the Kierkegaardian scheme, the ego is redeemed in its infinite eternal validity through the subject's relationship to God. Both irony and Kierkegaardian "humour" function within a system of vertical transcendence; the recuperation of the self in a transcendental Other remains as egotistical a theoretical gesture as the self-aggrandizement practiced by the ironist.

A final word on the irony/humor of the Kierkegaardian text is in order before turning to the fate of these concepts in literary theory. That Kierkegaard invites the identification of himself with Socrates is indisputable—*The Concept of Irony* is strewn with self-reflexive passages as well as personal allusions too complex to deal with in the present context.[26] I shall cite but one striking example of an intertextual thread linking Socrates to Kierkegaard. In the introductory paragraph of "The Conception Made Necessary," we read: "With Socrates the stream of the historical narrative plunges underground for a time like the river Guadalquivir, but only in order to burst forth again with renewed force" (*CI*, 222). A note informs us that the analogy recurs in Kierkegaard's 1849 journals: "As the river Guadalquivir at one place plunges underground for a time only in order to emerge once more, so now must I plunge into pseudonymity. But this time I have also understood where I will emerge again in my own name" (394–95, n.1). As editor-translator Lee M. Capel remarks elsewhere, there is justification for considering *The Concept of Irony* as the first of the pseudonymous works, though it of course must bear his name to fulfill its function—its *telos*—as an academic thesis. Indeed, in studying *The Concept* one is often led to ask if the Søren Kierkegaard inscribed on the title page is not itself a pseudonym for a nameless, faceless humorist. While the doctrine that the text preaches loudly and clearly is thoroughly ironic, culminating in a philosophical position of mastery, one cannot ignore the persistent heretical whisperings which punctuate it and undercut the theological principles it advertises. This subversion of Christian theology is effected via the interrelationship between the Hegelian and Kierkegaardian texts, the latter constituting both an endorsement and a rejection of teleological, apocalyptic philosophic systems. In this respect *The Concept of Irony* is a profoundly humorous work, not antithetic, but "non-thetic":[27] a nonoppositional confrontation with Hegelianism. Kierkegaard himself has aptly described his philosophical project as one of "appropriation": "In our age philosophy has come into possession of such an enormous result that all can scarcely be right with it. . . . The task of our age must surely be seen to be that of translating the results of philosophy into the personal life, personally to appropriate these results" (339–40).

The Concept appropriates Hegel's text while neither assimilating nor negating it. In a very current sense of the term, Hegel's work is a pretext out of which Kierkegaard generates another text that, while not an exegesis of the first, sheds new light on it through the play of resemblances and differences it sets up between itself and the other. The contrast between exegesis, or "interpretation" in the traditional sense, and the type of non-thetic interaction with another text currently termed a "reading" (or, by some, a "re-writing") serves to define the methodological differences separating what I shall hereafter refer to as "ironic" and "humorous" literary criticism. Chapter Two is devoted to the discussion of contemporary manifestations of the ironic and humorous critical stances adumbrated in *The Concept of Irony,* and presently at the center of an ongoing controversy concerning the status of literature and of language, and the future of humanism.

2 : Irony/Humor

If *The Concept of Irony* is of any interest to contemporary critics, it is because Kierkegaard's two Socrates and his two conceptions of irony correspond to two principal, and fundamentally irreconcilable, critical positions occupied by literary scholars today, which I shall term: the standpoint of *irony* and the standpoint of *humor.* Each entails a set of presuppositions about the nature of language and of literature, and therefore certain assumptions as to the means and ends to be pursued by literary criticism. It is not only justifiable, but even necessary, at this historical juncture, to define these standpoints in terms of the problematic of irony, because the use and abuse of irony has become a central issue in the critical controversies of recent years, and this, for a very good reason: the single most bitterly debated question has long been, and continues to be, in this country, the status of the subject. Irony has, since Plato, been indissociable from the problems of self-knowledge and of self-expression, along with all the ontological and epistemological questions (the nature of "true" reality, the adequation of sign to meaning, etc.) attendant thereon.

Thus the general tendency among Anglo-American critics to defend the Cartesian *cogito* and to practice a hermeneutics oriented toward the revelation of authorial intent is apparent in their inclination to treat irony primarily as a rhetorical device, specifically as a *trope* which consists of saying the opposite of, or something other than, what one really means.[1] On the other hand, contemporary Continental critics, in keeping with their current systematic questioning of metaphysical categories and their rejection or reformulation of such notions as subjectivity and intent, have tended to treat irony as a philosophical stance, while criticizing the classic dichotomies (reality/appearance, meaning/expression, etc.) upon which the concept of irony-as-trope is founded. I shall argue, then, that Kierkegaard's "second" Socrates, the justified, "dialecticized" Socrates, represents the type of teleological, dialectical thinking championed by the former group, in that he incarnates the trope, irony, as a sign whose appearance, or superficial meaning, conceals its true or essential meaning, while at the same time calling attention to that meaning by demanding interpretation. He is both the personification of the ironic literary text, in which expression does not correspond to meaning, and the archetypal serious critic, who conceives of himself as the midwife of truth. The sophistic, undialecticizable Socrates, devoid of positive content, who played upon his interlocutors' discourse in order to draw it out, to develop its possibilities in a dialogue destined to end in aporia, both incarnates the postmodern text and exemplifies the stance of the poststructuralist literary critic. Furthermore, the refusal on the part of Anglo-American critics to consider the philosophical implications of their approach to irony corresponds to the gesture of *dénégation* or denial, with which Kierkegaard, in Part 2 of his thesis, suddenly suppresses the infinite negativity of pre-Platonic irony in order to condemn romantic irony— existential and literary—on the grounds that it constitutes the unwarranted generalization and prolongation of what should be only a localized and temporary disparity between essence and phenomenon. This refusal expresses itself in a propensity for characterizing existential irony, or any prolonged use of verbal irony, as a morally reprehensible (deceitful) *extension* of the trope, while ignoring the fundamental problem posed by the history of the term, that is, how the concept came to be *restricted* to its tropological form. Thus, even though they call attention to the fact that in the time of Plato and Aristotle (that is, before it was defined as a trope), *eironeia* referred to an evasive or self-deprecating mode of behavior, critics D. C. Muecke, Norman Knox, and Wayne Booth all speak of nonlocalizable manifestations of irony—both existential irony and what they see as the pervasive irony of modern and postmodern literature—as though they constituted aberrations from a norm which is implicitly defined as the type of restricted, punctual phenomenon represented by irony used as a rhetorical ornament.[2] Booth, in particular, insists anachronistically that irony persisted in overstepping its rhetorical boundaries—even before those boundaries had been drawn: "From the earliest discussions of irony it has been seen as something that, like metaphor, will not stay graciously in an assigned position. . . . From the beginning, apparently, the word tended to get itself attached to a type of character— Aristophanes' foxy *eirons*, Plato's disconcerting Socrates—rather than to any one device."[3]

What has no "assigned position" can scarcely be accused of having gotten out of it. An uncritical reading of Quintilian—quoted by all three of the above-mentioned works on irony—may be partially responsible for this confusion. In his *Institutio Oratoria*, the Roman rhetorician draws the following distinction between the *trope* and the *figure:*

The name of the *trope* is applied to the transference of expressions from their natural and principal signification to another, or . . . the transference of words and phrases from the place which is strictly theirs to another to which they do not properly belong. A *figure*, on the other hand, as is clear from the name itself, is the term employed when we give our language a conformation other than the obvious and the ordinary . . . a figure does not necessarily involve any alteration either of the order or of the strict sense of the words.[4]

In the following chapter, he applies this distinction to irony, extending the notion of figure to include the ironic persona in terms which imply that the ironic figure is a later (and somewhat deceitful) development or proliferation of the ironic trope:

> As regards irony . . . in some of its forms it is a *trope*, in others a *figure*. . . . The *trope* is franker in its meaning and despite the fact that it implies something other than it says, makes no pretence about it. For the context as a rule is perfectly clear. . . . But in the figurative form of irony the speaker disguises his entire meaning, the disguise being apparent rather than confessed . . . nay, a whole man's life may be colored by *irony*, as was the case of Socrates, who was called an *eiron* because he assumed the role of an ignorant man lost in wonder at the wisdom of others. Thus, as continued *metaphor* develops into *allegory*, so a sustained series of *tropes* develops into this *figure*. (9: ii, 44–46)

Quintilian either influences or prefigures many contemporary scholars of irony in two respects. First, he apparently needs to make the less comprehensible, more ambiguous or polyvalent form of irony correspond to a *loss* of clarity resulting from the diffusion of an originally punctual discrepancy between signifier and signified, or form and content, throughout one's entire discourse or entire existence. Secondly, having asserted that Socrates is an ironic *figure*, he then proceeds to redefine this figure as a series of *tropes*, a reformulation which is incompatible with his earlier distinction between figure and trope; for the figure was defined (to use contemporary terminology) as a relationship among terms *in praesentia*, entailing no alteration of their "strict sense," whereas the trope consisted of the relationship between a present term and another term *in absentia*, thus involving a change in meaning. Theoretically, the difference between figure and trope is qualitative, not quantitative, and no accumulation of tropes would convert them into a figure. In "troping" Socrates, Quintilian is performing precisely the same interpretive gesture as that which Plato had before him, by endowing the master ironist with golden images, or which Kierkegaard will reproduce centuries later, in justifying Socratic irony as a pregnant moment in world history.

That gesture which consists of treating Socrates as the sign of a concealed meaning-to-be-revealed (and therefore as a text-to-be-interpreted) is repeated as well in recent critical works that treat the presumed "irony" of postmodern texts as a discrepancy between meaning and expression, or reality and appearance. To use the example of Knox, Muecke, and Booth once more, all three find that the literature of the past century has become progressively more ironic, and they define that evolution in terms of an increase and/or prolongation of the disparity between meaning and expression. Moreover, although they suggest that this recent irony is somehow akin to Socratic irony, they take pains to assure us that Socrates was no mere sophist or comedian. "He hid mystical ideas beneath ugliness and buffoonery," writes Knox (17), recalling the Alcibiades scene from the *Symposium*. Muecke, too, defends Socrates and other ironists, by implying that they knew to stop playing when truth was at stake:

> As there may be scientists who botanize upon their mothers' graves, so there may be ironists who find in Auschwitz only material for a flippant anti-Semitic joke. But I see no reason to suppose that the habit of irony prevents ironists from being serious when seriousness is called for. Socrates, on trial for his life, was ironic towards his accusers. But he was prepared to die rather than capitulate and afterwards make ironical jokes about the relative values of life and honesty. Voltaire did not take a detached ironical view of the Calas case. . . . Thomas Mann did not make ironical jokes about Hitler. (*Compass*, 245)

Booth's *Rhetoric of Irony* is organized so as to reflect the now-familiar logical progression from punctual, transparent irony to ubiquitous, irreducible irony, opening as it does with analyses of "stable" irony (e.g., Swift and Voltaire) and concluding with chapters on "local instabilities" and finally, "infinite instabilities" (e.g., Pinter and Beckett). Not surprisingly, Socrates turns up in the last chapter as the incarnation of virtually all the ironies discussed so far (*RI*, 269), and no less surprisingly, Booth launches into an impassioned defense of Plato-Socrates and dialectic:

> But Socrates (to leave Plato aside for a moment) believed in *something* sufficiently to give his life for it—the value of the city and its laws, the value of conversation with his fellow citizens, the value of (finally inaccessible) truth itself. And Plato, even more obviously, believes that it is possible to master the ironies of Socrates by fighting through them to a comprehensive vision that will encompass all negations. No one can read many Platonic dialogues without becoming convinced that both he and Socrates know a great deal. For one thing, they know how to discover error through rigorously thoughtful conversation: they know a method. (*RI*, 274)

The need to redeem Socrates by according him a positive value[5] (symbolized in Plato by Alcibiades' golden images) is of course the legacy of that metaphysical tradition which opposes meaning to expression as reality to appearance or sincerity to deceit, as I hope I have made abundantly clear in Chapter One. Thus sustained irony (and often any irony whatsoever) has long been considered immoral and even criminal because it constitutes a nonteleological (Kierkegaard would say: irreligious) use of language, both deceitful and wasteful. Those who condone only irony used as an end and not as a means, or who condemn its use when real values are at stake (lest one be guilty of botanizing on one's mother's grave!) can trace their moral lineage back at least two thousand years. Aristotle, in his *Ethics,* disapprovingly characterizes the *eiron* as a dissembler who conceals his true powers; Christianity took an even dimmer view of irony, as evidenced by a passage from *Thordynary of Chrysten Men* warning that self-deprecating dissimulation "may be mortall synne and such synne is named yronye."[6] In more recent years, the pervasive irony of twentieth-century literature has come under attack:

> Older writers used irony as a means of lending force to their creative beliefs. The Socratic irony takes wing into the Platonic myth, Swift's writing constitutes an inverted evangel of reason.
> Behind Voltaire's icy grin is the burning resolve, "Ecrasez l'infâme!" But the irony of the modern hero serves no ulterior purpose and reveals no creative thought. It is irony for its own sake; manner worn as a protective garment by a dissociative and neurotic personality.[7]

In these examples are mingled the major themes that run through all condemnations of the "illicit" use of language—that is, any discourse in which the signifier is not bound by the signified or concept (Kierkegaard would say: in which the speaker is negatively free). Thus the very same charges of immorality, perversity, and insanity that have so often been brought against *irony* reappear in moralists' harangues against *humor,* another gratuitous use of language. Bossuet, for example, warns his readers that "les plaisanteries" are but so many *"paroles oiseuses,* dont Jésus-Christ nous enseigne, qu'il faudra rendre compte au jour du jugement."[8] In an even more damning critique, Addison manages to ascribe every conceivable perversion to the punster: "To trifle with the vocabulary which is the vehicle of social intercourse is to tamper with the currency of human intelligence. He who would violate the sanctities of his mother tongue would invade the recesses of the paternal till without remorse, and repeat the banquet of Saturn without an indigestion."[9]

It is needless to multiply examples: my point is that a certain type of irony, when conceived of only as a divergence from the truth, with no subsequent moment of convergence, is metaphysically and ethically identical to *humor,* defined as wordplay, or as any non-truth-oriented mode of discourse. Irony becomes serious only when it is negated, when signifier once again coincides with signified. It is primarily because this relationship between *irony* and *humor* taken in the narrow, verbal sense exemplifies the relationship between the undialecticizable negativity, or irony, of the pre-Platonic Socrates and the serious, Messianic irony, or dialecticized negativity, of the *redeemed* Socrates that I have adopted the term *humor* to designate the former. Moreover, it will be recalled that Kierkegaard attributes to the sophist and to the romantic ironist—both avatars of the "bad" Socrates, purveyor of hollow rhetoric—all those evils which tradition has associated with the use of language as an end in itself: immorality (irreligiousness), sexual perversion (pederasty), fraudulent misrepresentation (the circulation of "bogus money").[10]

To return to contemporary literary criticism, the truthful, knowing Socrates has become the model for the critic whose prime criterion of literary value is that same "deep seriousness" with which Kierkegaard demanded that a writer relate to his work, so that however ironic a particular poetic production might be, it functioned as a positive moment within his personal development. Just as works in which the process of literary production takes precedence over the process of self-knowledge and self-expression are viewed as "mere playthings"—or unwarranted irony—by the author of *The Concept of Irony,* so those contemporary works in which the signifier takes priority over the signified have also been contemptuously dismissed as examples of "play" by those critics who perceive that "play" as meaningless, gratuitous irony. The motive for this dismissal is the fact that such texts cannot be read as tropes.

Booth's *Rhetoric of Irony,* which focuses more on the reading of ironic texts than on the classification of ironies, offers an excellent example of the type of critical method that is maladapted to the reading of postmodern literature and that has been at least partially responsible for the current popularity of the idea that postmodernism in literature and poststructuralism in criticism are but newer and more virulent manifestations of romantic irony, or modernism. In the opening chapters of his book, Booth proposes a four-step procedure for the interpretation of "stable" ironies: (1) the reader (hearer) realizes that the surface meaning is nonsense (contradictory, counter to known fact, etc.); (2) he is faced with alternatives: writer (speaker) is crazy, stupid, etc.—or he means something else. Choosing among alternatives entails (3) making a decision about the speaker's knowledge or beliefs, on the basis of which (4) the hearer constructs a meaning—a new statement—which eliminates any contradiction and is in harmony with known fact or context. This completes the process designated, significantly, as "reconstruction," or the rebuilding of the statement in another (and, Booth insists, *superior,* locus). In all cases, then, the comprehension of irony entails the elimination of a contradiction within the original utterance and/or between that utterance and its context, by transporting the true meaning of the expression *elsewhere*—that is, by treating it as a trope. In fact, the various examples of brief ironic statements that Booth uses to demonstrate his method correspond to a variety of the different tropes classified by rhetorical treatises,[11] but the method of interpretation remains the same: the replacement of an illogical or unacceptable utterance with an acceptable, logical one. When applied to literary texts, the process is of course more complex, but the object of the exercise is comparable: to phrase in logical, coherent language an original intention that unifies all parts of the text by subordinating them to a central core of meaning.[12]

A satirical work such as Swift's *Modest Proposal* lends itself rather well to such a method, for our understanding of the piece (despite complexities to which Booth accords ample attention) basically depends upon (1) incoherencies of tone or voice within the essay, and more importantly, (2) the contradiction between the explicit assertion that it is permissible, even desirable, to slaughter and eat children, and the universally (in Swift's culture) accepted maxim that cannibalism is monstrous and inhuman. Thus our interpretation of Swift relies on references to two types of context, one written, the other unwritten—that is, on a number of indignant "non-ironic" metadiscursive utterances within the text that provide us with clues to the "appropriate" response, as well as a social code or value system that we must share with Swift in order to detect his irony. Two observations are in order here. First, the "reconstruction" of Swift's meaning is actually the result of a destruction, or suppression of those elements that disturb the unity and coherence of the whole; that is, the elimination of the *figural* aspect of the text, or relationship among terms *in praesentia,* is prerequisite to the construction of the *in absentia* term of the trope. Secondly, the importance, for such a method, of the value system shared by author and reader cannot be overemphasized. Did I not share Swift's beliefs in regard to cannibalism (or assume that he shared mine), his text would be unreadable to me—and Booth's interpretation unacceptable. And of course I cannot be absolutely certain that Swift did share my values; should my assumption prove invalid, my critical edifice would crumble. Therefore Booth's choice of the term *reconstruction* (rather than recovery or rediscovery) has an appropriateness

which he would perhaps not care to emphasize: that of pointing up
the extent to which authorial intent is a critical fabrication.

Booth's reading of Beckett is a case in point. Confronted with a text
virtually devoid of meta-discursive directives, and which seems to
imply a world view that he does not share, Booth must choose between reducing the entire Beckettian text to one meaning, such as
"there is no truth" or "life is meaningless," and arguing that Beckett is
in fact ironically speaking up for all those values dear to him. Unable
to accept what he suggests is the prevailing view of the author "as inaccessible prophet of emptiness" (*RI*, 265), he opts for the latter approach
and proceeds, predictably, to produce a Beckett who could rival Alcibiades' Socrates: "Honesty, courage, generosity, prophetic wisdom, a
bitter passion for a justice that is denied us, and compassion—the only
traditional virtue he may lack is temperance!" (263). Booth draws this
conclusion less on the basis of what Beckett says (since none of that
supports his thesis) than on the fact that he says it, apparently reasoning that to write such depressing and nihilistic books must require a
great deal of courage, honesty, etc. Thus there is no methodological
difference between the "nihilistic" and the "redemptive" readings of
Beckett: both essentially involve ignoring most of his text. In more
Kierkegaardian terms, Booth's critical operation consists in this case of
displacing that negativity or groundlessness which the Beckettian text
evokes rather than names (or makes audible rather than visible, as the
text of history does the silence of Socrates) and by reinterpreting (*relo-
cating*) it as the *disparity* between what is and what should be—in
other words, as that discrepancy between the author's meaning or
belief as to what should be and his expression of what is. Having thus
redeemed so incorrigible an apostate entitles the critic to a certain
degree of beatitude as well: "Our reading of these 'indecipherable'
ironies depends, once again, on a silent act of reconstruction of the
author's superior edifice, and on our ascent to dwell with him in silent
communication while the 'meaningless' drama enacts itself below, on
the surface of things" (263).

The reconstruction method degenerates into a kind of self-parody
when applied to much recent literature because it provides no critical
apparatus (conceptual or terminological) for working on the surfaces
of texts: it lacks the analytical techniques to deal with a text whose
structuring principles are a function of the signifier rather than the signified (intention or diegesis), and above all, perhaps, it lacks the concepts with which to think of a text in terms other than intent versus
expression. For Booth, language is—or ought to be—always the (inevitably inadequate) representation of an anterior meaning, and it goes
without saying (though he says it often) that that meaning constitutes

one small contribution to a universal striving toward Truth. His criticism presupposes a potentially coherent universe (a divine design concealed in apparent disorder)—so that any literary text which does not promote or at least reflect such a world view can only be read as a lament on the fact that things are not as they should be in the phenomenal world or do not correspond to the author's idea of what they should be. That is, *difference* must be read as *disparity:* as the tragic alienation of the self from the world or from the Other, and the disparity between the ideal (unified, eternal) world and the real (chaotic, temporal) world—both of which are manifest in the disparity between sign and meaning.

To the concept of the logically ordered, teleologically directed universe corresponds, of course, the notion of a unified autonomous subject, whose conscious intent gives unity and meaning to his work as God's design does the universe.[13] Thus the truly multivalent text is unthinkable: discrepancies or incoherencies can only be interpreted as errors, as attempts to communicate anxiety over life's contradictions, as despairing demonstrations of the inadequacy of language as a vehicle of self-expression, or as gratuitous wordplay with intent to mystify. In any case, such a text does not really mean what it says; like the trope, it has an alibi—a true meaning that is elsewhere.

The same assumptions and preoccupations determine the current tendency to classify structuralist and poststructuralist criticism and its derivatives as recent developments in irony. Since much of the critical literature generated by critics of that persuasion focuses on textual "surfaces," emphasizing and analyzing the lacunae and incoherencies that are the stumbling blocks of the "reconstructive" reading—and therefore do not arrive at satisfactorily logical conclusions—they are judged ironic. This judgment is evidently founded upon the assumption that the complexity and irreducibility of many of these texts is either an attempt to disguise what the critic is really saying or a shameless display of nonsensical wordplay (which can only be the expression of severe anxiety over the duplicity of language). Once again, it is inconceivable that a writer could relinquish his authority over his own discourse to the extent of emphasizing its multivalence.

Yet it is precisely the disappearance of the postmodern author-critic in his text that likens him to the "invisible" Socrates whose *modus operandi* I have called humor, in contradistinction to the wise, superior Socrates who serves as Booth's role model. Therefore I have reserved the adjective *ironic* for the intention- or meaning-oriented critic because he presumes to occupy a position of superiority, to speak an objective metalanguage that enables him to step outside and beyond the language of the literary texts he interprets. This stance is ironic in another, complementary sense, as well, in that it incorporates a moment of self-critique, proclaiming its own lucidity as to its vulnerability to error, as Booth explains with self-congratulatory humility: "But even the few men who 'know that they do not know' are dealt with ironically by Truth itself. . . . Plato, Socrates, and the reader all know that the Discoverer of their errors looms above them observing in ironic wisdom as they all charge, *almost* as blind as Thrasymachus, into other unforeseen traps. Thus the true philosopher lives in self-corrective dialogue, in which the inadequacies of one attempt lead inevitably to another one, and then to another" (*RI,* 275).

A Rhetoric of Irony, of course, represents a fairly extreme example of what I have qualified as the "Anglo-American" trend in irony criticism, but as such it provides an excellent illustration of some of the pitfalls inherent in moralistic, "reconstructive" criticism. In *Horizons of Assent: Modernism, Postmodernism, and the Ironic Imagination,* published in 1981, Alan Wilde has proposed a more viable approach to postmodern literature than intent-oriented methods founded on the tropological formulation of irony as saying something other than what one means. Noting the tendency of most critics (e.g., Booth) "to regard irony as little more than a series of techniques and strategies," the author proposes to treat it "as a mode of consciousness."[14] Professedly working under the influence of phenomenology (Merleau-Ponty in particular), he brackets intent, in order to focus instead on studying in selected works the textual traces (themes and images as well as gaps and silences) left—whether intentionally or unintentionally—by the writer's structuring consciousness in the process of endowing the world with meaning. Wilde also criticizes Muecke for "defining irony essentially as a contrast between reality and appearance," on the ground that such a division "all too easily assumes and perpetuates a separation between consciousness and the world of which it is so inevitably a part" (*HA,* 4), and he suggests that the notion of a vertical separation be replaced by a horizontal conception of the discontinuity of experience. He further deplores Hayden White's "failure to see the potential for affirmation" in contemporary irony, insisting instead on the "creative and redemptive forces of consciousness" which manifest themselves in that irony (6).

What he gives with one hand, he takes back with the other, however, as he introduces the concept of the *anironic:*

> In locating modernist irony in a vision of things side by side and not (as Muecke does) one behind the other and in finding its essence in the articulation of disconnection, I don't mean to rob human beings altogether of their sense of doubleness, which may be, after all, the chief token of living in a fallen world. In fact, I want to argue that

all irony, regarded as a perceptual encounter with the world, generates in response to its vision of disparity (or in some cases is generated by) a complementary, more conceptual vision of wholeness or singleness, which I want to refer to as the *anironic*. (*HA*, 30)

This formulation constitutes a return to the vertical reality/appearance dualism in two senses. First, at the textual level, the assertion that the writer is harboring an ideal (idea) while portraying (expressing) a different reality implies a disparity between "covert" and "overt" meanings, to use Booth's terminology. This is not particularly crucial for Wilde's theory, though, since the content/form dichotomy that it seems to represent is undermined by the fact that he reads texts *as texts*, that is, by focusing on their figural aspect, or the interrelationship of copresent elements, without reference to absent or hidden meanings. Secondly, and more importantly, on a metaphysical level: in asserting that this is indeed a fallen world and assuming that the perception of discontinuity is necessarily accompanied by a desire for unity, he is himself taking a modernist position, according to which the phenomenal world (that which is) does not correspond to the ideal world (that which should be, and once was). He has every right to a modernist world view, of course, but he is belying his previous assertions about postmodernity (and, I believe, misrepresenting postmodernity) by attributing such a tragic vision to the postmoderns. On the other hand, the reversion to the vertical reality/appearance dichotomy is entirely appropriate in the case of modern literature, since the abandonment of that dualistic world view marks the turning point between modernity and postmodernity—as Wilde himself remarks.[15]

Wilde, like Booth, seems to be incapable of apprehending "the return to the surface" (*HA*, 70)[16] as anything but a *loss* of depth, or difference as anything but a *lack* of unity. His critique of Robbe-Grillet is telling:

> The business of the novelist, he [Robbe-Grillet] writes, is to record distances "and to insist further on the fact that these are *only distances* (and not divisions)." The implications of this statement are enormous. If there are no divisions, then all of the anguish of modernist literature is meaningless. Indeed, to see separation as disturbing is to assume that there is such a thing as depth or interiority or transcendence. But there is, in fact, only surface: "The world is neither significant nor absurd. It *is,* quite simply." The attitude is, again, one of acceptance, but the acceptance is achieved, not, as in the case of Merleau-Ponty or the later Virginia Woolf, by a restructuring of the relations between self and world but by a semantic sleight-of-hand, whereby the ominous "division" becomes the neutral "distance." (71)

It is difficult to see in what sense the affirmation that there are only neutral distances is more a matter of mere semantics than the assertion that those distances are in fact divisions. The only priority that the notion of "division" can claim over that of "distance" is that it has been parroted for two millennia, which is precisely what Robbe-Grillet was pointing out in *Pour un nouveau roman,* and what critics such as Barthes, Lyotard, Deleuze, and Derrida have, in more subtle terms, perhaps, been trying to demonstrate since the sixties. Wilde dismisses those attempts at ironic play,[17] himself refusing "to embrace uncritically such currently fashionable notions as absence and play, which one associates with the theoretical defenders of irony, who are, perhaps, its most avid practitioners as well" (6). Singling out Paul de Man as the most extreme of the supposed practitioners of irony, Wilde quotes the difficult concluding passage of *Allegories of Reading* as his example of deconstructive irony. I shall return briefly to that passage later; suffice it to remark, for the time being, that it is probably imprudent and doubtless unfair to evaluate deconstruction on the basis of the work of those whom one assumes to have embraced it uncritically; in any case, Wilde has certainly misconstrued the Derridean notion of play.

This is not the case for Gary J. Handwerk, author of *Irony and Ethics in Narrative: From Schlegel to Lacan.* Although he does not deal directly with Derrida, he does demonstrate, in his lucid pages on de Man, a better understanding of deconstruction and of its philosophical and social implications than does Wilde, even if Handwerk ultimately faults de Man for "persistently reduc[ing] the relationship between subjects to a narcissistic one."[18] Handwerk defines irony—or more specifically that strain of it which he terms "ethical irony"— much as I have humor, seeing it as the acknowledgment and assertion of the subject's fragmentation, a reaffirmation and exploration of the *inter*subjective nature of individual identity, rather than as a melancholic expression of frustration over the ineffability of the self. Thus he avoids disdainfully reducing postmodern irony to a form of despairing lamentation over a tragic loss of identity or unity, emphasizing instead its positive, dynamic aspect:

> More precisely, then, irony is a form of discourse that insists upon the provisional and fragmentary nature of the individual subject and thus forces us to recognize our dependence upon some mode of intersubjectivity that exceeds the furthest extension of any individual subject. Yet irony is more than an expression of the subject's incapacity, for it simultaneously acts to bypass the limits of that individual subjectivity by inciting pursuit of the verbal consensus on which a coherent and self-conscious community must rest—while never underestimating the hermeneutic obstacles to such consensus.

The same dynamics at work in the Lacanian subject or the Beckettian narrator can be traced back through hermeneutically self-conscious novelists such as Meredith to the initial Romantic posing of this problem—what, or where, is the subject? (*IEN*, viii)

As is evident from the above, however, Handwerk views postmodern irony (my "humor") as a direct descendant of romantic irony, whereas I have insisted here on the fundamental difference between romantic and postmodern mentality. This is not, however, because Handwerk considers contemporary "irony" to be a new and more virulent form of protest over the self-other dichotomy, resulting in an exacerbated egoism, but rather because he asserts that what he calls romantic irony (i.e., that of Friedrich Schlegel), is in fact already the kind of relinquishment of the ego that I hold to be characteristic of humor. Indeed, he describes Schlegelian irony in much the same terms as I have humor, as a "heuristic device" (*IEN*, 6) intended to explore the subject's situation in the world (in its relation to the Other), and as a "nonsynthetic dialectic," an ongoing process "without ontological or teleological aim" (15). Thus he argues quite persuasively for a reevaluation of the German romantics, criticizing readers such as Hegel, Kierkegaard, and many contemporary detractors of romantic irony of ignoring its philosophical foundations, thereby defining it in "reductively aesthetic terms"—whence the frequent, unjustified "charges of aesthetic solipsism" leveled at writers such as Schlegel and Novalis. Handwerk further traces the roots of postmodern, ethical irony back to Socrates, whom, interestingly, he characterizes as the elusive, infinitely negative "humorist" whose portrait Kierkegaard initially paints but ultimately retouches with shades of positivity in order to salvage teleology, and, of course, theology.

I could scarcely agree more with Handwerk's charge that many critics' failure to take into account the philosophical foundations of irony has led them to a woefully inadequate understanding of the phenomenon. This in fact constitutes my principal objection to Booth, who, not incidentally, remarks in his introduction that he has read and enjoyed Kierkegaard on irony, but that the philosopher's "wonderfully wild line" is of virtually no use to him (*RI*, xiii). Handwerk, too, reproaches Booth for restricting irony to a mere rhetorical device (*IEN*, 6–8), but he also accuses Kierkegaard of basing his condemnation of the romantics on an over-simplistic conception of Schlegelian irony as a form of solipsistic aestheticism. While one can hardly maintain that Kierkegaard disregards the philosophical implications of irony, Handwerk may be quite right when he claims that the author of *The Concept of Irony* misunderstood Schlegel, and I have neither the expertise nor the inclination to refute Handwerk's interpretation of the German

romantics. It is certainly possible that Kierkegaard and many others
have misread them, and that they were in fact harbingers of what we
consider to be a Lacanian, or primarily "postmodern" notion of subjectivity.

Assuming the correctness of Handwerk's thesis would not, however,
affect my own argument in the present work—namely, that there is an
essential difference between romantic-ironic or "modern" mentality
and "humorous" or "postmodern" mentality, particularly in regard to
their understanding of the relation of the human subject to language.
A qualification is doubtless in order, though: the romantic irony to
which I refer and from which I sharply distinguish the spirit animat-
ing such recent trends in literary and critical practice as the *nouveau
roman* or deconstruction is the romanticism that Kierkegaard sees,
rightly or wrongly, in Schlegel and Tieck—the cynical disillusionment
that informed much of late French romanticism—and which remains
today the prevalent conception of romanticism. I am objecting, not to
any suggestion that contemporary literature and criticism may have
had precursors in the other centuries, even among the ranks of the so-
called romantics, but rather to the notion that postmodernism is a
natural continuation and/or intensification of the past century's
anguish over the loss of meaning (be that loss defined in terms of the
death of God, the disintegration of the social order, the dissolution of
individual identity, or the disappearance of the referent).

I *am* somewhat suspicious of Handwerk's apparent readiness to
affirm a fundamental similarity among *all* "types" of irony, for there
are certainly important distinctions to be made, distinctions which are
not merely a matter of degree. I am also a little skeptical about his suggestion (which smacks of teleology) that ethical irony may lead to a
"future consensus" (*IEN*, 4). *Irony and Ethics in Narrative* nonetheless
remains one of the most interesting recent treatments of irony, especially for its non-tragic, non-nostalgic perception of the postmodern
subject.

A more useful basis for the development of my own thesis, however,
is a much earlier article by Paul de Man, "The Rhetoric of Temporality," which deals explicitly with the concept of irony in literature,
while implicitly raising a number of crucial questions concerning the
problematic status of literary critical discourse. De Man's discussion of
irony forms part of a larger investigation centering on the distinction
between allegory and symbol in romantic literature. The first part of
the essay establishes that the use of symbol, in which the relationship
between sign and meaning is perceived as necessary and continuous,
represented an attempt to suppress the difference between subject and
object, while the choice of allegory, in which the sign-meaning rela-

tionship was clearly arbitrary and discontinuous, constituted a refusal of any such illusion, formulated in temporal terms.[19] According to de Man, the opposition between these two forms of language reflected the romantics' simultaneous (or alternating) affirmation and denial of temporality:

> The dialectical relationship between subject and object is no longer the central statement of romantic thought, but this dialectic is now located entirely in the temporal relationships that exist within a system of allegorical signs. It becomes a conflict between a conception of the self seen in its authentically temporal predicament and a defensive strategy that tries to hide from this negative self-knowledge. On the level of language the asserted superiority of symbol over allegory, so frequent during the nineteenth century, is one of the forms taken by this tenacious self-mystification. (RT, 191)

Irony is like allegory "in that, in both cases, the relationship between sign and meaning is discontinuous. . . . In both cases, the sign points to something that differs from its literal meaning and has for its function the thematization of this difference," but as de Man's subsequent development of the topic demonstrates, the difference asserted by irony is within the subject itself. His analysis is based primarily on Baudelaire's essay "De l'essence du rire" ("The Essence of Laughter"), in which the author's major emphasis falls upon the poet-philosopher's ability to laugh at himself, that is, "to split rapidly into two persons [*se dédoubler*] and observe himself with the detachment of a disinterested spectator"[20]—an act of self-reflection which he frequently refers to as *ironie* in his other works. Baudelaire's key example in developing his thesis is that of a fall which, as is evident from the rest of the essay, represents *the* Fall. Explaining that laughter is essentially the expression of a feeling of superiority such as one experiences upon seeing a man stumble and fall in the street, he remarks that the source of laughter is not in the object itself but in the laugher, and that one does not usually laugh at oneself unless one has the philosopher's powers of self-reflection. The ability to laugh at oneself, or the capacity for irony, then, comes with the knowledge of one's own vulnerability (susceptibility to falling), and thus constitutes a kind of wisdom in relation to a naïve past self which thought itself incapable of falling, a wisdom which also provides a painful insight into the postlapsarian human condition. Therefore all laughter is akin to the diabolical laughter of Lucifer or of the Faustian Melmoth, for it is the expression of a fallen being's bitter awareness of his infinite superiority over common mortals and his infinite inferiority in relation to God. The parallel between Baudelaire's satanic irony and Kierkegaard's romantic irony, defined as despairing self-knowledge, is, I think, too evident to require further elaboration. Indeed, de Man's analysis, though it does not explicitly address Kierkegaard's theories,[21] develops the consequences of that self-*dédoublement* in rather Kierkegaardian (Hegelian-Sartrian) terms.

As de Man points out, the ironic disjunction can be effected only by means of language: "It transfers the self out of the empirical world into a world constituted out of, and in, language—a language that it finds in the world like one entity among others, but that remains unique in being the only entity by means of which it can differentiate itself from the world. Language thus conceived divides the subject into an empirical self, immersed in the world, and a self that becomes like a sign in its attempt at differentiation and self-definition" (RT, 196).

The new linguistic self enjoys a certain superiority relative to the subject's mystified self-in-the-world, but that lucidity as to the empirical self's mystification in no way constitutes an escape from that condition: "The ironic language splits the subject into an empirical self that exists in a state of inauthenticity and a self that exists only in the form of a language that asserts the knowledge of this inauthenticity. This does not, however, make it into an authentic language, for to know inauthenticity is not the same as to be authentic" (RT, 197). The ironic self is menaced with an even greater mystification, that of naïvely believing that its knowledge can have any effect in the empirical domain, that its superiority is operative in the "real" world. In order to avoid a new fall into mystification, "the ironic self at once has to ironize its own predicament and observe in turn . . . the temptation to which it is about to succumb" (RT, 199). So begins an endless series of renewed disjunctions by which the ironic self protects itself from reimmersion in the empirical world, by repeatedly "reasserting the purely fictional nature of its own universe and by carefully maintaining the radical difference that separates fiction from the world of empirical reality" (199).

The recurrent "self-escalating act of consciousness" described here as an endless spiraling effect is the spatial equivalent of the Kierkegaardian ironist's perpetual self-observation throughout an "eternity void of content." While both depict the plight of Hegel's "beautiful soul," which, with its vows to maintain its absolute purity, renounces all possibility of return to the empirical world, de Man's model is perhaps more elucidating as regards the status of ironic critical discourse. For the would-be objective critic finds himself in the same predicament as Baudelaire–de Man's ironic self. In order to maintain the metalinguistic status of his theoretical discourse, he must constantly monitor its purity, reasserting its radical difference from the metaphorical, literary languages or codes upon which he is commenting.[22] That is, if he is to objectively evaluate a work, the critic must be capable of stepping outside the conceptual, psychological, and linguistic categories that inform the text he is reading, an act that must be duplicated in a self-critical moment of stepping outside his own discourse to check it for blind spots; the objectivity of the self-critical discourse must then be assured by a new ironic disjunction, and so on, ad infinitum, with no possibility of return. "La méthode," Barthes has written, "accomplit le plus haut degré de conscience d'un langage *qui ne s'oublie pas lui-même*," with the result that the methodological critical text is ultimately only a discourse on its own method:

> Se posant comme un pur métalangage, [la Méthode] participe à la vanité de tout métalangage. Aussi il est constant qu'un travail qui proclame sans cesse sa volonté de méthode soit finalement stérile: tout est passé dans la méthode, il ne reste plus rien à l'écriture.[23]

> Method . . . realizes the highest degree of consciousness of a language which is not forgetful of itself. . . . Posing as a pure metalanguage, it partakes of the vanity of all metalanguage. The invariable fact is that a piece of work which ceaselessly proclaims its determination for method is ultimately sterile: everything has been put into the method, nothing is left for writing.

It should be evident, however, from Barthes's allusion to *écriture* that the sterility with which he is reproaching the champion of method has nothing to do with a failure to engender Truth. (Indeed, that type of sterility—the refusal to produce positive results—is valorized in the Barthesian text.) *Ecriture* is a term that will be widely adopted by French critics to designate a variety of attempts to avoid the impasse of "objectivity" by assuming a certain blindness and incorporating that blindness into their work as a necessary condition of textuality.

But I anticipate. De Man finally can propose no solution. In fact, he has not yet explicitly transferred the problematic that he is presenting to the domain of critical discourse, although he initiates that move in several references to Schlegel's "*permanente Parekbase*" (RT, 200). He returns to literature to see whether *allegory* offers the possibility of a demystified language that is not perpetually vulnerable to renewed mystification, using the example of one of Wordsworth's Lucy Gray poems in which the first stanza presents the subject's blissful obliviousness to mortality, and the second, his tragic wisdom following the loved one's death. De Man is obliged to conclude, however, that there is no essential difference between irony and allegory; allegory only presents the same *prise de conscience* of temporality[24] in narrative form:

The difference has been spread out over a temporality which is exclusively that of the poem and in which the conditions of error and of wisdom have become successive. This is possible within the ideal, self-created temporality engendered by the language of the poem, but it is not possible within the actual temporality of experience. . . . The fundamental structure of allegory appears here in the tendency of the language toward narrative, the spreading out along the axis of an imaginary time in order to give duration to what is, in fact, simultaneous within the subject. . . .

Both modes are fully demystified when they remain within the realm of their respective languages but are totally vulnerable to renewed blindness as soon as they leave it for the empirical world. Both are determined by an authentic experience of temporality which, seen from the point of view of the self engaged in the world, is a negative one. The dialectical play between the two modes, as well as their common interplay with mystified forms of language (such as symbolic or mimetic representation), which it is not in their power to eradicate, make up what is called literary history. (RT, 206–7)

The real subject of de Man's article is the impossibility of metalanguage, and the fundamental question that it poses is: how is it possible for one text to talk about another text? Is it possible to elaborate a critical discourse that is neither pure mimesis nor pure method (theory)—neither a simple paraphrase in the text's own language nor an irrelevant self-commentary on the critic's own philosophy of literature? Given that both modes of discourse are finally equally mystified, is there a third position (but not a synthesis, which would produce only the kind of vacillation between terms which, according to de Man, characterizes literary history)? Baudelaire himself hints at a solution, though in an ambiguous and fleeting fashion, a fact which de Man seems to miss, because he equates—erroneously, I believe—irony and *le comique absolu*. In "De l'essence du rire," laughter, and ironic wisdom, are more particularly associated with *le comique significatif*, the expression of "the idea of superiority . . . of man over man,"[25] which is in fact the kind of superiority implied in the allusions to the ironic *dédoublement*—and not, as de Man holds, the superiority of "man over nature" (*OC*, 985), which characterizes *le comique absolu*. *Le comique absolu* is the form of the *comique* that nearly transcends laughter, approaching the pure joy that Baudelaire says is accessible only (and then not fully) to the naïveté of childhood and the "contemplative innocence" of the true sage. Hence the designation *comique innocent* for those works which best approximate the *absolu*—most notably those of Hoffmann. Whereas the *comique significatif* presents itself as a kind of self-knowledge or superior wisdom, the essence of the *comique absolu* is "to be unself-conscious": it is a form of ignorance or self-forgetting. But that ignorance is only a feint, a lure:

> Quand Hoffmann engendre le comique absolu, il est bien vrai qu'il le sait; mais il sait aussi que l'essence de ce comique est de paraître s'ignorer lui-même et de développer chez le spectateur, on plutôt chez le lecteur, la joie de sa propre supériorité et la joie de la supériorité de l'homme sur la nature. (*OC,* 993)

> When Hoffmann engenders the absolute comic, it is quite true that he knows it; but he also knows that the essence of this comic is to appear unself-conscious and to develop in the spectator, or rather in the reader, a joyful sense of his own superiority and of the superiority of man over nature.

Despite the assertion that the reader of the "naïve" text experiences a certain *joie* (of man's superiority over nature), or relatively "innocent" pleasure, the passage implies as well that he enjoys a feeling of superiority over the apparent naïveté of the artist, thus walking into the textual trap—somewhat like the hubristic stroller who falls into a manhole while laughing at another slipping on a banana peel.

The feint—not unlike the apparent unself-consciousness of the absolute comic—is one of the strategies adopted by poststructuralist criticism to elude the master-slave dialectic that is inevitably instituted the moment a critic assumes a discourse of mastery. De Man, of course, encountered the feint in Derrida's works. It is not surprising, therefore, that the term *irony* later reappears in the passage of *Allegories of Reading* quoted by Wilde, where it has become "the permanent parabasis of an allegory (of figure) . . . the undoing of the deconstructive allegory of all tropological conditions, the systematic undoing, in other words, of understanding. As such, far from closing off the tropological system, irony enforces the repetition of its aberration."[26] Yet despite the resemblance that this irony, described as "permanent parabasis," or the "repetition of an aberration," might seem to bear with the "self-escalating act of consciousness" of "The Rhetoric of Temporality," it is engendered by a fundamentally different critical tactic and implies a different ontology. Whereas the earlier irony constituted a futile attempt to criticize discourse from the outside, that is, to find a language that could proclaim the vacuity of language without asserting its own futility as well, the latter irony is the mute affirmation of a critical step back inside, into language and into a certain blindness.

This irony is not a voice sagely acknowledging its own vulnerability in a vain attempt to dialecticize it into a strength ("I am wisest of all because I know that I do not know"). It is the irony—the *humor*—of language itself. It is, in a sense, the vulnerability or naïveté, both real and feigned, with which deconstruction proceeds to undermine its own foundations along with those of the discourse it criticizes. Furthermore, whereas "The Rhetoric of Temporality" implicitly affirms a Sartrian (Platonic, Hegelian, etc.) ontology by never questioning the assumption that language, or representation, does constitute a detour from presence, and that the coincidence of sign and meaning is the *telos* of all intellectual striving, the deconstructive stance of *Allegories* is postulated on the originary deferral of meaning. Whether or not de Man carries out the critical enterprise he evokes in the elusive reference to irony cited above is open to debate. But the deconstructive project represents an attempt, at least, to short-circuit the infinite spiraling of romantic irony. Furthermore, as I remarked earlier, it seems ill-advised to attack Derrida (and, as is often the case, contemporary Continental criticism in general) through the presumed (or even self-proclaimed) disciples of deconstruction.

What Derrida has sought to do is to critique the traditional discourses of philosophy and criticism from the inside—in other words, *without* resorting to irony, without futilely rejecting the sole conceptual language at his disposal in the name of some imaginary new form of serious discourse whose claim to difference would only constitute a new stereotype or discourse of mastery.[27] His strategy consists, therefore, of adopting the language of tradition (of the Master or of the Law, in Hegelian, Kierkegaardian, or Lacanian terms), feigning to speak it by really speaking it. Thus Derrida, in what Barthes might call a "parody that does not advertise itself as such,"[28] follows the logic of philosophy to its absurdest extremes, where it appears that the discourse of reason has always already born within it the possibility of unreason, as that which it must exclude or expel in order to establish its own hegemony.[29]

The term *play* or *game* (*le jeu*) of course figures prominently in Derrida (as well as in many of his contemporaries), a fact which Anglo-American criticism has not failed to proclaim loudly, while ignoring its function within his texts. Derrida's *jeu* is not "merely" a game (gratuitous irony) as opposed to serious, productive work. Nor is it a revalorized, productive play (mastered irony) that ultimately "turns out" to be serious because it is dialectically incorporated as a negative moment in the progress of reason (as when critics redeem the comic by solemnly affirming that it is "really serious," i.e., profoundly meaningful).[30] It is *un autre jeu:* the inter"play," complicity, or symbiosis of *le sérieux* and *le jeu* that undercuts their opposition. Derrida's game is always serious because the serious is always already affected by the nonserious. Derridean humor consists of this refusal—some would say failure—to assume a single voice. The self-conscious narrator of classical irony has been superseded by the self-conscious text; and the self-escalating act of consciousness, by the inward spiraling of language turning in upon itself.

While Derrida was seeking to elaborate a philosophical discourse without metalinguistic pretensions, Barthes was pursuing a similar end in the realm of literary criticism. It would not be an exaggeration to claim that the avoidance of irony has been a major preoccupation of Roland Barthes's career. As early as 1966 he was writing in *Critique et vérité:*

> L'ironie n'est rien d'autre que la question posée au langage par le langage . . . il y a une ironie des symboles, une façon de mettre le langage en question par les excès apparents, déclarés, du langage. Face à la pauvre ironie voltairienne, produit narcissique d'une langue trop confiante en elle-même, on peut imaginer une autre ironie, que, faute de mieux, l'on appellera *baroque,* parce qu'elle épanouit le langage, au lieu de la rétrécir. Pourquoi serait-elle interdite à la critique? Elle est peut-être la seule parole sérieuse qui lui soit laissée, tant que le statut de la science et du langage n'est pas bien établi—ce qui semble être encore le cas aujourd'hui. L'ironie est alors ce qui est donné immédiatement au critique: non pas de voir la vérité, selon le mot de Kafka, mais de l'être, en sorte que nous soyons en droit de lui demander, non point: *faites-moi croire à ce que vous dites,* mais plus encore: *faites-moi croire à votre décision de le dire.* (74–75)

> Irony is nothing other than the question that language poses to language . . . there is an irony of symbols, a way of putting language into question by the conspicuous, avowed excesses of language. In opposition to poor Voltairean irony, the narcissistic product of an overly self-confident language, one may imagine another irony, which, for want of better, we shall call *baroque,* because it expands language instead of contracting it. Why should it be forbidden the critic? It is perhaps the sole serious discourse left to him, as long as the status of science and of language is not firmly established, which seems still to be the case today. Irony, then, is that which is immediately given to the critic: not to see the truth, in Kafka's words, but to be it, so that we have the right to ask of him, not: *make me believe in what you say,* but rather: *make me believe in your decision to say it.*

What Barthes is calling for here, as an alternative to the discourse of mastery ("poor Voltairean irony")—that dominant censoring voice which restricts the possible interpretations of a text—is an *écriture* that will take full advantage of the polyvalence of language. How Barthes pursued the goal of plural writing in his own work, while fleeing the single-voiced dogmatism of ironic discourse, is the principal subject of Chapter Six. What concerns us here is his particular formulation of the problematic, which in many regards exemplifies poststructuralist theoretical approaches to irony. Three passages in *S/Z*–sections 21, 59, and 87–set forth the essential elements of a Barthesian conception of (classical) irony and the rudiments of a textual strategy for circumventing it. Significantly, Barthes avoids the classical tropological (meaning/ expression, reality/appearance) model of irony, insisting instead upon its status as a cultural code. The importance of this reformulation cannot be overemphasized: it entails more than a mere shift in emphasis from authorial intent to language (code), for it is ultimately a rejection of the primacy of intention altogether.

The code is, for Barthes, a stereotypical discourse, or one of the multiplicity of ready-made languages whose confluence determines and characterizes a given culture. The stereotype is also referred to as *la doxa*, or universally accepted belief(s) (what "they say"), hence another of its avatars, *la bêtise* ("stupidity"), or the parrotlike repetition of commonplaces. This is not to suggest, however, the possibility of an "intelligent" discourse that would avoid all recourse to stereotype; *l'intelligence* is itself a code, the stereotype that consists of denouncing the mystification or inauthenticity of all other codes: *l'Ironie*. Thus irony, like other codes, is a kind of citation, or repetition of a *déjà-dit*, but with one essential distinction: irony is a meta-citation, the quotation of other codes *as quotations*. Whereas other codes are commonly assumed by the speaker and repeated without attribution of origin, the function of the ironic code is to put the stereotypes it repeats in quotation marks, explicitly attributing them to the Other.

In other words, irony represents an attempt to create an authentic voice, the self-distinguishing strategy of "un sujet qui met son imaginaire dans la distance qu'il feint de prendre vis-à-vis du langage des autres, et se constitue par là d'autant plus sûrement sujet du discours" ("a subject that puts its imaginary elements at the distance it pretends to take with regard to the language of others, thereby making itself even more securely a subject of discourse" [*SZ*, 52/45]). In the case of the traditional novelist, irony served as a claim to originality, or, as Barthes says, as a panacea for the nauseating repetition of stereotypes: "Le remède classique, plus ou moins utilisé selon les auteurs, est de les ironiser; c'est-à-dire de superposer au code vomi un second code qui le parle avec distance . . . ; autrement dit, d'engager un processus de méta-langage" ("The classic remedy, more or less employed according to the author, is to make them ironical; that is, to superimpose on the vomited code a second code which expresses it at a distance . . . ; in other words, to engage a metalinguistic process" [145/139]). In the passage from Balzac that serves as Barthes's example, the *code passionnel* (what Sarrasine supposedly feels) and the *code romanesque* (the description of his romantic expectations for a meeting with Zambinella) are reduced to naïve stereotypes by the parodic tone of the *code ironique,* which emphasizes their conventionality.

But the inevitable irony of irony is that there is nothing original about pointing to the unoriginality of others. The ironic gesture is finally only the ostentatious assumption of another time-worn code: "Parody, which is in a sense irony at work, is always a *classic* language" (*SZ,* 52/45). The question then becomes, for the novelist and for the critic, how is it possible—is it possible—to criticize the stereotype without recourse to another stereotype, or "how can one pin down stupidity without declaring oneself intelligent?" (212/206). Hence the avoidance of irony constitutes the fundamental problem of the post-modern author[31]—how can one differ except by a banal proclamation of one's difference? "What could a parody be that did not advertise itself as such?" (52/45).

The inaugural gesture of postmodernity is the renunciation of all pretensions to a singular voice, by simultaneously *assuming* a multiplicity of discourses (without quotation marks):

> Un texte multivalent n'accomplit jusqu'au bout sa duplicité constitutive que . . . s'il n'attribue pas ses énoncés (même dans l'intention de les discréditer) à des autorités explicites, s'il déjoue tout respect de l'origine, de la paternité, de la propriété, s'il détruit la voix qui pourrait donner au texte son unité ("organique"). (*SZ,* 51/44)

> A multivalent text can carry out its basic duplicity only . . . if it fails to attribute quotations (even with the intention to discredit them) to explicit authorities, if it flouts all respect for origin, paternity, propriety, if it destroys the voice which could give the text its ("organic") unity.

Only in refusing to hierarchize the voices within his text, thereby relinquishing his own authority, or paternity, can the writer evade the stereotypical through the anonymity of writing: "The very being of writing . . . is to prevent us from ever answering the question: who is speaking?" (146/140). Whereas the function of classical irony was to "clos[e] off . . . the plurality of codes" (212/206) by pronouncing the last word (or having the last laugh: "I am not so stupid"), the *ironie baroque* invoked in *Critique et vérité* serves to preclude any possibility of reducing a text to a single voice or final meaning. The "individuality" of the subject of *écriture* subsists in his text only—but this is Foucault—as "the singularity of its absence."[32] To be different can only be to *différer,* in the Derridean sense: to forestall closure. To renounce *la parole* for *l'écriture:* such is the strategy of nonviolent confrontation ("to oppose without appeal to force" [212/206]) that Barthes, and others, propose for the postmodern writer. Or, in somewhat more Kierke-gaardian terms: to elaborate a new discourse that is not antithetical to the old, but non-thetic, by responding to irony—the jangling of spurs and the master's voice—with *une autre ironie:* humor.

In treating irony as a code or citation, Barthes is presupposing a Lacanian conception of the subject as a "self" always already pene-trated with otherness because it exists only insofar as it assumes the language imposed upon it by the Other. This presupposition invali-dates a priori the meaning/expression model of language in general and of irony in particular,[33] since it accords the subject no anteriority or priority over its discourse. In Barthes's formulation, therefore, irony is not the disparity between an anterior intention and a subsequent ut-terance, or between meaning and sign; it is the rejection of a mode of expression perceived to be Other, the refusal, finally, of all language as Otherness. It is the subject's futile attempt to defend an illusory ego (hence Barthes's allusion to the Lacanian *imaginaire*) against the on-slaught of alterity, by staking out its own territory, its personal prop-erty in the realm of discourse. Irony, in other words, is the chimerical project of inventing a *parole* outside of the *langue.*

Thus Barthesian *ironie,* as a negative assertion of Authority or differ-ence, is equivalent to Kierkegaardian romantic irony. Indeed, Barthes's ironist *is* the romantic ironist, the subject who clings to the illusion of his ipseity and autonomy and perceives his being in the world as a tragic one or a fallen condition: an exile into a phenomenal world incommensurable with his eternal ego. But Barthes is not Kierkegaard; and if Kierkegaard's critique of irony is conducted in the name of a superior irony, or superior ideal, Barthes's is not. Kierkegaard shares the tragic world view of his romantic ironist, who is but the philoso-pher's mystified past self. For Kierkegaard, the ego is not an illusion, it is a spiritual reality that can only be expressed by approximations in the phenomenal world, which in his system is the realm of *mere* ap-pearance. His religious "humour" is the resigned acceptance of a detour from presence in the hope of its future restoration.

Barthes's *autre ironie*—which I shall henceforth designate as *humor*—is not Kierkegaard's irony as a mastered moment (which itself is noth-ing but an escape from the prison of romantic irony via a leap of faith), nor is it a new manifestation of gratuitous romantic irony, as some of his critics have suggested. For Barthes, the way out of irony is not more irony. Barthesian humor—the affirmation of a self con-stituted in and out of language—is not a choice of appearance *instead* of reality, signifier *instead* of signified, "an effeminate ruse for sneaking oneself out of the world" (*CI,* 341). It is quite simply the assumption of a critical paradigm within which the dichotomies that ground the classical concept of irony have no pertinence.

The same may be said of postmodern literature, a category in which I would include those works that are free of nostalgia for a lost presence—whereas the kind of reluctant renunciation of a unified cosmos that de Man associates with the use of allegory and irony is characteristic of modernism.[34] I hasten to add that the distinction is seldom so clear in practice as in theory, but it does provide the critic with some paradigms on the basis of which to work. Often, of course, a text will present an admixture of irony and humor that eludes definitive classification. In any case, postmodernity is the product of an affirmation, not of a negation; the truly postmodern work (of literature or of criticism) is anything but an impotent wordplay symptomatic of the "sickly longing" of romanticism.[35]

This is why two contemporary French critics, Gilles Deleuze and Jean-François Lyotard, have defined their relationship to traditional philosophy and theory in terms of a nondialectical opposition between *ironie* and *humour*. For each, theorizing from the standpoint of humor entails an attempt to think negativity as such (Derridean *différance*), rather than as an absence of positivity, as well as the affirmation of the inherent otherness of the self and, with it, the elaboration of a non-thetic, non-teleological mode of critical discourse.

In "Le Non et la position de l'objet," Lyotard analyzes the relationship between negativity, language, and desire in the emergence of the speaking subject. Writing on Freud's article "Die Verneinung" (negation, or in French, *dénégation*), and on Benveniste's reading of it, Lyotard comments on the analyst's paradoxical claim that when the patient declares of a dream image, "No, that is not my mother," the statement must be taken as an assurance that it is indeed the mother. How is it that, as Benveniste observes, the No, negation, posits the very object it denies? Lyotard prefaces his response by first acknowledging "la portée universelle du négatif: avant d'être un rapport au sein du système, la négativité est constituante de tout rapport, serait-il de ressemblance, voire d'identité" ("the universal scope of the negative: before being a relationship within the system, negativity is constitutive of every relationship, be it one of resemblance, even of identity").[36] It is this negativity that subtends language as its "silent support," and is perceptible in the horizontal plane of discourse only as the play of differences that constitutes the various elements of the system as purely relative values. A second negativity constitutive of all discourse is the "vertical" distance between subject and object, which founds the function of designation, or reference. This is the negativity that institutes the difference between self and non-self and assures that ego, or *celui qui parle*, will never coincide with his discourse:

> La négation qui supporte le rapport de désignation est la scission qui s'ouvrant entre le discours et son objet, nous donne à parler puisque nous ne pouvons dire et n'avons qu'à dire que ce que nous ne sommes pas, et qu'il est assuré qu'à l'inverse ce que nous ne pouvons pas dire, nous le sommes. ("Le Non," 120)

The negation that supports the relation of designation is the split which, in opening up between discourse and its object, allows us to speak, since we can only say—and have only to say—what we are not; and since it is certain that, inversely, what we cannot say, we are.

In Benveniste's terms, the *je de l'énonciation* can never coincide with the *je de l'énoncé.*

But the essential point is this: the grammatical *no,* the *no* of signification, repeats, or names, the original negation or expulsion of the non-self that constitutes what will become "reality": "reality is what has been rejected" ("Le Non," 124). It is because language recalls or represents the other (of which the archetype is the mother) *as Other*— as reality, or that which is always already lost to the self—that it opens up the space of designation, and with it, the space of desire: "Reality and desire are born together when the subject enters language" (125). Furthermore, the space of desire is the space of knowledge, of a *discours de connaissance* seeking to grasp that very object which it posits as irretrievable:

> Il faut poser l'identité de vouloir savoir et désirer; Socrate l'a inaugurée, incarnée. Vouloir savoir est impliqué dans le discours: tournant *autour* de son object, dans l'espace profond, l'objet se dérobant toujours par quelque face. (128)

We must posit the identity between the will to know and desire; Socrates inaugurated it and incarnated it. The will to know is implied by discourse: moving *around* its object, in the depth of space, with some aspect of the object always escaping it.

Although highly schematic, this summary of Lyotard's article brings out two important notions or major themes common to Lyotard's work—and to that of a number of his contemporaries. First, the *distance* that separates subject from object is not conceived of as a prelinguistic disparity that discourse vainly seeks to suppress after the fact, nor is the ultimate inaccessibility of the object attributed to the *inadequacy* of language in bridging the gap between subject and objective reality; rather, subject, object, and the distance or distinction that separates them emerge simultaneously with the assumption of language. The "lost" object was never present; representation is the positing of a presence that never was, rather than a detour from that presence. In other words, representation mutely designates the unthinkable: originary absence or pure negativity, death. Furthermore, desire is not a negative longing for a lost origin, but the positive force of a will to knowledge—knowledge conceived not as recovery, but as production of a discourse that posits its referent. Secondly, discourse is anything but the *expression* (adequate or inadequate) of a subject's interiority ("we can only say . . . what we are not"). Subjectivity, or desire, speaks through language, but only in its silences and interstices. The subject does not "speak itself," yet it exists only insofar as it speaks; its ineffability is not the result of a division, the splitting of an originally unified ego into a prelinguistic self and a linguistic, alienated self.

That originary non-coincidence of the speaking subject with an objectified ego received its most famous formulation, of course, in Lacan's theory of the mirror stage, according to which the child's first apprehension of himself as a unified entity comes with his identification with his own mirror image. Thus the subject's conception of his self is from the outset that of an ideal, or imaginary ego, or Other. The mirror stage prepares the subject's entry into language via the assumption of the pronoun "je," which, as Benveniste, in particular, has emphasized, is an "empty" signifier, or shifter, serving only to indicate *celui qui parle* as the source of each separate instance of discourse. The speaking subject, or "je," in a perpetual process of becoming, is a dispersed self that can never coincide with its fictive ego:

> Cette forme [l'image spéculaire] situe l'instance du *moi*, dès avant sa détermination sociale, dans une ligne de fiction, à jamais irréductible pour le seul individu,—ou plutôt, qui ne rejoindra qu'asymptotiquement le devenir du sujet, quel que soit le succès des synthèses dialectiques par quoi il doit résoudre en tant que *je* sa discordance d'avec sa propre réalité.[37]

> This form [the specular image] situates the agency of the ego, before its social determination, in a fictional direction, which will always remain irreducible for the individual alone, or rather which will only rejoin the coming-into-being of the subject asymptotically, whatever the success of the dialectical syntheses by which he must resolve as *I* his discordance with his own reality.

Language—the language of the Other—names the non-self; the self speaks silently through its manipulation of that language. This is not simply to resituate the instance of individuality at a deeper level, in the recesses of the unconscious, for the Lacanian unconscious itself is structured like a language: as opposed to the content-laden unconscious of traditional Freudianism, Lacan's conception of the unconscious is eminently humorous.

Although Lyotard is not entirely in agreement with Lacan,[38] he shares with him a humoristic notion of the subject and of discourse— both "subjective" and "objective." If objective language is that which posits the objects of knowledge, subjective language is the silent disruption of the language of knowledge. A passage from *Dérive à partir de Marx et Freud* that articulates the two deserves to be quoted at length:

> C'est dans le langage de connaissance lui-même que le désir fait des déplacements, des condensations, des caviardages, subvertit les relations régulières, laisse des traces. . . . La vérité *ne parle pas, stricto sensu;* elle travaille. La connaissance parle, elle appartient à la distance, à la rupture avec la chose, que le discours exige. Elle produit une théorie dans l'espace du possible, délivré des choses, et s'enquiert ensuite de trouver dans les choses ce qui pourra servir de modèle de référence pour son discours, de domaine d'interprétation. La vérité n'est pas ce qui opère cette disjonction secondaire, mais elle opère *dans* cette disjonction. Elle laisse sa trace sur le discours, la fulgurance d'un lapsus, d'un silence, d'une métaphore interdite, d'un mot-valise, d'un non-sens, d'un cri; mais ces effets viennent d'*ailleurs,* signalent leur étrangeté en ce qu'ils font violence à l'ordre (de langage réglé) où ils s'inscrivent. ("Oedipe Juif," 167–68/35)[39]

> It is within the language of cognition itself that desire displaces, condenses, suppresses, subverts regular relations, leaves traces. . . . Truth *doesn't speak, stricto sensu;* it works. Cognition speaks, it belongs to distance, to the rupture with things that discourse requires. It produces a theory within the space of possibility, freed from things, and seeks afterwards to find in things what can serve as a referential model for its discourse, as a field of interpretation. Truth is not what operates this secondary disjunction, but it operates *in* this disjunction. It leaves its traces on discourse, the fulguration of a slip, a silence, a forbidden metaphor, a portmanteau word, a non-sense, a cry; but these effects come from *elsewhere,* signaling their strangeness in that they do violence to the order (of regulated language) in which they inscribe themselves.

The transcendental signified has disappeared, as it were, from both "ends" of discourse: at its origin, the person expressed, and as its *telos,* the object recovered. That double disappearance signals the demise of two types of mastery, or authority: paternity, or the author's status as creator of his own *parole,* as well as the self-possession or self-knowledge it implies, and sovereignty,[40] or the possession of the "objective" world through scientific discourse. Theoretical discourse, asserts Lyotard, must dispassionately relinquish its pretensions to truth;[41] classic theory must be countered by a nonteleological, "sophistic" discourse which "cares nothing for reasons and ends, but has a passion for means alone, and whose only strength, like that of the weak, consists in setting traps."[42] It is time criticism had both the humility to acknowledge the role of desire ("the despair of irony, which feeds the false modesty of the logician") in theoretical discourse and the audacity to affirm it, not as a lack (*Penia*), but as a means:

> L'humour procède d'un Eros qui est tout *Poros,* rien que moyen de moyenner, comme d'une logique sans aporie et d'une politique sans utopie. A ce désir il faut des dieux beaucoup plus retors que celui qui s'est proclamé la vérité, et des divinations sans péché. ("Humour en sémiothéologie," in *Rudiments,* 58)

> Humor comes from an Eros that is all *Poros,* nothing but a means of producing means, as from a logic without aporia or a politics without utopia. This desire demands gods far wilier than he who declared himself the truth, and divinations without sin.

The only effective strategy with which to confront a zealous *théorie-vérité* is an impious *théorie-fiction,* "not a derision of theory, but its parody," the freely wandering thinking of art and of scientific speculation ("Apathie," in *Rudiments,* 29).[43] Lyotard insists, however, that the recourse to fiction is not a retreat but a tactic of infiltration—a means of assuming the master's voice and daring to explore, *apathetically,* the logical consequences of his position to their most illogical conclusion:

> N'espérez donc pas que les artistes de la théorie-fiction laisseront le champ libre à la théorie-vérité: au contraire ils seront *aussi* présents dans cette vieille bataille, et ce sera pour argumenter. Ainsi la dissimulation sera complète, la parodie ne se laissant pas discerner (en termes de vrai et de faux) de son prétendu "modèle." Seuls n'y perdront pas la tête et le coeur ceux qui sont guéris du pathos théorique, les apathiques. ("Apathie," in *Rudiments,* 30)

> Do not hope, then, that the artists of theory-fiction will leave the field open to theory-truth: on the contrary, they will *also* be present in this ancient battle, and they will be there to argue. Thus the dissimulation will be complete, the parody being indistinguishable (in terms of true and false) from its alleged "model." Only the apathetic—those who are cured of theoretical pathos—will neither lose their heads nor lose heart.

It should be remarked, if it is not evident from the preceding, that Lyotard's stance is first and foremost a political one, a position vis-à-vis the language of power. It is based on the conviction that, given the universality and homogeneity—and particularly the dialectical prowess—of the discourse of power, the only viable means of opposition is subversion from within by attacking the *forms* of representation through which that power is exercised (represented); art, literature, and philosophy are among those forms. The direct confrontation of a power structure in its own terms is infinitely less threatening to the System, which has an inexhaustible capacity for dialectically absorbing its opponents and in fact needs them, as the master needs the slave's recognition; but a slave who is resolutely disinterested in mastery is a troublesome thing indeed. The accuracy of this theory has, I might add, been well born out in the violently defensive responses that poststructuralist criticism has elicited from traditional theoreticians who find themselves incapable of disarming a logic that quite simply escapes their apprehension. American critics have, on the whole, been surprisingly slow to recognize the fundamentally political nature of what might be most aptly qualified as a "guerrilla criticism," in that it does not openly attack a type of ideology that could only be strengthened by such a confrontation. However diverse the tactics of its various practitioners—not only Lyotard, but Derrida, Barthes, Deleuze, Foucault, and others—"humorous" critical discourse is the product of a politics of subversion.

Lyotard's notion of humor, as he himself acknowledges ("Humour," in *Rudiments,* 58, n. 3) owes much to Gilles Deleuze's *Présentation de Sacher-Masoch,* in which he opposes *l'ironie sadique*—the will to overthrow the law, or paternal instance—to *l'humour masochiste:*

> Simplement le masochiste attaque la loi par l'autre côté. Nous appelons humour, non plus le mouvement qui remonte de la loi vers un plus haut principe, mais celui qui descend de la loi vers ses conséquences. Nous connaissons tous des manières de tourner la loi par excès de zèle: c'est par une scrupuleuse application qu'on prétend alors en montrer l'absurdité, et en attendre précisément ce désordre qu'elle est censée interdire et conjurer. On prend la loi au mot, à la lettre; on ne conteste pas son caractère ultime ou premier. . . . La loi n'est plus renversée ironiquement, par remontée vers un principe, mais tournée humoristiquement, obliquement, par approfondissement des conséquences.[44]

> It is just that the masochist attacks the law from the other side. We call humor, not the movement that ascends from the law toward a higher principle, but that which descends from the law toward its consequences. We all know ways of getting around the law through excessive zeal: it is by the scrupulous application of the law that one

proposes to show its absurdity and to anticipate precisely that disorder which it is supposed to forbid and avert. One takes the law literally, follows it to the letter; one doesn't contest its ultimate or fundamental status. . . . No longer is the law overturned ironically, through an ascent to a principle, but humorously, obliquely circumvented, through the development of its consequences.

The ironist identifies with the paternal instance ("L'ironie, . . . c'est l'exercice d'un surmoi dévorant"—"Irony is the exercise of a voracious superego" [*SM,* 106]) who incarnates the immutable and absolute form of authority which is the Institution; the masochist displaces authority onto the figure of the mother by means of the *contract,* or pact, thus substituting the conventional for the absolute. It is not difficult to translate the Freudian language of *Sacher-Masoch* into the structuralist language of *Logique du sens,* where irony, "the art of depths or heights," is associated with a meaning/expression, depth/surface model of discourse and the traditional depth- or meaning-oriented criticism founded upon it, while humor, "art of surfaces,"[45] refers to Saussure-inspired critical approaches that appeal to the conventional, differential aspects of language.

For his reading of Lewis Carroll in *Logique du sens,* Deleuze adopts the Stoic theory of language according to which a statement brings four types of relationships into play: it designates a thing or state of being, expresses a belief, signifies a conceptual order, and produces a meaning. The theory is of particular interest to the reader of postmodern literature and criticism in that it distinguishes between *signification* and *meaning (sens).* The term *signification* refers to the relationship of a statement to general universal concepts. The signifying function of language always entails a logical ordering of propositions leading up to a conclusion (*LS,* 24). Thus signification works only "dans le bon sens," that is, in one direction, the "right" direction, and admits of only one meaning, the "good" one. Logical thought always moves "from the most differentiated to the least differentiated," in order to arrive at a final unity. As "good sense," *le bon sens* is indissociable from "common sense" (94–95); the two together constitute *la doxa*—which we have already met through Barthes, in the stereotype, or *la bêtise.* To the *doxa* Deleuze opposes the *paradoxe,* the proposition having a double or contradictory meaning, which, as everyone knows, violates common sense. However, *le sens,* which is neither signification nor designation nor expression, but the pure "expressed" ("l'exprimé de la proposition" [30]), is pure meaning, independent of all logical conditions (e.g., the law of noncontradiction) or grammatical modalities (e.g., negation, tense, etc.). Even a statement devoid of signification is not meaningless. Hence the paradox of "impossible objects—the round square, matter without extension, *perpetuum mobile,* the mountain without a valley, etc.":

> Les propositions qui désignent des objets contradictoires ont elles-mêmes un sens. Leur désignation pourtant ne peut en aucun cas être effectuée; et elles n'ont aucune signification, qui définirait le genre de possibilité d'une telle effectuation. Elles sont sans signification, c'est-à-dire, absurdes. Elles n'en ont pas moins un sens, et les deux notions d'absurde et de non-sens ne doivent pas être confondues. (*LS,* 49)

> Propositions that designate contradictory objects have a meaning themselves. Their designation cannot, however, be effectuated under any circumstances; and they have no signification, which would define the genus of possibility of such an effectuation. They are without signification, that is, absurd. They nonetheless have a meaning, and the two notions of the absurd and of nonsense must not be confused.

Neither a principle nor an origin, meaning is produced at the surface of the text by the interplay of relations among signifiers which are meaningless in themselves. It is the mechanisms of this production of meanings—*dans tous les sens*—which have been the primary preoccupation of much recent literature and criticism:

> Les auteurs que la coûtume récente a nommés structuralistes n'ont peut-être pas d'autre point commun, mais ce point est l'essentiel: le sens, non pas du tout comme apparence, mais comme effet de surface et de position. . . . Et lorsque le structuralisme montre de cette façon que le sens est produit par le non-sens et son perpétuel déplacement, qu'il naît de la position respective d'éléments qui ne sont pas par eux-mêmes "signifiants," on n'y verra en revanche nul rapprochement avec ce qui fut appelé philosophie de l'absurde: Lewis Carroll oui, Camus non. Car, pour la philosophie de l'absurde, le non-sens est ce qui s'oppose au sens dans un rapport simple avec lui; si bien que l'absurde se définit toujours par un défaut de sens, un manque (il n'y en a pas assez . . .). Du point de vue de la structure, au contraire, du sens, il y en a toujours trop: excès produit et surproduit par le non-sens. (*LS,* 88–89)

> The authors that recent custom has named structuralists may have no other point in common, but this point is the essential one: [they conceive of] meaning [sense], not at all as appearance, but as an effect of surface and position. . . . And when structuralism shows in this manner that sense [meaning] is produced by nonsense and its perpetual displacement, that is, is a product of the respective position of elements that are not in themselves "meaningful," one should not attempt to draw any parallel with what was called the philosophy of the absurd: Lewis Carroll yes, Camus no. Because, for

the philosophy of the absurd, nonsense is that which is opposed to sense, in a simple relationship with it: so that the absurd is always defined as an absence of meaning, a lack (there is not enough of it ...). From the standpoint of structure, on the contrary, there is always too much meaning: an excess produced and overproduced by nonsense.

If the influence of Freud on recent criticism has been as great as that of Saussure—and so complementary to it—it is because psychoanalysis too is an exploration of surfaces, and not of murky depths, as many have complained. The processes of the unconscious, free of the constraints of logic and of referentiality, have offered a privileged domain of reference for the study of how texts produce meanings. Those who decry the superficiality of postmodern literature and of poststructuralist criticism generally do so in the name of meaning. They confuse, it seems, *signification* and *sens*, in assuming that what cannot be reduced to a sole signification is meaningless, that an excess constitutes a lack. Hence the "pseudo-sense of the tragic" that Deleuze abhorred in so many critical writings on postmodernity.[46] This tragic outlook is doubtless partly responsible, as well, for the failure of many critics to perceive the extent to which much great literature of all periods (and this may be a criterion for its greatness) not only acknowledges but even affirms the absence of Transcendence (as ground for meaning and for the writing subject), turning that absence to the benefit of art.

The following chapters constitute attempts to read selected works from both the modern and postmodern periods with an eye to whatever traces of an ironic or a humorous world view may be discernible in each text. The results vary widely from author to author, for the paradigm irony/humor provides only the loosest critical parameters within which to work; this has the advantage, however, of allowing the critic to respect as much as possible the specificity of diverse works. I have found, no doubt predictably, some rays of humor in each of them. But that humor manifests itself in very different forms and of course to greater or lesser degrees, at times being overshadowed by irony; it is the distinctive interplay of irony and humor in each text that I have sought to bring out in my readings.

3 : Stendhal
Nostalgia

The novel tells the story of two lovers who, like Eros and Psyche, are never allowed to come into full contact with each other. When they can see each other they are separated by an unbreachable distance; when they can touch, it has to be in a darkness imposed by a totally arbitrary and irrational decision, an act of the gods. The myth is that of the unovercomable distance which must always prevail between the selves, and it thematizes the ironic distance that Stendhal the writer always believed prevailed between his pseudonymous and nominal entities. As such, it reaffirms Schlegel's definition of irony as "permanent parabasis" and singles out this novel as one of the few novels of novels, as the allegory of irony. (RT, 209)

So de Man concludes "The Rhetoric of Temporality," inviting the reader to consider *La Chartreuse de Parme* as an exemplary work on irony—irony, defined as a distance between selves: both between self and other and between the essential and phenomenal selves of a single individual. But if *La Chartreuse* is the allegory of that irony, might not then the moment of mystification to which it refers be the *Vie de Henry Brulard*, Beyle's earlier attempt to fuse his phenomenal and essential selves into a single being through an act of writing?

Qu'ai-je été, que suis-je, en vérité, je serais bien embarrassé de le dire. . . . Je devrais écrire ma vie, je saurai peut-être enfin, quand cela sera fini dans deux ou trois ans, ce que j'ai été, gai ou triste, homme d'esprit ou sot, homme de courage ou peureux, et enfin au total heureux ou malheureux.[1]

What have I been, what am I, in truth I would be hard put to say. . . . I ought to write my life; perhaps I will know at last, when I've finished, in two or three years, what I have been, cheerful or sad, a man of wit or a fool, brave or timorous, in short, on the whole happy or unhappy.

Imagine Sartre's Garcin in good faith, seeking to "put his life in order," to sift out his *être-en-soi* from the confusion of an unfinished existence. Naïve perhaps, but in good faith, Beyle is acutely aware from the outset that "hell is other people," whence his oft-reiterated distrust for the judgments of others: "What have I been? I couldn't say. What friend, however enlightened, can I ask? . . . To what friend have I ever said a

word of my disappointments in love?" (*HB*, 7). Even the author's closest friends have not been privy to his most intimate feelings; *a fortiori,*
the casual acquaintance can scarcely have penetrated the surface of his
social persona. It is of little use, then, to consult the writings of others
in a quest for self-knowledge:

> Dernièrement, j'ai appris en le lisant dans un livre . . . que quelqu'un
> avait pu me trouver brillant. Il y a quelques années j'avais vu la
> même chose à peu près dans un livre, alors à la mode, de lady Mor-
> gan. J'avais oublié cette belle qualité qui m'a fait tant d'ennemis. Ce
> n'était peut-être que l'apparence de la qualité. (17)

> Recently, I read in a book . . . that someone had found me brilliant.
> A few years ago I read nearly the same thing in a then-popular book
> by Lady Morgan. I had forgotten that fine quality which has made
> me so many enemies. Perhaps it was only the appearance of the
> quality.

A sole solution remains: to write one's own life, a book of *Confessions,* an examination of conscience (*HB*, 10), with utter and complete
candor, "without lying . . . , without deluding myself" (11). The project
is of course an eminently romantic one, positing as it does an essential
self defined as pure interiority, soul, sentiment, à la Rousseau, à la Chateaubriand; yet these are precisely the authors whom Beyle singles out
as negative models, or predecessors in the genre *not* to be imitated. His
repugnance for their collossal egotism translates into a formal
dilemma: to write in the first or the third person?

> Cette idée [d'écrire ma vie] me sourit. Oui, mais cette effroyable
> quantité de *Je* et de *Moi*! Il y a de quoi donner de l'humeur au lecteur
> le plus bénévole. *Je* et *Moi,* ce serait, au talent près, comme M. de
> Chateaubriand, ce roi des *égotistes.* . . .
> On pourrait écrire, il est vrai, en se servant de la troisième per-
> sonne, *il* fit, *il* dit. Oui, mais comment rendre compte des mouve-
> ments intérieurs de l'âme? (8)

> This idea of writing appeals to me. Yes, but what an appalling
> amount of *I*'s and *Me*'s! It's enough to annoy the most benevolent
> reader. *I* and *Me*—apart from the talent, it would be like M. de Cha-
> teaubriand, that king of *egotists.* . . . One could write, it's true, using
> the third person, *he* did, *he* said. Yes, but how would one account for
> the inner impulses of the soul?

Consistent with his overriding concern for sincere and candid self-
expression, Beyle feels constrained to adopt the same narrative voice as
Jean-Jacques, though not without considerable discomfiture, to which
he periodically gives vent:

Mais qui diable aura le courage de couler à fond, de lire cet amas ex-
cissif de *je* et de *moi*? Cela me paraît *puant* à moi-même. C'est là le
défaut de ce genre d'écrit où, d'ailleurs, je ne puis relever la fadeur
par aucune sauce de charlatanisme. Oserais-je ajouter: *comme les*
Confessions *de Rousseau*? (*HB,* 224)

But who the devil will have the courage to go through with it, to
read this mass of *I*'s and *me*'s? It seems *revolting* even to me. That is
the drawback of this kind of writing, whose insipidity I cannot even
spice up with a sauce of charlatanism. Dare I add: *like Rousseau's*
Confessions?

The reference to "charlatanism" alludes to what Beyle considers to be
Rousseau's most unforgivable fault: his ultimate dishonesty, his failure
to be totally sincere, all the *I*'s and the *me*'s notwithstanding. For the
author of the *Confessions* did not hesitate to rework, supplement, or
embellish the materials supplied to him by his memory in order to
produce a well-ordered, seamless narrative—not to mention a flattering
self-portrait.[2] Thus Beyle will remind himself as he writes that he must
not "lie with artifice like J.-J. Rousseau" (391).

In the interest of absolute veracity, he proposes to recount only
what he has witnessed with his own eyes, rejecting secondhand reports
or representations as mere hearsay; as he easily forgets this self-
imposed constraint, however, the text of *Brulard* is punctuated with
self-admonishments: "But all this is history, in truth recounted by eye-
witnesses, but which I didn't see. In the future, I only want to tell . . .
what *I saw*" (*HB,* 52; Beyle's italics). Furthermore, Beyle, who abandoned *Brulard* after four months of daily writing, never edited, re-
vised, or refined the text; that he may, in fact, have never intended to,
so as not to vitiate the candor of the first draft, is suggested by an early
marginal note: "Perhaps, by not correcting this first draft, I will
manage not to lie out of vanity" (68).[3] In any case, Beyle rarely erased
or deleted material, although he reread daily what he had written the
previous day, often adding clarifications or qualifications as well as reflections on the difficulties he encountered in the execution of his
project, and prescriptions as to how to proceed. Thus the result is far
more than an engaging collection of personal reminiscences; it is an
intriguing document on the problems and pitfalls inherent in the writing of autobiography, as that genre is traditionally defined.

The traditional definition of autobiography as self-representation
depends upon an essentialist conception of the self, or, in more contemporary terms, upon the conviction that "I," the speaking subject,
has a single, stable referent. Moreover, the appearance of the term *autobiography* at the end of the eighteenth century and the rise in popularity of the confessional genre during the late eighteenth and early nine-

teenth centuries coincide with the emergence of the romantic notion of personhood [4] and the simultaneous development of the concept of the author as the sole authority, or single individual responsible for (and therefore expressed through) his writings.[5] The determination of the private subject (rather than the universal) as the object of knowledge is therefore a modern phenomenon. However, the notion of truth involved here remains a fundamentally Platonic one, that of an abstract eternal essence to be glimpsed in a dazzling vision or a brilliant insight; which is to say that seeing (what is hidden behind a veil of appearance) remains the only valid mode of knowing. Thus the passionate assertion of veracity with which Rousseau introduces his *Confessions,* claiming that he therein unveils his soul as only God has seen it ("I have shown myself such as I was . . . I have unveiled my inmost self [*dévoilé mon intérieur*] such as You Yourself have seen it. Eternal Being . . .")[6] epitomizes the pretensions of romantic autobiography.

In according a privileged status to the faculty of vision, then, Beyle follows, however unwittingly, the example of Jean-Jacques. In announcing his intention to "look back a moment" (*HB,* 93) in order to comprehend his life, he is in fact proposing to effect that romantic-ironic *dédoublement* which consists of stepping outside oneself to constitute the *moi* as an object of knowledge. Nonetheless, his initial skepticism regarding the feasibility of that project ("What eye can see itself?" he worries in chapter 1), combined with his stubborn refusal to "cheat" à la Rousseau, will work to undermine his autobiographical enterprise. This is inevitable, for the autobiographical project he has designed for himself is in fact impossible to execute without resorting to narrative sleight. To weave a discontinuous series of experiences into a continuous narration is to impose a unity or meaning upon them in retrospect, a meaning which itself can only emanate from a writing subject seeking to order the disparate moments of his past in a logical—hence teleological—sequence, the culmination of which is a predetermined ego-ideal. However, the desiring (writing) subject can never coincide with the self-image it has thusly ratified; or, to recall the Sartrian (Hegelian, etc.) categories evoked earlier, the *être-pour-soi* can never exist in the mode of an *en-soi.* Translated into linguistic-psychoanalytic terminology, then, the unrealizable goal of the traditional autobiographer would be to fuse the "*je*" *de l'énonciation* (that discontinuous speaking subject "I" which is never signified, only designated as the source of an individual instance of discourse) and the "*je*" *de l'énoncé* (which is, in autobiographical narrative, an objectified entity, or "*il*").[7] Beyle has said as much in affirming that the source of vision cannot be its own object.

Nevertheless, he sets out to write his life on the assumption that by so doing he will simply be reproducing (representing) a past which has an inherent "objective" order, and which, once set forth on paper, may then be probed for its subjective significance. The result is an inherently paradoxical autobiographical project which in effect constitutes an attempt to synthesize the traditional autobiographical narrative as defined by Philippe Lejeune in *Le Pacte autobiographique*[8] with the more "modern" *autoportrait* described in Michel Beaujour's *Miroirs d'encre* as a montage of autobiographical fragments organized according to a system of analogical, spatial relationships, rather than a linear, temporal logic.[9] It will soon become apparent to Beyle that his memory enables him to "see" only disparate, isolated, and often incomplete scenes from his past, and that if he is to bestow upon them any logical continuity, he will have to "novelize" (*faire du roman*).[10] What will gradually emerge in the *Vie de Henry Brulard* is an implicit understanding that any recovery of lost time can only be a fiction, or myth, and that furthermore, that myth, however personal its author might presume it to be, is always also a product of his culture.[11]

The opening "scene"/inaugural passage of *Brulard*—a panoramic view of Rome—serves as an emblem of Beyle's conception of autobiography; in retrospect, however, it also foreshadows, both thematically and formally, the fate of the text. From a vantage point of the type favored by romantic heroes, the narrator apprehends, in a sweeping glance, all of the eternal city, past and present:

> Je me trouvais ce matin, 16 octobre 1832, à San-Pietro *in Montorio,* sur le mont Janicule, à Rome, il faisait un soleil magnifique. Un léger vent de sirocco à peine sensible faisait flotter quelques petits nuages blancs au-dessus du mont Albano, une chaleur délicieuse régnait dans l'air, j'étais heureux de vivre. Je distinguais parfaitement Frascati et Castel-Gandolfo qui sont à quatre lieues d'ici, la villa Aldobrandini où est cette sublime fresque de Judith du Dominiquin. Je vois parfaitement le mur blanc qui marque les réparations faites en dernier lieu par le prince F[rançois] Borghèse, celui-là même que je vis à Wagram colonel d'un régiment de cuirassiers, le jour où M. de Noue mon ami eut la jambe emportée. Bien plus loin, j'aperçois la roche de Palestrina et la maison blanche de Castel San-Pietro qui fut autrefois sa forteresse. Au-dessous du mur contre lequel je m'appuie sont les grands orangers du verger des capucins, puis le Tibre et le prieuré de Malte, un peu après sur la droite le tombeau de Cécilia Metella, Saint-Paul et la pyramide de Cestius. En face de moi j'aperçois Sainte-Marie-Majeure et les longues lignes du Palais de Monte-Cavallo. Toute la Rome ancienne et moderne, depuis l'ancienne voie Appienne avec les ruines de ses tombeaux et de ses aqueducs jusqu'au magnifique jardin du Pincio bâti par les Français, se déploie à la vue.
>
> Ce lieu est unique au monde, me disais-je en rêvant, et la Rome

ancienne malgré moi l'emportait sur la moderne, tous les souvenirs
de Tite-Live me revenaient en foule. Sur le mont Albano, à gauche
du couvent j'apercevais les prés d'Annibal.

Quelle vue magnifique! c'est donc ici que la *Transfiguration* de Ra-
phaël a été admirée pendant deux siècles et demi. Quelle différence
avec la triste galerie de marbre gris où elle est enterrée aujourd'hui au
fond du Vatican! Ainsi pendant deux cent cinquante ans ce chef-
d'oeuvre a été ici, deux cent cinquante ans! . . . Ah! dans trois mois
j'aurai cinquante ans, est-il bien possible! (*HB,* 5-6)

This morning, October 16, 1832, I was at San-Pietro *in Montorio,* on
Mount Janicule, in Rome; it was a magnificent sunny day. A light si-
rocco, scarcely perceptible, was wafting a few little white clouds over
the Mount Albano, a delightful warmth filled the air, I was happy to
be alive. I could distinguish perfectly Frascati and Castel-Gandolfo,
which are four leagues from here, [and] the villa Aldobrandini, where
the sublime fresco of Judith, by Il Domenichino, is located. I see perfectly the white wall that marks the recent reparations done by the
prince F[rancesco] Borghese, the very same whom I saw at Wagram
as colonel of a regiment of mounted soldiers the day that Mr. Noue,
my friend, had his leg blown off. Much farther off, I see the rock of
Palestrina and the white house of Castel San-Pietro which used to be
its fortress. Above the wall on which I am leaning are the tall orange
trees of the Capucine orchards, then the Tiber and the priory of Mal-
ta, [and] a little further on, on the right, the tomb of Cecilia Metella,
Saint Paul, and the pyramid of Cestius. Opposite me, I see Santa-
Maria-Maggiore and the long lines of the Palace of Monte-Cavallo.
All of ancient and modern Rome, from the former Appian Way
with its ruins of tombs and aqueducts, to the magnificent gardens of
Pincio built by the French, is spread out under my view.

This place is unique in the world, I said to myself dreamily, and
despite myself, ancient Rome prevailed over the modern, all the
memories of Titus Livius were crowding in upon me. Upon the
Mount Albano, to the left of the convent, I could make out the
fields of Hannibal.

What a magnificent view! so it is here that Raphael's *Transfiguration* was admired for two and a half centuries. What a difference
from the gloomy gallery of gray marble in the depths of the Vatican
where it is buried today! Thus for two hundred and fifty years this
masterpiece was here, two hundred and fifty years! . . . Ah! in three
months I will be fifty, is it really possible?

The totalizing gaze that Beyle casts upon the city of Rome and its history from a position above and beyond it is analogous to that which
he will seek to turn upon his own life; the written transcription of the
panorama he supposedly beholds leads directly, by an associative process ("two hundred and fifty years . . . fifty years"), into a reflection

on the author's advancing years and the idea that it is time he initiate a quest for self-knowledge. The figure fifty is evidently associated with death in the narrator's mind, a fact which he will later reaffirm in re-iterating that it was at San Pietro in Montorio that he first had "the brilliant idea that I was going to be fifty and that it was time to think about my departure, and, beforehand, to give myself the pleasure of looking back for a moment" (*HB,* 93). Therefore, the opening passage of Brulard, which moves logically from a celebration of life in the luminous atmosphere of what will later prove to be an edenic space, to an allusion to the narrator's mortality inspired by the memory of Raphael's *Transfiguration* (now "buried" in a "gloomy gallery of gray marble"), serves as a matrix, or pre-text, for the autobiography. Indeed, it serves as a pretext in more than one sense, for not only, it seems, was the passage actually written in 1835, but on October 16, 1832, Beyle was not in Rome.[12] The panoramic vision of Rome, witnessed by a "dying" ("I am going to be fifty") man, is a writer's artifice, his solution to a fundamental problem of autobiography: How do I begin? The prob-lem of closure will solve itself. In fact, then, all the "je vois" and "j'aper-çois" are not literally true; presumably, however, the terms may be taken figuratively, as referring to objects of the mind's eye, and in this respect they have the same status as those memory-objects which Beyle will represent to himself in the course of his writing. Further-more, the passage exemplifies a textual mechanism which operates throughout *Brulard:* a vision, or supposed vision, evokes a memory, or supposed memory, which the author transcribes in writing. Thus the "sight" of the Villa Aldobrandini reminds Beyle of Il Domenichino's Judith fresco, which is actually a tondo, and located elsewhere; he con-fuses it with the Cavalier d'Arpino's fresco of Judith, which adorns a ceiling of the villa (see *HB,* 418, n. 7). The white wall repaired by Fran-cesco Borghese evokes another tableau from the narrator's past, an image of the prince "whom I saw at Wagram," although Beyle was not at the battle of Wagram (418, n. 8). Finally, all of ancient Roman his-tory comes back to the narrator, in a flood of "memories" which, need-less to say, he could only have acquired indirectly. Scene one does not constitute a terribly auspicious prelude to a "veracious journal" (397), if it portends anything of the accuracy of the narrator's memory, his reliability, and the nature of his sources.

Of course, the only real falsehood in the passage is the insinuation that the author was at Wagram, a sophism of which he hastens to repent:

Mais combien ne faut-il pas de précautions pour ne pas mentir!

Par exemple au commencement du premier chapitre, il y a une chose qui peut sembler une hâblerie: non, mon lecteur, je n'étais point soldat à Wagram en 1809.

Il faut que vous sachiez que quarante-cinq ans avant vous il était de mode d'avoir été soldat sous Napoléon. C'est donc aujourd'hui, 1835, un mensonge tout à fait digne d'être écrit que de faire entendre indirectement et sans mensonge absolu (*jesuitico more*) qu'on a été soldat à Wagram. (*HB*, 11)

But how many precautions are needed not to lie! For example, at the beginning of the first chapter, there is something that may seem to be a boast: no, my reader, I was never a soldier at Wagram in 1809. You should know that forty-five years before you it was fashionable to have been a soldier under Napoleon. Thus today, in 1835, it is a lie perfectly worthy of being written to imply indirectly and without an absolute lie (*jesuitico more*) that one was a soldier at Wagram.

Thus it is that Beyle becomes aware from the outset that writing is a seductive process, that what is "worthy of being written" may not correspond to objective truth, as he defines it. Writing has a disconcerting way of engendering more writing according to its own logic, a process of association of signifiers that shows little respect for the presumed referentiality of the text. "But I'm getting carried away, I digress," grumbles Beyle scarcely a page after his retraction of the Wagram account. "I will be unintelligible if I don't follow chronological order" (12). "Will I have the courage to write these confessions in an intelligible fashion?" he wonders a few pages later. "I am supposed to be narrating, and I am writing *considerations*" (21). Narrative, as he conceives of it, should serve to represent a real referent or series of referents ordered according to their own logic, that is, a linear, chronological, causal logic. Much of the second chapter is devoted to prescriptions for maintaining his ironic detachment by resisting the seductions of writing, not infrequently associated with the remembered charms of his mistresses:

Pour les considérer le plus philosophiquement possible et tâcher ainsi de les dépouiller de l'auréole qui me fait *aller les yeux*, qui m'éblouit et m'ôte la faculté de voir distinctement, j'*ordonnerai* ces dames (langage mathématique) selon leurs diverses qualités. . . .

Je cherche à détruire le charme, le *dazzling* des événements, en les considérant ainsi militairement. C'est ma seule ressource pour arriver au vrai. (19; Beyle's emphasis)

To consider them as philosophically as possible and to divest them of the halo that makes my eyes pop, that dazzles me and deprives me of the faculty of seeing distinctly, I *will order* these ladies (mathematical language) according to their divers qualities. . . . I seek to destroy the charm, the *dazzling* of events, by considering them so militarily. It is my only expedient for arriving at the truth.

In hopes of containing the excesses of Beyle the sentimentalist, Beyle the rationalist appeals to the sciences of mathematics, philosophy, and finally botany, to discipline his text:

A force d'employer des méthodes philosophiques, par exemple à force de classer mes amis de jeunesse par *genres*, comme M. Adrien de Jussieu fait pour ses plantes (en botanique), je cherche à atteindre cette vérité qui me fuit. . . .
Donc, en classant ma vie comme une collection de plantes, je trouverai:
Enfance, et première éducation, de 1786 à 1800.................. 15 ans
Service militaire de 1800 à 1803... 3 —
Seconde éducation, amours ridicules...........................
                                                                            (*HB*, 21)

By using philosophical methods, for example, by classifying my childhood friends by *genuses*, as M. Adrien de Jussieu does for his plants (in botany), I seek to reach that truth which eludes me. . . .
Thus, by classifying my life like a collection of plants, I find:
Childhood and early education, from 1786 to 1800......... 15 years
Military service from 1800 to 1803.................................... 3 —
Second education, ridiculous love affairs....................

But the device that Beyle will exploit most consistently throughout the autobiography in his efforts to attain objective truth is the *sketch* (unquotable, alas), which enables him to literally inscribe an image in his text, that is, to import empirical evidence ("seeing is believing") to ensure the veracity of his memoirs. By drawing for himself and for the reader what he pictures in his mind's eye, Beyle apparently supposes, he guarantees a minimal distortion of perceived reality. Yet the sketches themselves require clarification and explanation by a written text which therefore becomes incomprehensible without them, so that, as Gérard Genette has aptly observed, writing and image are inextricably interwoven to constitute the text of *Brulard*.[13] Despite their intended function, then, as guarantors of objective truth, Beyle's sketches, as well as the related "memorative inscriptions"–*J. vaisa voirla5* ("Je vais avoir la cinquantaine"), scribbled inside his waistband, lists of his mistresses scratched in the sand, etc.–which he reproduces in his text, bear even more persuasive witness to the "pleasure of writing" that is the author's ultimate justification for indulging in an orgy of *I*'s and *me*'s.[14] In so privileging the "pleasure of the text," the author of *Brulard* is jeopardizing his ironic mastery of his discourse.

Nevertheless, Beyle clings, for a time at least, to his conviction that images do not lie, reserving all his skepticism for the accuracy of his interpretations:

> Mais le lecteur, s'il s'en trouve jamais pour ces puérilités, verra sans peine que tous mes *pourquoi*, toutes mes explications peuvent être très fautives. Je n'ai que des images fort nettes, toutes mes explications me viennent en écrivant ceci, quarante-cinq ans après les événements. (*HB*, 44)

> But the reader, if there ever is one for all these puerilities, will easily see that all my *why*'s, all my explanations may be quite faulty. I only have very sharp images, all my explanations come to me as I write this, forty-five years after the events.

To supplement his memory, and as if to palliate the distortive effects of his subjective contributions, he promises himself repeatedly to verify historical and biographical information, particularly dates, in the Grenoble archives and other presumably reliable documents. A favorite figure for the author's past is that of the time-worn fresco, which he struggles to restore to its original state:

> En écrivant ma vie en 1835, j'y fais bien des découvertes . . . ce sont de grands morceaux de fresques sur un mur, qui depuis longtemps oubliés apparaissent tout à coup, et à côté de ces morceaux bien conservés sont comme je l'ai dit plusieurs fois de grands espaces où l'on ne voit que la brique du mur. L'éparvérage, le crépi sur lequel la fresque était peinte est tombé, et la fresque est à jamais perdue. A côté des morceaux de fresque conservés il n'y a pas de date, il faut que j'aille à la chasse des dates actuellement en 1835. Heureusement, peu importe un anachronisme, une confusion d'une ou de deux années. A partir de mon arrivée à Paris en 1799, comme ma vie est mêlée avec les événements de la gazette, toutes les dates sont sûres. (*HB*, 120)

> By writing my life in 1835, I am making a good many discoveries . . . they are large pieces of frescoes on a wall, which, long forgotten, suddenly appear, and next to the well-preserved pieces are, as I have already said several times, large spaces where you can only see the brick of the wall. The plaster on which the fresco was painted has fallen away, and the fresco is lost forever. Next to the well-preserved pieces there is no date; I shall have to hunt up the dates now, in 1835. Fortunately, an anachronism, a confusion of one or two years, matters little. After my arrival in Paris in 1799, since my life is mingled with the events in the newspaper, all the dates are certain.

In seeking to avoid imposing order and signification on the fragments of his past, Beyle is in effect shunning the type of autobiographical project defined by Beaujour as *l'autoportrait*—that is, a reflection

or projection of the writing subject in a present state of constant
becoming (a continually renewed "I am") in favor of a Rousseauian
essentialist autobiography ("I was, therefore I am.")[15] If the author of
Brulard repeatedly renews his caveats regarding the validity of his explicatory hypotheses, he nevertheless continues to proffer them. Moreover, at a relatively early stage in his enterprise, he begins to devalorize
the objective status of events in favor of their subjective, affective
value: "I beg the reader, if I ever have one, to remember that I only
claim veracity insofar as my sentiments are concerned; as for facts, I
have always had a poor memory" (*HB*, 105); "I protest once more that
I don't claim to depict things in themselves, but only their effect on
me" (134).[16] Indeed, despite his frequent protestations that the images
he "sees" are "*very sharp*," Beyle is already entertaining doubts as to
their reality:

> A côté des images les plus claires je trouve des *manques* dans ce sou-
> venir, c'est comme une fresque dont de grands morceaux seraient
> tombés. Je vois Séraphie se retirant de la cuisine et moi faisant la
> conduite à l'ennemi le long du passage. . . . Il me semble que je
> pleurais de rage pour les injures atroces (impie, scélérat, etc.) que
> Séraphie m'avait lancées, mais j'avais une honte amère de mes larmes.
>   Je m'interroge depuis une heure pour savoir si cette scène est bien
> vraie, réelle, ainsi que vingt autres qui, évoquées des ombres, reparais-
> sent un peu, après des années d'oubli. (107–8)

> Next to the clearest images I find *gaps* in this memory; it's like a
> fresco of which large pieces have fallen away. I see Seraphie retreat-
> ing from the kitchen and me driving the enemy down the corri-
> dor. . . . It seems to me that I was crying with rage over the dreadful
> insults (impious wretch, scoundrel, etc.) that Seraphie had flung at
> me, but I was bitterly ashamed of my tears. I have been questioning
> myself for an hour to know if this scene is really true, real, as with
> twenty others which, called up out of the shadows, are reappearing
> a little after years of oblivion.

Beyle will convince himself that this particular memory is indeed
authentic, but when he comments that "the act of writing my life
makes great scraps of it appear" (109), one cannot help but wonder if
these fragments of the past ressurrected through the act of writing have
not the same status as the briefly evoked Wagram scene, that is, if they
are not projections of the author's desire, and products of his culture—
things "worthy of being written" in 1835.

In fact, Beyle seems to be slowly drifting toward a position of pure
subjectivism as, midway through the book, he emphatically declares
his disdain for chronology, historical accuracy, and narrative coherence:

J'aurais peut-être dû placer ce détail bien plus haut, mais je répète que pour mon enfance je n'ai que des images fort nettes, sans *date* comme sans *physionomie.*
Je les écris un peu comme cela me revient.
Je n'ai aucun livre et je ne veux lire aucun livre, je m'aide à peine de la stupide Chronologie . . . [de] . . . M. Loeve-Veimars. . . . Je ne prétends nullement écrire une histoire, mais tout simplement noter mes souvenirs afin de deviner quel homme j'ai été: bête ou spirituel, peureux ou courageux, etc., etc. C'est la réponse au grand mot: Gnoti seauton. (*HB,* 195–96)

Perhaps I should have placed this detail much earlier, but I repeat that for my childhood I have only very sharp images, without *date,* as without *physiognomy.* I write sort of as things come to me. I have no books, and want no books, I am hardly using the stupid Chronology . . . [by] M. Loeve-Veimars. . . . I am by no means claiming to write a history, but simply to jot down my memories in order to tell what sort of man I have been: stupid or witty, timorous or courageous, etc., etc. It's the answer to the great dictum: Gnoti seauton.

Even this conception of his project is soon to be significantly modified, however, when he renounces all pretensions to definitive self-classification:

Mais au fond, cher lecteur, je ne sais pas ce que je suis: bon, méchant, spirituel, sot. Ce que je sais parfaitement, ce sont les choses qui me font peine ou plaisir, que je désire ou que je hais. (260)

But actually, dear reader, I don't know what I am: good, wicked, witty, foolish. What I know perfectly are the things that cause me pain or pleasure, what I desire or hate.

It would appear that Beyle has abandoned narrative in favor of free association, self-representation in deference to self-expression, so that writing can take over. He digresses with increasing nonchalance—"The memories multiply under my pen. Now I realize that I forgot one of my closest friends, Louis Crozet" (*HB,* 264)—and blithely discounts vast portions of his text: "Thus I don't really have much confidence in all the judgments with which I've filled up the last 536 pages. Only *sensations* are infallibly true" (312). He is nevertheless plagued by lingering scruples about misrepresenting the truth, however subjective. Even after having relinquished his claims to objective truth, he continues to conceive of the self as a static *être,* rather than a dynamic *devenir,* much less as a structuring intentionality whose truth lies in its very "distortion" of the real. He troubles over his inability to distinguish "real" subjective events from those dreamed, desired, imagined, or otherwise mediated: "I believe I've discovered while writing that

Cardon wore [this uniform]. . . . At this distance, for matters of vanity . . . things imagined and things seen become confused" (372). Worse yet, it is at times impossible to discriminate between one's own perceptions and those filtered through the Other. Long alerted to the dangers of reporting hearsay as personal experience, he now discovers its equivalent in the visual domain:

> Il me semble que nous entrâmes, ou bien les récits de l'intérieur de l'Hospice qu'on me fit produisirent une image qui depuis trente-six ans a *pris la place de la réalité.*
> Voilà un danger de mensonge que j'ai aperçu depuis trois mois que je pense à ce véridique journal.
> Par exemple je me figure fort bien la descente. Mais je ne veux pas dissimuler que cinq ou six ans après j'en vis une gravure que je trouvai fort ressemblante, et mon souvenir n'est *plus* que la gravure.
> C'est là le danger d'acheter des gravures des beaux tableaux que l'on voit dans ses voyages. Bientôt la gravure forme tout le souvenir, et détruit le souvenir réel.
> C'est ce qui m'est arrivé pour la Madone de *San-Sisto* de Dresde. La belle gravure de Müller l'a détruite pour moi, tandis que je me figure parfaitement les méchants pastels de Mengs. (397–98; Beyle's emphasis)

> It seems to me that we went in, or perhaps the accounts I heard of the inside of the Hospice produced an image that, in thirty-six years, has *taken the place of reality.* There is a danger of falsehood that I've noticed in the three months that I've been thinking about this veracious journal. For example, I can imagine the descent very well. But I don't want to hide the fact that five or six years later, I saw an engraving of it that I found to be an excellent likeness, and now my memory is *no more* than the engraving. That is the danger of buying engravings of the beautiful scenes one sees in one's travels. Soon the engraving forms the whole memory, and destroys the real memory. That is what happened to me for the Madonna of *San-Sisto* in Dresden. Müller's beautiful engraving has destroyed it for me, whereas I can picture perfectly Meng's miserable pastels.

Is no experience truly immediate? This is a possibility which haunts the text of *Brulard*, even more so than the author's own avowed doubts as to the "reality" of his memories would suggest. For Beyle's life has a remarkable tendency to imitate art. Not only do secondhand stories and images threaten to vitiate the authenticity of his memoirs, but works of art, literature, and music determine Beyle's "sincerest" passions ("what I desire or hate"), express his most "intimate" feelings, and color his vision of "reality." The Stendhalian soul manifests itself via the medium of art; as Beyle explains in a favorite analogy, "a novel is like a bow; the body of the violin, *which produces the sounds,* is the reader's soul" (*HB,* 159; Beyle's italics). His love for the arts, he writes, was born of his adolescent sexual desires—or vice versa; the two passions, which fueled each other mutually, were first awakened as he read forbidden novels stealthily borrowed from his uncle's library:

> Je ne saurais exprimer la passion avec laquelle je lisais ces livres. Au bout d'un mois ou deux je trouvai *Félicia ou mes fredaines.* Je devins fou absolument, la possession d'une maîtresse réelle, alors l'objet de tous mes voeux, ne m'eût pas plongé dans un tel torrent de volupté.
>
> Dès ce moment ma vocation fut décidée: vivre à Paris en faisant des comédies comme Molière. (160)

> I could not possibly express the passion with which I read these books. After a month or two I found *Felicia, or My Escapades.* I became absolutely insane; the possession of a real mistress, then the object of all my desires, would not have plunged me into such a torrent of voluptuousness. From that moment on, my vocation was decided: to live in Paris and write comedies like Molière.

His imagination thus prepared, he was ready to become a devotee of painting, upon beholding a landscape depicting three near-nude women bathing in a stream, a scene that immediately became for him "*the ideal* of happiness" and simultaneously a sort of artistic ideal, a valorization which he admits was "quite independent of the value of the landscape, which probably looked like a dish of spinach, with no aerial perspective" (*HB,* 151). Furthermore, his memory of the painting will heighten his pleasure years later when he will have occasion to watch his mistress bathing nude in the Huveaune (150). Similarly, a young actress, Mlle Kubly, will introduce him to the ecstasies of music by singing the lead role in "that tremulous little stream of vinegar called *Le Traité nul*" (220), which Beyle afterwards learned by heart. If his passion for the opera was apparently inspired by his desire for the actress in this instance, elsewhere the reverse seems to hold, as is the case with his adoration for the gap-toothed Caroline, who reigned over Beyle's enraptured discovery of Italian opera (to become a lifelong passion) in Milan (406–7).

Like Julien Sorel and Mathilde de la Mole, young Brulard inhabits a universe mediated by art, music, and particularly literature. From them he draws the models to which he expects (and sometimes forces) reality to conform; when at a loss to depict reality, he will turn to the arts for examples. Indeed, it often seems that the existence of a literary reference is a condition *sine qua non* for experience. Thus, characteristically, Brulard, as though to awaken his senses to the spectacle before him, announces to himself upon crossing the Italian border: "I am in

Italy, that is, in the country of *Zulietta,* whom J.-J. Rousseau found in
Venice; in Piedmont, the country of Mme Bazile" (*HB,* 399).

But literature is more than a source of ideas and images; it is also a
vast reserve of words and phrases from which Beyle borrows liberally,
in order to better "express" himself. From the opening scene of *Brulard,* in which he invokes Grétry ("I'm going to be fifty and I was singing Grétry's tune 'When You're Fifty'" [*HB,* 6]), to the final page, on
which, at a loss for words, he simply copies a passage from a book
before him (415), the autobiographer takes words from the mouths of
others—Molière, Corneille, Shakespeare, and even Stendhal: "I would
say, like Julien: 'Scum! Scum! Scum!'" (131).[17] Thus, despite Beyle's continued insistence that "This book, made only from my memory, will
not be made with other books" (373), it becomes increasingly apparent
that *Brulard* is, in at least two senses, composed of other books, other
stories, other images. It is so, first of all, because the author's perceptions of "objective" reality constantly prove to be adulterated by otherness (i.e., procured second- or thirdhand) and, secondly, because not
only are his desires and sentiments mediated by art, but to communicate those feelings, he resorts repeatedly to allusions and quotations.
Involuntarily, no doubt, Beyle succeeds in demonstrating that autobiographical writing, whether defined as historical narrative or as pure
expression of affect, as the representation of the *être-en-soi* of the past
or of the *être-en-soi* of the subject, can have only a tangential relationship to the being (*dasein*) of the author. The autobiographer's intermit-
tent commentary on the work in progress betrays his anxious awareness of the gap which persists between the word and the intent, the
dire and the *vouloir-dire* of his text, between the representations of the
self and the consciousness which presides over the act of representation. The images of his past which fill the pages of *Brulard,* are but so
many portraits of alter egos in whom the author seeks to recognize
himself; the same is true for the literary characters with whom he
identifies, in vain hope of a future coincidence. In the *Vie de Henry Brulard,* the famous Stendhalian *chasse au bonheur,* or pursuit of happiness,
is thematized as a pursuit of self; *le bonheur* is explicitly equated with
the suppression of the ironic distance that separates the selves, as well
as self and other (*moi* and *soi, je* and *il*)—an experience invariably
described as a state of total blindness and oblivion, a blissful annihilation of the self.

Beyle refers to this sensation of momentary loss of self (i.e., of self-
consciousness) quite early in *Brulard,* albeit more or less in passing,
since he is anticipating his future experience: "I was with them as I was
later with the people I loved too much—mute, immobile, stupid, not

very likable and sometimes offensive out of devotion and absence of ego [*moi*]. My self-esteem, my self-interest, my self [*moi*] had disappeared in the presence of the beloved; I was transformed into that person" (*HB,* 21). The proximity of the desired object and the concomitant suppression of desire entail a loss of lucidity resulting in a state of mutism. Thus having barely begun his account of Henry's stay at les Echelles with his amiable uncle Romain Gagnon and the passionately admired aunt Camille ("She greatly resembles those charming women from Chambéry . . . so well portrayed by J.-J. Rousseau"), Beyle suddenly finds himself incapable of continuing: "The difficulty, the profound regret over depicting things so badly, and thereby spoiling a divine memory in which the *subject* too far *surpasses* the *saying* [le *sujet surpasse* trop le *disant*], actually causes me pain instead of the pleasure of writing" (122; Beyle's italics).[18] Happiness, or the absence of desire, is ineffable: "I could only depict this delightful, pure, fresh, divine happiness by enumerating the sorrows and troubles of which it was the total absence" (121). A banal discovery, really; any child knows that once the prince and princess are united, the story must end. Brulard, however, has yet to endure many trials and tribulations, and once Beyle has stammered through the most difficult moments, he will recover from his attack of verbal impotence and resume his writing, for the *Vie de Henry Brulard* is the story of an errant and insatiable desire in pursuit of an undefined object, which is why the autobiography is fated to end in Milan. No sooner has our hero crossed the Saint Bernard pass into Italy than does the narrative begin to founder:

Je me dis: je suis en Italie, c'est-à-dire dans le pays de la *Zulietta* que J.-J. Rousseau trouva à Venise. . . .

Je serais obligé de faire du roman et de chercher à me figurer ce que doit sentir un jeune homme de dix-sept ans, fou de bonheur en s'échappant du couvent, si je voulais parler de mes sensations d'Etroubles au fort de Bard.

J'ai oublié de dire que je rapportais mon innocence de Paris, ce n'était qu'à Milan que je devais me délivrer de ce trésor. Ce qu'il y a de drôle, c'est que je ne me souviens pas distinctement avec qui.

La violence de la timidité et de la sensation a tué absolument le *souvenir.* (399)

I said to myself: I'm in Italy, the country of *Zulietta*, whom J.-J. Rousseau found in Venice. . . . I would have to novelize and try to imagine what a young man of seventeen, deliriously happy and having just escaped from the convent must feel, if I were to talk about my feelings from Etroubles to the fort of Bard. I forgot to say that I had brought my innocence with me from Paris; it was only

in Milan that I would relieve myself of this treasure. What is funny
is that I don't exactly remember with whom. The violence of the
timidity and of the sensation has absolutely killed the *memory*.

It is no mere coincidence that Beyle suddenly "remembers" having
lost his virginity in Milan at the moment when he first evokes his ineffable happiness upon crossing into Italy, for that bliss can only be
expressed in terms of the ecstatic oblivion he experiences in the arms
of his mistresses—an oblivion which is itself, of course, indescribable:
"The present sensation absorbed everything, exactly like the memory
of the first evening when Giulia treated me as a lover. My memory is
nothing but a novel made up on that occasion" (*HB,* 406). Henceforth,
Beyle will do little more than elaborate on the impossibility of continuing his narrative (that is, without "novelizing")—for this time,
Brulard is destined to live happily ever after, as the author has just remarked: "I had an execrable lot from age seven to seventeen, but since
crossing Mount Saint Bernard . . . I no longer have reason to complain
about fate, but rather to be very pleased with it" (404). Indeed, Milan
is the *locus amoenus* par excellence, a garden of delights, the space of
a happiness which the protagonist had vainly sought in France: "I had
just seen clearly where happiness was" (407).[19] "This city became for
me the most beautiful place on earth. I feel none of the charm of my
fatherland [*patrie*]; I have, for the place where I was born, a repugnance bordering on physical disgust" (412).

"I thought I had died and gone to heaven"—the popular expression
comes irresistibly to mind upon reading Beyle's superlative-laden
attempts to express the "divine, complete happiness" (*HB,* 413) he discovered in Italy. His efforts at introspection produce, not clear images,
but a blinding heavenly light: "One cannot see clearly that part of the
sky which is too close to the sun; by a similar effect, I will have great
difficulty narrating in a reasonable fashion my love for Angela Pietragrua" (413).[20] On the following page he will reiterate his dilemma one
last time before falling silent:

> Comment peindre le bonheur fou?
> Le lecteur a-t-il jamais été amoureux fou? A-t-il jamais eu la for-
> tune de passer la nuit avec cette maîtresse qu'il a le plus aimée en sa
> vie?
> Ma foi je ne puis continuer, le sujet surpasse le disant. . . .
> Ma main ne peut plus écrire, je renvoie à demain. . . .
> Voici le sommaire de ce que, à trente-six ans d'intervalle, je ne puis
> raconter sans le gâter horriblement.
> Je passerais dans d'horribles douleurs les cinq, dix, vingt ou trente
> ans qui me restent à vivre qu'en mourant je ne dirais pas: Je ne veux
> pas recommencer.

D'abord ce bonheur d'avoir pu faire à ma tête. Un homme mé-
diocre, au-dessous du médiocre si vous voulez, mais bon et gai, ou
plutôt heureux lui-même alors, avec lequel je vécus.
Je suis très froid aujourd'hui, le temps est gris, je souffre un peu.
Rien ne peut empêcher ma folie.
En honnête homme qui abhorre d'exagérer, je ne sais comment
faire. . . .
On gâte des sentiments si tendres à les raconter en détail. (414–15)

How can you describe insane happiness? Has the reader ever been
madly in love? Has he ever had the good fortune to spend the night
with the mistress whom he loved the most in his life? My word, I
can't go on, the subject surpasses the saying. . . . My hand cannot
write, I'll put it off until tomorrow. . . . Here is the summary of
what, after thirty-six years, I cannot recount without spoiling it hor-
ribly. If I were to spend my five, ten, twenty or thirty remaining
years of life in horrible sufferings, I wouldn't say, upon dying: I don't
want to start over. First of all, there is the good fortune of having
been able to do as I please. A mediocre man, less than mediocre if
you wish, but kind and cheerful, or rather happy himself then, with
whom I lived. I'm very cold today, it's gray out, I'm not feeling too
well. Nothing can stop my madness. As an honest man who abhors
exaggeration, I don't know what to do. . . . You spoil such tender
feelings by recounting them in detail.

Thus concludes, abruptly, the *Vie de Henry Brulard.* It is more appropriate, perhaps, to speak of an indefinite interruption than of a
conclusion, for Beyle had most certainly intended to narrate his life
beyond the age of seventeen; yet in respect to narrative technique, at
least, the final pages of the text constitute an eminently logical ending
for the Stendhalian autobiography: the closing paragraphs echo the
opening passage by suggesting a reversal of the narrator's situation, a
reversal which is itself inscribed in the overture. Having begun his life
story bathed in brilliant sunlight, "happy to be alive," atop the Janicu-
lum, overlooking the city of Rome which emblematizes his past, he
ends it alone, enclosed in his room, on a gray afternoon, in a melancholy humor. "I am very cold"–"je suis très froid," instead of the customary "j'ai très froid"–is a strangely morbid expression, particularly
in the light of the preceding linguistic anomaly, "je vécus"–or "I lived,"
in the *passé défini,* normally reserved for events of a bygone past. It is
as though Beyle the autobiographer, in referring to his life in the past
historic, wished to articulate his death, already evoked in the initial
scene through his references to Raphael's *Transfiguration,* buried in the
somber depths of the Vatican. The final pages of the *Vie de Henry Brulard* represent a kind of death and transfiguration of the protagonist,
who in a sense will "live" on, in another form. For if Beyle abandons

his autobiography because of the impossibility of continuing "sans faire du roman" ("without novelizing"; the expression recurs with increasing frequency near the end of the work), he will go on to write a novel which, as Genette has observed, begins with the arrival of the French troops in Milan, "linking without break fiction to autobiography, the destiny of Lieutenant Robert to that of Second-Lieutenant Beyle—with all the consequences that follow."[21] That novel is, of course, the same which de Man characterized as an allegory of irony—*La Chartreuse de Parme.*

More importantly, perhaps, the figurative blinding of the narrator marks the death of an illusion, that is, of a certain concept of the self which had engendered the autobiographical project. Consciously or not, Beyle has had to accept the consequences of an axiom for which the pages of *Brulard* offer abundant proof: that insight equals blindness. That is to say, that the im-mediate self (unmediated by the Other), which the author sought to glimpse in his writing, is a myth; that writing is precisely the opposite of insight, and even presupposes the Oedipal blindness so transparently symbolized by Beyle's bedazzlement in the presence of his mistresses. Despite all his pretensions to the contrary, Beyle has written a novel about "the man with whom he lived," a *roman familial,* or "family romance"[22]—which, as Roland Barthes will remark a century and a half later, in the preface to his own "autobiography," can only be the tale of some defunct "he" who is, precisely, *not* the writer: "The time of the narrative (of the imagery) ends with the subject's youth: the only biography is of an unproductive life" (*RB,* 6/3). In *Brulard,* that tale is the story of a young *Grenoblois* who adored his mother and abhorred his father, and who, having lost the former, set out to recover that maternal presence from which he had been exiled—via a return to his mythical origins. It is also the story of Everyman, a fact for which the traces of *Brulard*'s mythological intertext will serve as a reminder.

Once again, the text of the opening scene contains the germs of what is to come, as a retrospective reading of the passage reveals. Not only does the edenic atmosphere evoked here through the references to the luminous skies, the balmy air, and the orange groves foreshadow the role that Italy is to play in Beyle's family romance, but the allusion to the Judith fresco introduces, indirectly, the Oedipal theme, which will soon become almost obtrusively apparent. For the Judith whose portrait Beyle so admired is she who seduced Holofernes to save her people, returning with his severed head as a symbol of her triumph. In Il Domenichino's tondo (which Beyle mistakenly "sees" in the Villa Aldobrandini), she appears to present her macabre trophy to a small child in the foreground. It is hardly necessary to elaborate on the symbolism of such a figure, at once mother and mistress, virgin and whore, *protectrice* and *castratrice,* both Mme de Rênal and Mathilde de la Mole. In fact, the paradoxical image of the castrating mother/mistress is a recurrent one in Stendhal's personal writings, as Louis Marin has demonstrated in *La Voix excommuniée,*[23] citing yet another such figure who haunts the inaugural scene of the autobiography: that of Beatrice Cenci, who, raped by her father, induced a henchman to drive a stake through his eye as he slept, and died by the guillotine. Beatrice Cenci, notes Stendhal in *Chroniques italiennes,* "stipulated that her body be at San-Pietro *in Montorio,*"[24] but adds in the margin that the tomb bore no inscription—hence, perhaps, Beyle/Brulard's silence in respect to her "presence" in that first scene.

In the second chapter of *Brulard* (the same which is largely devoted to questions of method), Beyle will pursue the thematic just evoked via his allusions to "real" women—"real," but nonetheless endowed with a mythical aura. This time the dominant figure is Métilde, because of whom, the author recalls, he *left* Milan:

> En 1821 je quittai Milan, le désespoir dans l'âme à cause de Métilde. . . . J'écrivis pour me distraire; Métilde mourut, donc inutile de retourner à Milan. J'étais devenu parfaitement heureux, c'est trop dire mais enfin fort passablement heureux, en 1830, quand j'écrivais *le Rouge et le Noir.* (*HB,* 14)

> In 1821, I left Milan, with despair in my soul, because of Métilde. . . . I wrote to distract myself; Métilde died, so there was no use in returning to Milan. I had become perfectly happy—that's saying too much, but quite tolerably happy anyway, in 1830, when I was writing *Le Rouge et le noir.*

This narrative which, in quintessential Stendhalian style, collapses a decade into two sentences, virtually summarizes Beyle's autobiography, as he himself will comment on the following page. Recalling the list of his mistresses' names he recently scribbled in the sand during a solitary promenade, he muses: "Most of these charming creatures did not honor me with their favors; but they have literally occupied my whole life. They were succeeded by my works" (16). If *Le Rouge et le noir* was Métilde's novel, then the *Vie de Henry Brulard* is in a sense Giulia's, since she has recently married (in 1833—that is, in the interval between 1832, when Beyle supposedly began writing his life, and 1835, from which the manuscript most likely dates). Yet the autobiography is of course dedicated to all those whose names appear here, as well as to those evoked in the opening paragraphs, and finally—or first of all—to one whom he has yet to name, but who haunts all these pages: Henriette Gagnon.

It is not until chapter 3 that Beyle will actually begin to narrate his life, that is, the misfortunes which marked his seventh through seventeenth years. "This is where my troubles begin," he announces, ostensibly referring to his initiation to Latin, but the sentences which follow thereupon attest to the real source of his unhappiness:

> Mais je diffère depuis longtemps un récit nécessaire, un des deux ou trois peut-être qui me feront jeter ces mémoires au feu.
>   Ma mère, madame Henriette Gagnon, était une femme charmante et j'étais amoureux de ma mère.
>   Je me hâte d'ajouter que je la perdis quand j'avais sept ans. . . .
>   Elle périt à la fleur de la jeunesse et de la beauté en 1790, elle pouvait avoir vingt-huit ou trente ans.
>   Là commence ma vie morale. (*HB,* 29–30)

> But I have been deferring for a long time a necessary account, one of two or three perhaps that will make me throw these memoirs into the fire. My mother, madame Henriette Gagnon, was a charming woman and I was in love with my mother. I hasten to add that I lost her when I was seven. . . . She died in the flower of youth and beauty in 1790; she must have been twenty-eight or thirty. There begins my moral life.

The mother's death, rather than Brulard's birth, marks the true beginning of the autobiographical narrative, for it is only upon being banished from paradise that the narrator will be plunged—to use a Poulettian metaphor—into Time, with all the consequences that that fall implies: "It so happened that with my mother's death, all the joy of my childhood ended" (38).

It is impossible to overlook the Freudian reverberations of Beyle's passion for his mother. Genette, in particular, cites such passages as the following, observing that they leave precious little to interpret:

> Je voulais couvrir ma mère de baisers et qu'il n'y eût pas de vêtements. Elle m'aimait à la passion et m'embrassait souvent, je lui rendais ses baisers avec un tel feu qu'elle était souvent obligée de s'en aller. J'abhorrais mon père quand il venait interrompre nos baisers. . . . Un soir, comme par quelque hasard on m'avait mis coucher dans sa chambre par terre, sur un matelas, cette femme vive et légère comme une biche sauta par-dessus mon matelas pour atteindre plus vite à son lit. (*HB,* 29–31)[25]

> I wanted to cover my mother with kisses and I wanted there to be no clothing. She loved me passionately and kissed me often; I returned her kisses with such fervor that she was often obliged to leave. I abhorred my father when he came along to interrupt our kisses. . . . One evening, when I happened to have been put to bed

on her bedroom floor, on a mattress, this woman, as lively and nimble as a doe, leapt over my mattress to reach her bed more quickly.

There is, however, still a trace of the characteristic Stendhalian reticence, reminiscent, for instance, of the ellipsis which serves as sole testimony to Julien and Mathilde's first night of love-making. As ever, the unutterable coincides with the obscene (that which cannot or should not be seen); the lacunae in the text correspond to the unmediated, blinding presence of the desired object. Louis Marin has demonstrated the relevance of Freud's remarks on the Medusa complex to the above passage from *Brulard:* the terror of the Medusa, according to the psychoanalyst, "occurs when a boy, who has hitherto been unwilling to believe the threat of castration, catches sight of the female genitals, probably those of an adult, surrounded by hair, and essentially those of the mother." Freud further notes that the virgin goddess Athena wears "this symbol of horror [Medusa's head]... upon her dress.... And rightly so, for thus she becomes a woman who is unapproachable and repels all sexual desires."[26]

Although the narrator never explicitly associates the gentle and nurturing Henriette Gagnon with his various mistresses (real or fantasized), nor does he complain of any "dazzling" effect produced by his memories of her, she quite obviously belongs to the series of *femmes fatales* before whom the narrator is dumbstruck, *méduse*. Indeed, she is the original incarnation of that love-object, as one might guess without even reading the autobiography; it is more interesting, and more important, to note how, in the text of *Brulard,* she is also the incarnation of the author's Origins, so that Beyle/Brulard's quest for self-knowledge is represented as a ten-year odyssey in search of his "motherland." Nostalgia derives from the Greek *nostos,* "return home," and it is precisely in that sense that the narrator/protagonist of *Brulard* plays out his nostalgia for his long-lost mother.

For young Brulard, we are told, the homeland of his maternal ancestors was surrounded by a utopian aura. His grandfather, he had heard, was born in Avignon, of which he knew only that it was "much closer to Toulon than to Grenoble" and that there "orange trees grow outside in the ground"—enough for him to visualize it as a "land of delights" diametrically opposed to the banal here and now of Grenoble, where "the great splendor of the city was sixty or eighty orange trees in tubs" (*HB,* 71–72). It is Beyle the author of *Brulard* who interprets this family legend in concrete terms: "With what I know of Italy today, I would translate thus: that a Mr. Guadagni or Guadaniamo, having committed a little murder in Italy, had come to Avignon, around 1650, with some legate" (71). This line of reasoning enables Beyle to establish his roots far from his fatherland, dissociating himself entirely from the detested Cherubin Beyle ("For I considered myself a Gagnon and I never thought of the Beyles without a repugnance that endures in 1835" [71]), and furthermore, to claim the Italian language as his ancestral mother tongue:

> Ce qui me confirmerait dans cette idée d'origine italienne, c'est que la langue de ce pays était en grand honneur dans la famille, chose bien singulière dans une famille bourgeoise de 1780. Mon grand-père [Gagnon] savait et honorait l'italien, ma pauvre mère lisait le Dante, chose fort difficile même de nos jours. . . .
> Mon respect pour le Dante est ancien, il date des exemplaires que je trouvai dans le rayon de la bibliothèque paternelle occupé par les livres de ma pauvre mère. (72)

What seems to confirm this idea of an Italian origin is that the language of that country was held in great esteem in the family, a most unusual thing in a bourgeois family of 1780. My grandfather [Gagnon] knew and esteemed Italian; my poor mother read Dante, something quite difficult even these days. . . . My respect for Dante is longstanding; it dates from the copies I found on the shelf of my father's library occupied by my poor mother's books.

In Beyle's mythological genealogy, then, Henriette Gagnon is a (spiritual) sister to Beatrice—to Beatrice Cenci, and even more manifestly, to Beatrice Portinari, muse of the revered Dante. Moreover, she is the female counterpart of the autobiographer (who, significantly, divests himself of his father's name, but retains the Henri which he shares with his mother), that other self with which he longs to be reunited.

It is in his mother's room (need one elaborate on the connotations?), to which he alone was allowed access, that Brulard sequestered himself to work—to study mathematics (*HB,* 31) and to write: "Tranquil in the parlor with the handsome chair embroidered by my poor mother, I began to work with pleasure. I wrote my comedy called, I think, *M. Piklar*" (173). For if Henry's sole ambition, since discovering *Félicia ou mes fredaines,* was to "live in Paris and write comedies like Molière" (160, 331), he recognized early on that the study of mathematics was the "only means I had of getting out of this city I despised and that I still hate" (65; see also 79, 101, 229). Hence Henriette Gagnon is both his muse and the patron saint who will ensure the success of her son's strategy for escaping from the paternal space. He does, in fact, win first prize in mathematics in 1799, and sets off for Paris. Frustration: "Upon my arrival in Paris, two great objects of my constant and passionate desire suddenly crumbled" (331). Paris is muddy and inhospitable;

math is boring. Brulard tries to write, falls ill, despairs: "Good Lord! what a disappointment! but then what should I desire?" (33).

Brulard's journey is not over, but a final stage is about to begin. "I am going to be born, as Tristram Shandy says," announces Beyle on page 364, "and the reader will be done with all this childishness." Henry is soon to go to work for Martial and Pierre Daru at the Ministry of War, eventually following them to Italy. And the rest is history, or rather, novel. The entry into Milan marks the demise of the character Brulard, and that of the autobiographical project conceived as self-representation. The quest for self which is allegorized here (intentionally or no) as a return to the origin—a reunion with the mother, and hence the rediscovery of a prelapsarian state of candid, immediate self-knowledge[27]—has ended in blindness. And if that blindness is a form of knowledge, it is only the knowledge that the subject has no *en-soi.* Such is the message of the Medusa (or of her avatars in *Brulard*): that the *ungrund,* absence of ground or death, can neither be contemplated nor expressed. Writing is a perpetually substitutive activity, a "solitary debauchery," as Michel Beaujour has said of the *autoportrait,* in a passage which recalls uncannily young Brulard at work in his deceased mother's room—or Beyle alone, writing his life, in Civitavecchia:

> [Si l'autoportrait] est texte de divertissement, il s'écrit dans le repos d'une chambre et ce divertissement ne se distingue guère de l'apprentissage de la mort. L'écriture ponctue, structure, rachète une débauche solitaire, sans en sortir, sans jamais viser, ne fût-ce que par l'imagination, un ailleurs réel. (*Miroirs d'encre,* 24)

> [If the self-portrait] is a text of diversion, it is written in the tranquility of one's room and this diversion is hardly distinguishable from an initiation to death. Writing punctuates, structures, expiates a solitary debauchery, without going beyond that, without ever—even in the imagination—aiming at a real *elsewhere.*

Beyle's difficulties have all arisen from the fact that, unlike the *autoportraitiste,* he was seeking to represent an "ailleurs réel," a reality outside his text.

Writing serves both to affirm the absence of that *elsewhere* (i.e., of a transcendent signified), and to compensate for it—and here again, Freud's interpretation of the Medusa's head comes to mind: "The hair upon Medusa's head is frequently represented in works of art in the form of snakes. . . . It is a remarkable fact that, however frightening they may be in themselves, they nevertheless actually serve as a mitigation of the horror, for they replace the penis, the absence of which is the cause of the horror" (*Standard Edition,* 18: 273). The text as substitutive penis is a common enough theme in contemporary criticism;

Barthes, it will be remembered, evokes the image of braided pubic hairs as an emblem of the text/phallus (*SZ*, 166/160). In the case of Stendhal, one hardly need extrapolate to construe writing as a substitutive activity in the most literally sexual sense; the author of *Brulard* openly declares that his works succeeded his mistresses. And it is only after leaving the maternal space of Milan (and Métilde) that Beyle (or is it Brulard?) will write *Le Rouge et le noir*, which, lest we forget, ends with Julien's decapitation, "by" Mme de Rênal. Likewise, the author of *Le Rouge* will, after losing Giulia, begin his autobiography, which ends as we know. It is tempting and plausible to see *La Chartreuse de Parme* as the primary manifestation, among Stendhal's works, of writing as compensation for the absence or loss of self (ultimately inseparable from its more explicitly sexual function), as de Man's commentary suggests. Nevertheless, it would be misleading to imply that the protagonist of *La Chartreuse*, of all Stendhal's characters, somehow has a privileged relationship to the author, for Fabrice is finally but one of an astounding number of pseudonymous personae who populate the pages of his novels, notes, journals, and correspondence—in *Brulard* alone, "I" calls himself Beyle, Brulard, Stendhal, Dominique, T. Human, and me (the English pronoun).[28] There is little basis (i.e., evidence for the nature of the "real" Stendhal—er, Beyle) upon which to hierarchize those personae, in respect to their resemblance to their creator, or to the sincerity of the sentiments they convey. And it is certainly not the *Vie de Henry Brulard* that will put an end to this confusion. Therefore in a sense de Man, and numerous others, are absolutely right to speak of Beyle's perpetual irony; yet the term may be inappropriate, for it presupposes a being, a self, hiding behind the masks. While it is quite reasonable to suppose, as I have in these pages, that Beyle's pronouncements regarding the ultimate goal of his autobiographical enterprise are sincere, and that he himself believed in a Cartesian *cogito* (at least at the outset), it is difficult to suppress a lingering suspicion that Beyle "knew all along," and that a great part of his "pleasure of writing" was the pleasure of playing a role (yet another) and of playing with the reader. Should one speak of the irony or of the humor of a passage such as the following?

> Où se trouvera le lecteur qui, après quatre ou cinq volumes de *je* et de *moi*, ne désirera pas qu'on me jette . . . une bouteille d'encre? Cependant, ô mon lecteur, tout le mal n'est que dans ces sept lettres: B,R,U,L,A,R,D, qui forment mon nom, et qui intéressent mon amour-propre. Supposez que j'eusse écrit *Bernard*, ce livre ne serait plus, comme le *Vicaire de Wakefield* (son émule en innocence), qu'un roman écrit à la première personne. (*HB*, 264)[29]

Where is the reader who, after four or five volumes of *I*'s and *me*'s, won't wish someone would throw . . . a bottle of ink on me? And yet, dear reader, all the trouble merely comes from these seven letters: B,R,U,L,A,R,D, which form my name, and which involve my pride. Suppose I had written *Bernard*, this book would be no more, like the *Vicar of Wakefield*, its rival in innocence, than a novel written in the first person.

Beyle is difficult to classify, I think, because he does not take himself "seriously enough." His works exude all the ontological yearnings of a Rousseau, or a Kierkegaard, or a Baudelaire, but lack the dimension of a metaphysical despair which is the hallmark of romantic irony. A product of his time, he speaks the language of a soul-searcher, but the religious fervor is wanting. An ironist in 1835, he might have been a humorist among the *happy few* of 1900 or 1935 to whom *Brulard* is addressed, *a fortiori* among the critics/novelists of today.[30]

The *Vie de Henry Brulard* is, finally, a novel, a *Bildungsroman,* like all of Stendhal's novels, but it has the particular distinction, not only of being in the first person, but of being the story of a writer's apprenticeship. Scrutinized with a hundred and fifty years of hindsight, it appears to the critic of today to occupy an important niche among the antecedents of Proust and of all those who, in the twentieth century, thematize the act of writing in self-conscious works whose fundamental problematic is the relationship of the subject to language. This much said, it is convenient to suggest, as indeed I already have, that the text of Roland Barthes's autobiography will begin where Beyle's leaves off, at the close of the family romance. But before plunging headlong into humor, self-consciousness will have to assume, and exorcise, metaphysical despair.

4 : Baudelaire
Lequel Est le Vrai?

"Baudelaire is the man who chose to see himself as if he were another; his life is merely the story of this failed attempt."[1] Once again, irony becomes the scapegoat of philosophy. It is 1963, the critic is Sartre, the poet is French, and irony has become bad faith, but the discourse echoes uncannily Kierkegaard's condemnation of the German romantics. Sartre's Baudelaire incarnates the hyperreflective consciousness for whom all existence is vanity: "For the reflective person, every enterprise is absurd. Baudelaire steeped himself in that absurdity" (S, 36–37). Henceforth his existence, and his work, will be but a continually renewed refusal to overcome that absurdity by means of an existential choice, an *engagement,* or self-creative act. "He scorned usefulness and action . . . precisely, every act that uses means in order to attain a predetermined end" (85), playing instead an ineffectual role of rebel which is merely a series of "empty sterile acts . . . a game with Evil . . . a game without consequences" (97).

The famous Baudelairean Evil is in no way a value adopted, affirmed, and upheld in opposition to the value system that the poet has inherited; on the contrary, it serves only to reaffirm that system, for Baudelaire must constantly invoke the Good of his masters in order to define his own position as a rejection of it. His would-be acts of revolt are mere histrionics performed before those mirrors which are the eyes of the Other in order to draw down upon himself the condemnation of his judges (S, 68), thus assuring himself of his singularity. "He seeks to be an *object* for great, stern consciences" (69), writes Sartre; hence the masochism that characterizes his relationship with his parents, with authority, as well as with his mistresses, whose coldness and cruelty his poems celebrate (see S, 150–167). Constantly preoccupied with appearances, intent on projecting an image that, in Kierkegaardian terms, is "poetically correct," Baudelaire is an equally severe self-critic; in a perpetual state of *dédoublement,* or consciousness of consciousness, his only experience is the spectacle of himself experiencing: "This turning in on himself . . . prevents him from submerging himself in pleasure. He never lets himself sink in to the point of losing his senses" (93). Thus he abhors "the spontaneous exuberance of nature" (94) for the loss of self-awareness and self-control it entails. He must "maintain self-control in the midst of his pleasures" (238); "even during coitus, he would have remained solitary, an onanist" (96).

This spiritualized, narcissistic pleasure which Baudelaire calls *volupté* is a form of perversion: "In normal pleasure, one enjoys the object and forgets oneself, whereas in this irritating titillation, one enjoys one's desire, that is, oneself" (S, 239).[2] In his sterile self-containment, his flight from contact with the Other, his futile game of self-creation, the poet exists in that state of "self-willed impotence" characteristic of Hegel's "beautiful soul," for "the difference that grounds him is an empty universal form" (25). This "eternity without content, this bliss without enjoyment, this hungry satiety" (*CI*, 302)—this is Baudelaire's "sheer boredom [*ennui*] with living" (S, 33).

It follows that Baudelaire's ideal is the dandy—"the reader can establish for himself its connections with anti-naturalism, artificialism, and frigidity" (S, 167)—and that his poetic production is but a form of intellectual dandyism:

> The constraints of rhyme and verse oblige him to pursue in this area the *askesis* that he practices in his manner of dressing and his dandyism. He imposes a form on his sentiments as he has imposed a form on his body or his attitudes. There is a dandyism to Baudelaire's poems. Finally the object he produces is only an image of himself, a restoration in the present of his memory, which offers the appearance of a synthesis of being and existence. (242)

The analogy between dandyism and poetry serves the needs of a not-so-implicit polemic against formalist art, which Sartre judges as gratuitous and ineffectual as the merely symbolic revolt constituted by the dandy's cult of a purely superficial individuality:

> In a certain sense, he creates: in a universe in which every element is sacrificed to contribute to the grandeur of the whole, he introduces singularity, that is, the rebellion of a fragment, a detail. Thereby something has been produced that did not exist before, that nothing can efface and that was in no way provided for in the rigorous economy of the world: a work of luxury, gratuitous and unforeseeable. Let us note here the relationship between Evil and poetry: when, on top of it all, poetry takes Evil for its object, and the two kinds of creation with limited responsibility come together and merge, then we get a flower of Evil. (S, 89)

The allusion to the relationship between poetry and evil is telling,[3] as is Sartre's recourse to an economic metaphor. The passage seals the resemblance between Sartre's onto-theological position and that of Kierkegaard in indicating the values that are at stake in the condemnation of Baudelaire—essentially Platonic-Christian values, despite Sartre's

vehement atheism. In its very gratuitousness, Baudelairean irony is in
fact troublesome, because it represents a moment of undialecticizable
negativity, or irrecoupable expenditure (hence onanism). That is, as a
pseudo-revolt that does not represent a true opposition and "that was
in no way provided for in the rigorous economy of the world," it cannot be incorporated into the "established order"—but here I quote
Kierkegaard—and cannot be assigned a value or meaning in terms of a
totality. Baudelaire's poetry represents the same aberration in the linguistic domain: Sartre's disdain for intransitive, nonutilitarian language
is well known.[4] Therein lies the real relationship between poetry and
evil—that is, Sartrian "evil," or bad faith, which Sartre declines to elucidate: poetic language is perverse in that it is sterile, that is, does not
bear meaning; like the sophistic discourse that Kierkegaard (Aristotle,
et al.) so abhorred, it is a kind of "bogus money." As I have remarked
earlier, this non-coincidence of signifier and signified, appearance and
essence, traditionally associated with irony, has at least since Plato
been regarded as the most contemptible form of deceit. In Christian
theology, the misuse of language qualifies as a mortal sin because it
diverts it from the truth-bearing function for which God created it,
and ultimately casts doubt upon the validity of language; in Sartrian
theology, the notion of sin has been displaced by that of evil—and evil
which, for all its supposed relativity, is nonetheless definable in the
abstract as a refusal of teleological activity. In short, Sartre is situated
squarely within Western metaphysical tradition, and to summarize the
values affirmed by his reading of Baudelaire is to recite the litany of
terms valorized by that tradition: presence, nature, truth, etc.

Furthermore, this adherence to Platonico-Christian teleological tradition is precisely what makes Sartre's interpretation eminently defensible. Maurice Blanchot has pointed out "how little the philosophical
terminology of the commentary innovates in respect to the attitude
upon which it comments, and consequently could not betray it."[5]
Blanchot's observation in fact refers to Baudelaire's anguished awareness of the absurdity of existence, and the resulting existential *angoisse*
expressed in such poems as "Le Gouffre" ("The Abyss"): "–Hélas, tout
est abîme,—action, désir, rêve, / Parole!" ("Alas, all is abyss—action,
desire, dream, language!" [*OC,* 172]), but it is also an accurate assess-
ment of Sartre's critical enterprise in the sense that all of the existen-
tialist's philosophical categories and dichotomies (good/evil, self/other,
nature/culture, essence/appearance, seriousness/play, the useful/the
gratuitous, etc.) are readily discernible in Baudelaire's language, doubtless because existentialism itself is an outgrowth of romanticism.
Hence Sartre has no trouble discovering in the poet's work evidence of
his adherence to "the most banal and rigorous morality" (S, 17).

He rarely needs to read between the lines. In the *Journaux intimes* alone there is ample material to corroborate Sartre's claim that Baudelaire is characterized by "a tension resulting from the application of two opposing forces," good and evil, or God and Satan, as is clear from the poet's famous dictum: "Il y a dans tout homme à toute heure deux postulations simultanées, l'une vers Dieu, l'autre vers Satan" ("There are in every man at every moment two simultaneous postulations, one toward God, the other toward Satan" [*OC*, 1277; quoted by S, 45]), and that he extolled comportments that he associates with the satanic, even while holding up the contrary as model. Indeed, Sartre quotes extensively from *Fusées* and *Mon Coeur mis à nu*, citing most of the passages I shall indicate here. But let us leave *Baudelaire* for Baudelaire.

"Etre un homme utile m'a paru toujours quelque chose de bien hideux" ("Being a useful person has always seemed to me quite a hideous thing" [*OC*, 1274]). The useful is repeatedly defined in Baudelaire's journals as work: "Le travail, force productive et accumulative, portant intérêts comme le capital, dans les facultés comme dans les résultats" ("Work, productive and accumulative force, bearing interest like capital, in the faculties as well as in the results" [1257]). Economic productivity is equivalent to artistic fecundity: "Plus on produit, plus on devient fécond" ("The more one produces, the more fecund one becomes" [1265]). On the same page, work is explicitly associated with God, in an attempt to dialecticize it into its opposite, *volupté:* "Que de pressentiments et de signes envoyés par Dieu, qu'il est *grandement temps* d'agir . . . et de faire ma *perpétuelle volupté* de mon tourment ordinaire, c'est-à-dire du Travail!" ("How many presentiments and signs sent by God, that it is *high time* to act . . . and to make a *perpetual pleasure* of my habitual torment, that is, of Work!" [1265]). But "la volupté" as we read elsewhere, "gît dans la certitude de faire le *mal*" ("voluptuous pleasure . . . lies in the certainty of doing *evil*" [1249–50]), and a complex network of associations running throughout the journals links gratuitousness, sterility, *volupté,* and evil with art and the artist. At the center of the network is "the ideal type of the Dandy," whose air of "sensuousness [*volupté*] and sadness," combined with a "vengeful insensitivity" liken him to "the most perfect type of viril Beauty," which is "*Satan*—in the style of Milton" (1255).

The dandy's impassiveness, refinement, and spiritualized ardor situate him at the opposite pole from woman, who incarnates Nature: "La femme est le contraire du dandy. . . . Elle est en rut et veut être foutue. . . . La femme est naturelle, c'est-à-dire abominable" ("Woman is the opposite of the dandy. . . . She is in heat and wants to be screwed. . . . Woman is natural, that is abominable" [*OC*, 1272]). "Natural" sexuality is in turn associated with the philistine masses: "Plus l'homme cultive les arts, moins il bande. ... La brute seule bande bien, et la fouterie est le lyrisme du peuple. Foutre, c'est aspirer à entrer dans un autre, et l'artiste ne sort jamais de lui-même" ("The more man cultivates the arts, the less he can get hard. ... Only a brute can get a good hard-on, and screwing is the lyricism of the masses. To screw is to desire to enter another, and the artist never comes out of himself" [1295–96]). The artist's asexuality is thus a mode of self-containment, one aspect of the narcissistic configuration characteristic of the dandy, which Baudelaire comments on at length elsewhere, and which is summarized in *Fusées:* "Du culte de soi-même dans l'amour, au point de vue de la santé, de l'hygiène, de la toilette, de la noblesse spirituelle et de l'élégance. *Self-purification and anti-humanity*" ("On the cult of self in love, from the point of view of health, hygiene, grooming, spiritual mobility and elegance" [1257]).[6] An allusion to the dandy's need for perpetual self-observation and self-criticism—"he must live and sleep before a mirror" (1273)—further confirms his likeness to the figure of the romantic ironist–beautiful soul. Finally, a related pair of entries suggests that Baudelaire enjoyed the kind of rarified experience-to-the-second-degree that is procured through self-reflection; furthermore, the passage adds a hint of sadomasochism, which apparently attests to the accuracy of Sartre's portrait of the artist: "Je comprends qu'on déserte une cause pour savoir ce qu'on éprouvera à en servir une autre. Il serait peut-être doux d'être alternativement victime et bourreau" ("I understand how one might desert a cause to find out what it will feel like to serve another. It might be pleasant to be both the victim and the torturer" [1271]).

These passages of the *Journaux intimes* establish relationships among a number of elements that recur throughout Baudelaire's other writings—his poetry in verse and in prose as well as his critical essays—and that give his works their romantic-ironic tenor. Furthermore, Baudelaire himself frequently uses the term *ironie* in his poetry in conjunction with the themes adumbrated above: satanism, revolt, singularity, impassivity, sterility, self-criticism, and so on, so that an appropriately oriented reading of *Les Fleurs du mal* supports the conclusion that they are exemplary representatives of romantic irony and that they reflect the romantic-ironic self-ideal that Baudelaire seems to confide to the reader in *Fusées* and *Mon coeur mis à nu.*

Baudelaire's two most famous "irony poems" appear at the end of the *Spleen et idéal* section of *Les Fleurs du mal,* in a series of poems thematizing malediction and fall, which seems to counterbalance the "benediction-elevation" poetry that opens the collection. "L'Irrémédiable" begins:

Une Idée, une Forme, un Etre
Parti de l'azur et tombé
Dans un styx bourbeux et plombé
Où nul oeil du Ciel ne pénètre (*OC, 75*)

An Idea, a Form, a Being, out of the azure, fallen into a muddy,
leaden Styx, where no heavenly eye can penetrate.

And it develops the theme of the fall through the figures of "un Ange
pirouettant dans les ténèbres . . . un malheureux ensorcelé cherchant la
lumière . . . un damné descendant sans lampe" and finally of "un navire
pris dans le pôle . . . Emblèmes nets, tableau parfait / D'une fortune ir-
remédiable" ("an Angel . . . whirling down through the darkness
. . . wretched, spellbound, seeking the light . . . a condemned soul de-
scending without a lamp . . . a ship frozen in the pole . . . clear emblems, a perfect image of an irremediable fate" [75–76]). The concluding
lines constitute a commentary that interprets the paradise lost motif in
terms of an awakening of self-consciousness; the heavenly light of the
oeil du Ciel has become the infernal lucidity of self-observation:

Tête-à-tête sombre et limpide
Qu'un coeur devenu son miroir!
Puits de vérité, clair et noir,
Où tremble une étoile livide,

Un phare ironique, infernal,
Flambeau des graces sataniques,
Soulagement et gloire uniques,
—La conscience dans le Mal! (*76*)

Somber and limpid tête à tête, a heart become its own mirror! Well
of truth, clear and black, where a pallid star trembles. An ironic,
infernal beacon, torch of satanic graces, our sole solace and glory—
consciousness in Evil!

Despite the predominantly Christian imagery of the concluding
stanzas, then, the myth most strongly evoked here is that of Oedipus
plunged into the darkness of insight. The knowledge of good and evil
is explicitly defined as self-knowledge. In the preceding poem, "L'Héautontimorouménos," the emphasis is less on the concept of a fall than
on that of an exile, a difference which sets the narrator "je" apart from
the cosmos, that difference residing in his self-reflective nature. The
four final verses:

Ne suis-je pas un faux accord
Dans la divine symphonie
Grâce à la vorace Ironie
Qui me secoue et qui me mord?

Elle est dans ma voix, la criarde!
C'est tout mon sang, ce poison noir!
Je suis le sinistre miroir
Où la mégère se regarde!

Je suis la plaie et le couteau!
Je suis le soufflet et la joue!
Je suis les membres et la roue,
Et la victime et le bourreau!

Je suis de mon coeur le vampire
—Un de ces grands abandonnés
Au rire éternel condamnés
Et qui ne peuvent plus sourire! (*OC,* 74)

Am I not a dissonant chord in the divine symphony because of the voracious Irony that shakes me and gnaws at me? Her shrillness is in my voice! Her dark poison is my blood! I am the sinister mirror in which the Fury sees herself! I am the wound and the knife! I am the slap and the cheek! I am the limbs and the rack, both the victim and the torturer! I am the vampire of my own heart—one of the abandoned hordes condemned to eternal laughter and who can no longer smile!

The motif of guilt and retribution is brought to the fore here through the allusion to the *mégère* (Mégère being one of the three Furies); and importantly, "je" is here "le miroir où la mégère se regarde"—the reflection of that vengeance, that is, guilt. Thus the succeeding verse follows with impeccable logic: the subject is both guilt and vengeance—desire and the Law, in Lacanian terms ("the law is the same thing as repressed desire," [*SM,* 74]). In fact, the Lacanian schema of the mirror stage is highly pertinent here, since it identifies the awakening of self-consciousness with an irremediable split in the subject generating the ego-ideal that enters into the formation of the judgmental superego. We shall return to the relationship between irony and desire in Baudelaire, which appears more clearly in other poems. "L'Héautontimorouménos" concludes upon an allusion to a satanic outcast whom other Baudelairean texts (principally "The Essence of Laughter") identify as Melmoth, the hero of Maturin's novel *Melmoth the Wanderer,* the tale of a Faustian character who gives up his soul to the devil in exchange, essentially, for knowledge: superhuman faculties, immortality, and an ability to travel the world at will and to divine the innermost thoughts of those he encounters. His diabolical laughter is emblematic of his tragic knowledge of the human condition.[7]

Thus irony and ironic laughter are explicitly linked to temporality

and death, as in "L'Examen de minuit": "La pendule, sonnant minuit, /
Ironiquement nous engage / A nous rappeler quel usage / nous fîmes
du jour qui s'enfuit" ("The clock, striking midnight, ironically advises
us to recall what use we made of the fleeing day" [OC, 168]). In "Danse
macabre," the ironic judgmental faculty is incarnated (or in this case,
décharné) in the skeletal figure of Death: "En tout climat, sous tout so-
leil, la Mort t'admire / En tes contorsions, risible Humanité / Et souvent, comme toi, se parfumant de myrrhe, / Mêle son ironie à ton
insanité" ("In all climes, under every sun, Death admires you in your
contortions, ludicrous Humanity, and often, like you, perfuming itself
with myrrh, mingles its irony with your insanity" [94]). There is no
need to point out that one of the most frequently recurring motifs in
Baudelaire's poetry is time,[8] source of that *ennui* from which intoxication—via wine, opium, or poetry—offers the only escape: "Pour ne pas
être les esclaves martyrisés du Temps . . . enivrez-vous sans cesse! De
vin, de poésie ou de vertu, à votre guise" ("So as not to be the martyred
slaves of Time . . . intoxicate yourselves without cease! With wine,
poetry, or virtue, as you please" [286]). It is fitting, then, that in the
third edition of *Les Fleurs du mal*, "L'Horloge" should have been placed
at the end of the *Spleen et idéal* section, immediately following "L'Irre-
médiable."[9] As in "L'Examen de minuit," the clock here becomes the
impassive, ironic, and accusing representative of Time: "Horloge! dieu
sinistre, effrayant, impassible, / Dont le doigt nous menace et nous dit:
Souviens-toi! / . . . Souviens-toi que le Temps est un joueur avide / qui
gagne à tout coup! c'est la loi" ("Clock! sinister god, fearsome, impassive, who points at us menacingly and says: *Remember!* . . . remember
that Time is an avid gambler who always wins! that is the law" [76–77]).

In the same edition, "Le Voyage" has been placed last in the final section of the *Fleurs, La Mort*. While there is no explicit reference to irony
in "Le Voyage," the poem weaves together the themes of ennui, time,
desire, intoxication, poetry, and death. The quintessential voyage is
that of the poetic imagination, inebriated with visions of illusory paradises: "O le pauvre amoureux des pays chimériques! / . . . ce matelot
ivrogne, inventeur d'Amériques / Dont le mirage rend le gouffre plus
amer" ("Oh the poor lover of chimerical countries! . . . that drunken
sailor, inventor of Americas whose mirage makes the abyss even more
bitter" [OC, 123]). For the poetic voyage is the endless quest of an infinite, formless, errant desire; "les vrais voyageurs sont ceux-là seuls qui
partent pour partir":

Ceux-là dont les désirs ont la forme des nues
Et qui rêvent, ainsi qu'un conscrit le canon,

De vastes voluptés, changeantes, inconnues,
Et dont l'esprit humain n'a jamais su le nom!
....
Singulière fortune où le but se déplace,
Et n'étant nulle part, peut être n'importe où! (122–23)

The true travelers are those alone who leave simply to leave ...
those whose dreams have the shape of clouds and who dream—as a
conscript does of cannon—of vast, changing, unknown pleasures,
for which the human mind has never had a name. ... Singular
destiny whose destination changes, and being nowhere, may be
anywhere!

The object of our desires being anywhere and nowhere, we (for the
third-person "travelers" have suddenly become "we") know that it is
finally indifferent whether we leave or stay; like Melmoth (who represents, in a sense, the "astonishing travelers" who recount their voyages),
we are privy to the "Amer savoir, celui qu'on tire du voyage! / Le
monde, monotone et petit, aujourd'hui, / Hier, demain, toujours,
nous fait voir notre image." Whence the attraction of that most utopian of destinations, that most stationary of voyages, death:

Entendez-vous ces voix, charmantes et funèbres,
Qui chantent: "Par ici! vous qui voulez manger

Le Lotus parfumé! c'est ici qu'on vendange
Les fruits miraculeux dont votre coeur a faim;
Venez vous enivrer de la douceur étrange
De cette après-midi qui n'a jamais de fin!" (*OC*, 126)

Bitter knowledge that we acquire from our travels! The world, mo-
notonous and small, today, yesterday, tomorrow, always, is only an
image of ourselves. ... Do you hear those voices, charming and funereal, that sing: "Come, you who would eat the fragrant Lotus! Here
is harvested the miraculous fruit your heart hungers for; come par-
take of the strange intoxicating sweetness of this endless afternoon!"

The ultimate "trip," then, is an eternal Nirvana-like state of immobil-
ity, of forgetfulness, of suspended desire.[10]
    This is why the voyage is central to some of Baudelaire's most erotic
poetry. The *extase* of the narrator in "La Chevelure" ("The Head of
Hair" [*OC*, 25–26]) is evoked as an immobile voyage away from the object of desire that is ultimately a split in the desiring subject himself insofar as the Other is never present to him except as a projection of his
own desire. In the opening stanza the narrator declares that he intends
to awaken the "memories dormant in this hair" by waving it "in the air
like a handkerchief." The expression conjures up a somewhat amusing

image of the departing narrator waving farewell to his mistress, but in fact this is precisely what he is doing, since the second verse finds him (or his imagination) in "La langoureuse Asie et la brûlante Afrique / Tout un monde lointain, absent, presque défunt" ("languorous Asia and burning Africa, a faraway, absent, nearly defunct world")—though the following line reminds us that he has never really left, by asserting that this exotic world "vit dans tes profondeurs, forêt aromatique!" ("lives in your depths, aromatic forest"). This is a highly ambiguous "return," however, given that the hair has become an aromatic forest— an element of the faraway world that it is said to contain. The first line of the third verse effects a curious reversal of the temporality suggested in the preceding lines: while it has been up to this point a question of reliving a remembered voyage, suddenly that voyage is projected into the future: "J'irai là-bas où l'arbre et l'homme, pleins de sève, se pâment longuement sous l'ardeur des climats" ("I shall go there where trees and men, full of sap, swoon in the ardor of these climates"). While this could be read as a return to the remembered sites, the use of "I shall go" rather than a verb such as "return" weakens this interpretation, and seems rather, as does the vague "there," to anticipate the intimation that these memories are but an "éblouissant rêve," a dazzling dream— in which a past that was never present merges with a future that never will be.

It is an intoxicating dream of "Un port retentissant où mon âme peut boire / A grands flots le parfum, le son et la couleur"—of an un-differentiated and atemporal universe "où frémit l'éternelle chaleur" ("A resounding port where my soul can drink in the torrents of per-fume, sound and color; . . . where the eternal heat shimmers"). Simi-larly, the difference between self and other is apparently effaced between the fifth stanza, which begins "Je plongerai ma tête amou-reuse d'ivresse / Dans ce noir océan où l'autre est enfermé / Et mon esprit . . . Saura vous retrouver, ô féconde paresse!" ("I will plunge my head, in love with drunkenness, into this dark ocean where the other is contained, and my spirit . . . will find you, O fertile lethargy")—and the sixth, in which the narrator shifts to the present tense:

> Cheveux bleus, pavillon de ténèbres tendues,
> Vous me rendez l'azur du ciel immense et rond;
> Sur les bords duvetés de vos mèches tordues
> Je m'enivre ardemment des senteurs confondues
> De l'huile de coco, du musc et du goudron.

> Blue hair, canopy of darkness, you restore to me the azure of the im-mense domed sky; on the downy fringes of your twisted locks, I fer-vently drink in the intoxicating scents of coconut oil, musk, and tar.

The expression "you restore to me the azure of the immense domed sky" relates the state of oblivion described here to the unself-conscious state of grace evoked at the beginning of "L'Irrémédiable" and which precedes the fall into irony ("a Being, out of the azure, fallen . . ." [*OC*, 75]), thus implying that the narrator, through his *extase*, has been reintegrated into the "divine symphony" ("L'Héautontimorouménos," 74). However, the movement of the poem implies that this ecstasy is the masturbatory *volupté* of solipsism. "La Chevelure" is not atypical in this respect; Baudelaire's obliging muses have launched, if not a thousand, at least enough ships for critics to remark with some consistency on the fact that his love poetry tends to transport us away from its supposed object. Moreover, as Barbara Johnson puts it in *Défigurations du langage poétique*, the "emotional transports" are invariably conveyed by "rhetorical transports,"[11] that is, the kind of analogical language that characterizes "La Chevelure." Thus "L'Invitation au voyage" has come to epitomize, along with "Correspondances," Baudelaire's symbolist vein. A number of other love poems in *Les Fleurs du mal*—e.g., "Le Serpent qui danse," "Le Poison," "Parfum exotique," or "Le Beau navire"— might be classed with "La Chevelure" and "L'Invitation," in that the woman to whom they are addressed metaphorically becomes a vessel who bears the poet (and the reader) away on an intoxicating sea of memory/forgetfulness that ultimately extends to "the shores of death" ("Le Poison," 47).

That distancing which is the condition of *volupté* is *thematized* in another series of poems that celebrate the inaccessibility and glacial indifference of the beloved, thereby functioning as a sort of theoretical counterpoint to the *volupté* poems. These texts speak of the titillating effects of deprivation or deferral:

> Je t'adore à l'égal de la voûte nocturne,
> O vase de tristesse, ô grande taciturne,
> Et t'aime d'autant plus, belle, que tu me fuis,
> Et que tu me parais, ornement de mes nuits,
> Plus ironiquement accumuler les lieues
> Qui séparent mes bras des immensités bleues.
>
> Je m'avance à l'attaque, et je grimpe aux assauts,
> Comme après un cadavre un choeur de vermisseaux
> Et je chéris, ô bête implacable et cruelle!
> Jusqu'à cette froideur par où tu m'es plus belle! (*OC*, 26)

I adore you as I do the vaulted nocturnal sky, O urn of sadness, O silent one; and I love you all the more, my beauty, because you flee my embrace and because, ornament of my nights, you seem ironically to magnify the distance that separates my arms from the blue expanses. I advance to the attack, I clamber to the assault, like a chorus of vermine after a corpse; and I cherish, O cruel and implacable beast, even this coldness which makes you more beautiful to me!

The ironic distance that separates subject from object (and therefore subject from self) is the space of desire.[12] Indeed the woman herself is merely the emblem of a more abstract object, "the blue expanses"–the Baudelairean *azur* or *infini*. In "La Beauté," the immortal Ideal herself ironically asserts that her inaccessibility exacerbates desire:

Je suis belle, ô mortels! comme un rêve de pierre,
Et mon sein, où chacun s'est meurtri tour à tour,
Est fait pour inspirer au poëte un amour
Eternel et muet ainsi que la matière.
Je trône dans l'azur comme un sphinx incompris . . . (20)

I am beautiful, O mortals, like a dream of stone, and my breast, where each has bruised himself in turn, inspires in the poet a love as eternal and mute as matter itself. Enthroned in the azure like an impenetrable sphinx . . .

The allusion to the sphinx, metonymically representing the *azur*,[13] introduces the Oedipal theme and alerts us to the fact that the ironic configuration established here is essentially identical to that which we have observed in "L'Irrémédiable" and "L'Héautontimorouménos." Although there is only one reference to Oedipus in the *Oeuvres Complètes*,[14] there are a number of allusions to the sphinx from which we can infer, as we can in "La Beauté," that the poet occupies the position of Oedipus. The sphinx, like the Fury ("voracious Irony") evoked in "L'Héautontimorouménos," is an instrument of divine justice; she devours all those who fail to solve her enigma, and if Oedipus is wise enough to outwit the sphinx, it is in fact that apparent triumph which precipitates his fall and prepares him for his real punishment: the torment of self-knowledge, the knowledge of desire and guilt. In this sense, the voracious sphinx is only an alter ego of Oedipus, since she represents both the scourge of self-knowledge (it will be remembered that Oedipus solves her riddle by recognizing himself–man–in it) and the monster that Oedipus will discover in himself. Likewise, the sphinx of "La Beauté" fascinates poets because her eyes are "pure mirrors."

Here the ironic distance is represented as the incommensurability of the self with an ideal that it believes to exist outside itself but that is really only a projection of an ego-ideal with which it is perpetually striving to coincide. The self is guilty both because it does not coincide with that ideal and because it desires to do so–i.e., to usurp the role of the Law, or in Christian theology, to become the equal of God.[15] If in "L'Héautontimorouménos," irony is perceived from the point of view of the fallen self which knows that its *Evil* is only the reflection of the divine *Good* ("I am the sinister mirror in which the Fury sees herself!"), in "La Beauté," irony is presented from the point of view of the Ideal which knows that the Good is only the illusory projection of the self's desire for an ontological ground. The pursuit of the ideal is always presented as a fruitless enterprise in Baudelaire insofar as it can never produce a concrete result, namely truth. The only kind of knowledge it can yield is a knowledge of the search itself; the "austere studies" in which the bruised poets of "La Beauté" "will consume their days" will be mere reflections on reflection—or, yes, consciousness of consciousness. It is no mere coincidence that philosophical discourse so often resorts to birth metaphors to represent dialectical thought (witness Socrates' midwifery, and Kierkegaard's seduction of a fertile phenomenon); Sartre is of course absolutely correct in associating Baudelaire's "taste for the infinite" (S, 43; OC, 348) with his cult of sterility (and his onanism), and finally with his choice of an intransitive mode of artistic expression.

Like the sphinx, the women portrayed in *Les Fleurs du mal* are invariably impenetrable, in every sense of the word, and the logical consequence of that impenetrability is infertility. The majestic figure of "Avec ses vêtements ondoyants et nacrés" is exemplary:

Et dans cette nature étrange et symbolique
Où l'ange inviolé se mêle au sphinx antique,

Où tout n'est qu'or, acier, lumière et diamants,
Resplendit à jamais, comme un astre inutile,
La froide majesté de la femme stérile. (OC, 28)

And in this strange, symbolic nature, where the inviolate angel mingles with the antique sphinx, where all is gold, steel, light, and diamonds, there shines forever, like a useless star, the cold majesty of a sterile woman.

However, the granite-skinned subject (presumably corporeal beauty) of "Allégorie" (109), "cette vierge inféconde / Et pourtant nécessaire à la marche du monde" ("this infertile virgin, nonetheless necessary in the course of the world" [110]), is accorded a mysterious usefulness, a niche in the scheme of things. One can only guess that she shares that niche with the somewhat less virginal woman addressed in "Tu mettrais l'univers entier dans ta ruelle, / Femme impure!" ("You would have the whole world in your bed, slut!" [26]), whom the poet warns that "la nature, grande en ses desseins cachés, / De toi se sert, ô femme, ô reine

des péchés . . . pour pétrir un génie" ("nature, grand in its hidden de-
signs, is using you, O woman, O queen of sins . . . to mold a genius"
[27]). The double oxymoron (a figure dear to the romantics because it
effected the union of opposites) of the final line—"O fangeuse grandeur! sublime ignominie!" ("O mire of grandeur! sublime ignominy!"
[27])—serves to underscore the paradoxical fecundity of this sterile
creature who is in the process of engendering a genius. The virgin and
the whore are essentially identical in Baudelaire, for both represent
forms of sterility, or unproductive sexuality; their self-sufficiency and
indifference (whether it take the form of promiscuity or frigidity)
nourish the desire that is both the impetus for and the subject of Baudelaire's verse. There is no more explicit commentary on the *volupté* of
deprivation than the sonnet "Une nuit que j'étais près d'une affreuse
Juive":

> Je me pris à songer près de ce corps vendu
> A la triste beauté dont mon désir se prive.
>
> Je me représentai sa majesté native,
> . . . dont le souvenir pour l'amour me ravive. (32)

> One night when I was with a hideous Jewess . . . I found myself
> dreaming, near that hired body, of the sad beauty of which my
> desire deprives itself. I imagined her native majesty . . . whose mem-
> ory revives me for love.

It is not the fact that the Jewess's body is "hideous" or "hired" that
makes her undesirable; it is her proximity. That the *referent* of a work
of art is indifferent is a fundamental tenet of Baudelaire's aesthetics,
which received its most famous formulation in his announced project
to "extract beauty from evil" (185). Not only do poems like "Une
Charogne" ("Carrion") or even "Un Voyage à Cythère" represent attempts to do so, but poems such as "La Muse vénale" thematize the
interchangeability of referents, as does "Hymne à la beauté": "Que tu
viennes du ciel ou de l'enfer, qu'importe, / O Beauté!" (What does it
matter if you come from heaven or hell, O Beauty!" [24]).

Yet the theme of the alchemic power of poetry, the poet's ability to
transmute ugliness into beauty, or mud into gold ("I kneaded mud and
I made it into gold" [OC, 177]) can be tinged with a nostalgia for a time
when poetry was not necessary, when things were beautiful in themselves and did not need the embellishment of language:

> Nous avons, il est vrai, nations corrompues,
> Aux peuples anciens des beautés inconnues:
> Des visages rongés par les chancres du coeur,
> Et comme qui dirait des beautés de langueur;

Mais ces inventions de nos muses tardives
N'empêcheront jamais les races maladives
De rendre à la jeunesse un hommage profond,
—A la sainte jeunesse. . . . insouciante
Comme l'azur du ciel, les oiseaux et les fleurs. (12)

We have, it is true, corrupted nations, beauties unknown to ancient
peoples: faces eaten away by the cankers of the heart, and what you
might call the beauties of languor; but these inventions of our be-
lated muses will never prevent our sickly races from paying profound homage to youth, to sacred youth. . . . carefree as the azure of
the sky, the birds and the flowers.

The prelapsarian paradise thus evoked in "J'aime le souvenir de ces
époques nues" ("I cherish the memory of those naked ages") is a pre-
Christian utopia of unself-conscious, guiltless, and asexual beings,
where "man and woman played together [*jouissaient*] without lies and
without anxiety," free of "all the horrors of fecundity" (*OC,* 11–12).[16]
The mythical past of mankind is a universe without difference, that is,
without temporality and without discontinuity (between beings, between "action and dreaming,"[17] and between essence and appearance,
or sign and meaning). Poetry is the elixir of a sickly race longing to return to that undifferentiated bliss conjured up in "Correspondances,"
where "the transports of the mind and the senses" are one, or in "Elévation," where the spirit is united with nature in wordless communication, "the language of flowers and mute things" (10).
Nostalgia is the particular form of *volupté* that accompanies the
temporalization of that distance between self and other, or difference
between self and self, which the voyage represents in spatial terms.
Nostalgia (derived, it will be recalled, from the Greek *nostos,* "return
home") transforms "over there" into "back then," locating the yearned-
for state of plenitude in an edenic past, or "vie antérieure": "J'ai longtemps habité sous de vastes portiques / . . . . j'ai vécu dans les voluptés
calmes, / Au milieu de l'azur" ("I lived a long time under vast porti-
coes. . . . I lived in voluptuous tranquillity, surrounded by the azure"
[*OC,* 17]). Hence the equivalence of the temporal (*des souvenirs*) and
spatial (*un monde lointain*) dimensions in "La Chevelure," and the
intimation, in "L'Invitation au voyage," that *là-bas* is the country
where "Tout y parlerait / A l'âme en secret / Sa douce langue natale"
("Everything would speak to the soul in secret her sweet mother
tongue" [51]). Yet if some poems tend to make us forget that the past is
irrecoverable, others allegorize that irretrievability. Thus the narrator
of "Le Cygne" (81–83), confronting the changing Parisian landscape,
laments that "everything becomes an allegory for me": the swan be-
seeching an arrid sky to restore "its beautiful native lake" and the

Negress longing for the "absent coconut trees of splendid Africa" are reminders of "whoever has lost that which can never be recovered, never!" In the place of the watery (and alcoholic) *azur* of *volupté*,[18] an ironically, cruelly blue sky" becomes the sign of a "relentless desire."

The "infinite longing" which for Kierkegaard was the wellspring of romantic irony is thematized throughout *Les Fleurs du mal* as a difference or discontinuity that finds its expression in the themes of the disparity between the ideal, or essential, and the real, or phenomenal, worlds—the ideal world being conceived as a lost golden age or a future reward. This sense of disparity manifests itself as well in the motif of the ineffability of the self, that is, the impossibility of communicating essence through appearance (language), and therefore of projecting an adequate self-image; hence the anguish of the divided subject. Viewed from a post-Saussurean perspective, the romantic crisis is essentially a crisis of language, that is, an uneasy awakening to the arbitrary nature of the relationship between signifier and signified. However, while the arbitrary nature of the linguistic sign is, for contemporary criticism, a neutral given, for mainstream nineteenth-century thought the relationship of sign to meaning was implicated in a value system that privileged signified over signifier as the ideal over the material, truth over mere appearance, etc., and for which the introduction of a schism between sign and meaning could have disastrous epistemological and moral consequences.

The romantic ironist—essentially a disillusioned romantic idealist—made this schism into his personal tragedy via a revolt that consisted in the defiant assumption of an ethic and an aesthetic of superficiality, a self-imposed exile into the world of appearances, of empty signs, or deceit ("better to reign in hell than serve in heaven").[19] Hence art for art's sake and its existential equivalent, dandyism. Insofar as romantic irony did represent such a revolt, it of course upheld the predominant hierarchy of values; furthermore, any attempt to evaluate romantic irony from within that hierarchy will inevitably result in a condemnation of the ironist for immorality, or bad faith, as Sartre's *Baudelaire* attests.

There is another way of reading Baudelaire through the same interpretive grid: one can make of him not a romantic ironist but a sincere romantic: the Catholic interpretation of his works makes him a faithful Christian, rather than a Christian in bad faith. One reading is the mirror image of the other; which image appears to be faithful depends upon which texts one privileges. Thus, the "Catholics" read poems such as "Bénédiction" as sincere expressions of suffering, accept Baudelaire's claims that his *Fleurs du mal* in no way constitute an attack on morality, and dismiss his blasphemous poems as expressions of horror over the depths to which humanity can sink.[20]

Sartre, on the other hand, doubts that "Baudelaire suffered for real" (S, III), and claims that the poet accepted "the secret shame of lying about the meaning of his work" (57), by denying before the court that the *Fleurs* were indeed the expression of his deep hostility toward existing values. Despite their apparent incompatibility, both readings are of the man-behind-the-work variety; both are based on the presupposition that the poet's works are the expression of a potentially unified subject and that the purpose of interpretation is to cancel out the contradictions in the works to determine what (who) is ultimately expressed there, be that interpretation formulated in terms of a heart of hearts or of a fundamental project. Moreover, both readings are faithful to Baudelaire's text in that they are written in the same conceptual language as that upon which the poet's rhetoric draws and make no assumptions that cannot be supported in Baudelaire's "own" words. Does he not write in *Fusées:* "To find subjects, γνωθί σεαυτον [know thyself]" (*OC,* 1267)? What more valid authorization to read his poems as attempts at sincere self-expression – if not perhaps the famous letter to Ancelle in which he claims that "in this *atrocious* book I put all *my heart,* all my *tenderness,* all my *religion* (travestied), all my *hatred.* It is true that I shall write the opposite, that I shall swear the opposite, . . . that it is a book of *pure art,* of *trickery,* of *jugglery,* and I shall lie through my teeth" (letter of February 18, 1866, quoted in S, 58). Yet if we are to take Baudelaire's word as the key to his work, we have a number of mutually incompatible words among which to choose, and ultimately, which one we determine to be valid will depend on a foregone conclusion as to which of the many voices in Baudelaire is "sincere," for even a dialectical reading that eliminates contradictory utterances as ironic (or in bad faith) can only do so by first discerning a nonironic (or authentic) voice, if only a potential one (i.e., what the author would have said had he been sincere).

The most obvious (and probably the most defensible) way of pinning down Baudelaire is to conclude that he identifies with the dandy-satan figure in his texts, a conclusion comfortably supported by his essay "De l'essence du rire," for instance, which characterizes the poet-philosopher as he who, perpetually aware of man's "contradictory double nature," that is, his "infinite wretchedness relative to the absolute Being of whom he has the conception, infinite grandeur relative to animals," has acquired "the ability to split rapidly into two persons and to observe himself with the detachment of a disinterested spectator" (*OC,* 981–82) – and is thus subject to fits of Melmoth-like laughter. If this is the case, we can assume that the more pious or idealistic romantic poems of *Les Fleurs du mal* represent his heart of hearts and that the satanic or ironic ones (as well as many of the prose poems) represent his disillusioned rejection of a religious-romantic ideal. But even if, as we shall see, it is virtually impossible to positively identify an "idealist" poem among the *Fleurs,* Baudelaire's own comments on his work leave considerable doubt as to whether he is speaking seriously about ironic poems or ironically about serious ones. For instance, he claims in a note that "Le Reniement de saint Pierre" ("Saint Peter's Denial") is ironic in the sense that it represents a pastiche of another voice:[21] "Faithful to his painful design, the author of *Flowers of Evil* has, just like an actor [*en parfait comédien*] had to adapt his mind to all sophisms, as to all kinds of corruption" (1557). It seems reasonable, given the context, to assume that the comment, rather than the poem, is ironic, but it is considerably more difficult to qualify the tone of Baudelaire's letter to Victor de Mars, secretary of the *Revue des deux mondes,* concerning his plan for a new poem, which will become the self-castigating "Héautontimorouménos": "As you can see, that makes a lovely fireworks display of monstrosities [*un feu d'artifice de monstruosités*], a veritable *Epilogue,* worthy of the prologue to the reader" (letter of April 7, 1855). Furthermore, whatever conclusion we draw in either case will set off a domino effect that could potentially overturn our readings of all the *Fleurs du mal.*

As for those texts in which Baudelaire seems to be speaking ironically about irony, the encounter of the ironic voices, rather than producing any certitude, only engenders—to borrow Schlegel's words—another generation of little ironies.[22] *La Fanfarlo,* often considered to be Baudelaire's ironic self-portrait, is a case in point. While the portrait of Samuel Cramer is the epitome of the romantic ironist (and begs comparison with Baudelaire), the relationship of the narrative voice—which proclaims that Samuel is "one of the last romantics France possesses" (*OC,* 503)—to the protagonist entails complexities which preclude any simple formulation.[23] Similarly, the essays of *Les Paradis artificiels,* after describing in apparently laudatory detail states of self-conscious intoxication which are in every respect identical to romantic-ironic *volupté,* conclude upon a condemnation of such "artificial" means of acceding to "a suprasensual existence," in favor of a presumably authentic (but surely not *natural?*) means, poetry: "Great poets, philosophers, and prophets are beings who, through the pure, free exercise of will, can attain a state in which they are at once cause and effect, subject and object, hypnotizer and hypnotized" (343). Not only does the passage raise questions as to how poetry is a less artificial intoxicant than drugs—are not the literal and figurative strangely reversed here?—but it inspires considerable doubt as to the authenticity of the statement. Even if we are prepared to take the narrator's word for his rejection of intoxicants (*real,* that is, *artificial* ones), it is not in the

least clear whose word we are taking, for the passage just cited is a quotation from Barbereau. The narrator chimes in after giving us Barbereau's word: "I think exactly as he does."²⁴ Is *this* Baudelaire's word?
Michel Butor, for one, implies that it is, claiming that the *Paradis* constitute a "defense and illustration of poetry,"²⁵ despite the fact that he
has quoted Baudelaire's commentary on *Un Mangeur d'opium*, in
which the poet avows that his voice is so mingled with De Quincey's
that he would be incapable of distinguishing the two: "I made such an
amalgam that I would not be able to recognize the part that comes
from me, and which, besides, can only be quite small" (463; quoted by
Butor, 14). Surely one should hesitate to take Baudelaire-Barbereau's
conclusion at face value after reading Baudelaire–De Quincey's skeptical commentary on the denouement of the *Confessions of an English
Opium Eater*, according to which De Quincey cured himself of his
addiction. Judging such a cure unlikely, the narrator of *Un Mangeur*
speculates that it was an invention, "a sacrifice in which truth was
immolated in honor of decency and public prejudice . . . the public
doesn't like *impenitents*" (436).²⁶

Yet if Baudelaire's own condemnation of hashish is a concession to
public taste, what status are we to accord to his glorification of poetry?
There is one certitude to be extracted from all this: Baudelaire changes
voices with the ease of a *parfait comédien*. The Baudelairean self incorporates the Other with a nonchalance reminiscent of the Protean *moi*
of Samuel Cramer: "After an impassioned reading of a fine book, his
involuntary conclusion was: now there's something good enough to be
by me!—and from there, it takes nothing to conclude: then it *is* by me"
(*OC*, 486). Hence the danger of accepting any voice as authentically
Baudelairean, perhaps least of all the words of texts so seductively candid as the *Journaux intimes*. If the γνωθί σεαυτον (a quotation, of
course) of *Fusées* seems to testify to the fact that Baudelaire's works are
a reflection of his *moi*, other entries attest to the reverse. The famous
maxim of *Mon Coeur mis à nu*, often cited as an expression of the
poet's inner conflicts—"Even as a child, I felt in my heart two contradictory sentiments, the horror of life and the ecstasy of life" (1296)—
bears a suspicious resemblance to an utterance attributed, as it happens,
to De Quincey in *Un Mangeur d'opium*: "Already in my early childhood, the horror of life mingled with the heavenly sweetness of life"
(461). It is impossible to determine whether Baudelaire has appropriated the language of the Other²⁷ or if that language has appropriated
Baudelaire, but the effect is a blurring of the boundaries between self
and other, authenticity and inauthenticity, truth and fiction. It is less
appropriate to speak in terms of reflections and influences than in
terms of a generalized citationality that affects Baudelaire's texts, so

that the original or authoritative source of any given utterance is unlocalizable.

The resulting disintegration of the authorial voice and the dispersion (as opposed to a simple splitting or duplication) of the ego that it implies is also thematized in Baudelaire, a fact that tends to undermine the traditional romantic-ironic interpretations founded on the "double postulation" motif. For example, a more "humoristic" world view is implied in the portrait of the artist as a "*self* with an insatiable desire for the *non-self*" (OC, 1161) in the critical essay *Le Peintre de la vie moderne*, in the prose poem "Les Foules" ("Crowds"), celebrating the *poète-promeneur* who revels in a "holy prostitution of the soul" (1244), or in numerous journal entries associating art, prostitution—"Qu'est-ce que l'art? Prostitution" (1247)—and a kind of pagan religiosity with a joyful relinquishment of the ego: "Ivresse religieuse des grandes villes. —Panthéisme. Moi, c'est tous; tous, c'est moi" ("Religious intoxication of big cities.—Pantheism. I am everyone; everyone is me" [1248]). Such texts invite a reading of Baudelaire that favors the dispersion term[28] of another of his most-cited aphorisms: "De la vaporisation et de la centralisation du *Moi*. Tout est là" ("Of the vaporization and the centralization of the *Ego*. Everything depends on that" [1271])—whereas the traditional *homo duplex* (658) reading privileges the concentration term, in characterizing Baudelaire as the disillusioned romantic for whom the illusion of unity and totality created by poetic language is the sole consolation and compensation for an irretrievable past, a lost ideal, and an alienated self. Insofar as his work entails a questioning of language, but remains tied to a dualistic thematics of presence and absence, the "ironic" Baudelaire epitomizes the aesthetic of *modernity*, as it is defined by Jean-François Lyotard: "Modern aesthetics is an aesthetics of the sublime, though a nostalgic one. It allows the unpresentable to be put forward only as the missing contents; but the form, because of its recognizable consistency, continues to offer to the reader or the viewer matter for solace or pleasure."[29]

An "other," non-nostalgic Baudelaire which both assumes and affirms the arbitrariness of the sign is in fact emerging in the works of some contemporary critics who seek an alternative to a dialectical, totalizing method that must resort to ignoring, obfuscating, or finessing the problems posed by an attempt to synthesize a unified Baudelairean voice. The "postmodern" Baudelaire is of course not a previously unrecognized or misunderstood individual (hence my *which*, above), but a text; for it is by rejecting the presupposition of a unified subject and therefore by shifting the emphasis from intentions to the languages— or "codes"—which compose a text, that contemporary theoreticians have sought to elaborate a critical language capable of taking into account the incoherencies and contradictions inherent in literary texts. The postmodernist approach to Baudelaire is therefore essentially a reading based on the notion that the text, rather than the subject, is self-reflexive, and which proposes to describe the manner in which the different voices of the text function as commentaries and counter-commentaries on one another.

Two particularly notable efforts at nonbiographical, nonreductive readings of Baudelaire that have appeared in recent years are Leo Bersani's *Baudelaire and Freud* and Barbara Johnson's *Défigurations du langage poétique*. For Bersani, the primary interest of Baudelaire lies in the tension between two voices or types of language, that which "gives us images of . . . psychic fragmentation" and that which "documents a determined resistance to all such ontological floating."[30] The former manifests itself in the vague, abstractly sensuous language of those love poems such as "La Chevelure," "L'Invitation au voyage," or "Le Beau navire," which capture the spiritualized sensuality of "mobile desiring fantasy" (*BF,* 35); the latter is apparent in such bitterly ironic poems as "L'Irrémédiable" and "L'Héautontimorouménos," but is predominant in the more realist poems of *Tableaux parisiens* and the *Petits Poèmes en prose,* in which the narrator constantly seeks to reappropriate himself as a totality in the self-images (the artist, the prostitute, the beggar, etc.) that he projects into his fiction. Whereas the earlier Baudelaire is roughly assimilable to the "unanchored self" of the artist-prostitute ("l'homme des foules"), he later comes to identify with the ironic prince-dandy.

Johnson's book focuses on the manner in which the presumed distinction between poetry and prose, figurative and literal language, is undermined by a simultaneous reading of the verse and prose versions of "La Chevelure" and "L'Invitation au voyage," as well as in certain prose poems—e.g., "Le Thyrse," "Le Gâteau," and "Le Galant tireur"—that thematize the notions of duality and/or figuration. The *Petits Poèmes en prose* are found to function as deconstructive readings of the verse poems, in that they throw into relief the conventional, coded nature of a poetic diction that was traditionally valued as original or "priceless"—the antithesis of the banal, commonplace currency of social exchange.

While both works are nonreductive and nondialectical in that they avoid reading Baudelaire in terms of a series of vertical dichotomies (high/low, good/evil, God/Satan, etc.), they also rely heavily on a horizontal dichotomy, corresponding roughly in both cases to a distinction between the earlier and the later Baudelaire, and between the poetry and the prose, with Bersani emphasizing the former division, Johnson the latter. They nonetheless arrive at antithetical conclusions:

for Bersani, the "postmodern" Baudelaire is the fragmented self of the sensuous love poetry, while for Johnson it is the poet of the *Petits Poèmes en prose*. Johnson's conclusion is particularly relevant to the present study, since it essentially establishes a division between a non-ironic, mystified voice, and an ironic, demystifying (deconstructing) voice in Baudelaire.[31] According to her reading, the prose poems constitute an ironic commentary on and an implicit rejection of the poetic rhetorical style assumed in *Les Fleurs du mal*. Bersani, too, finds the later poems to be more ironic than the first, but he does not propose that the later works ironize at the expense of the earlier ones, since they are, if anything, more "mystified" than the "psychic fragmentation" poetry.

The fact that it is possible for two responsible readers to draw such diametrically opposed conclusions says much about the difficulty of distinguishing between a mystified and a demystified language, or an inauthentic and an authentic voice in Baudelaire, for a great deal depends upon the value which the reader accords to poetic language—or rather, which he or she assumes that the poet accords it within the context of his work. If we find that romantic-poetic language is treated as "authentic"—i.e., original, priceless, etc.—within a given work, then it will appear that the use of such language represents a mystified self.

If, on the other hand, we find that the poetic language of a text flaunts its own inauthenticity (its artificiality or figurativeness), then the adoption of that language seems to constitute a demystified gesture of self-abandonment. Now, Johnson has demonstrated very nicely in *Défigurations* that in economic terms, the "deconstruction" of poetic language consists of rendering manifest "its status as a pure linguistic value, arbitrary and contingent" (*DLP,* 152), that is, reinserting it into an economy of exchange, of *valant-pour.* Moreover, despite the emphasis that her argument lays on "form," by defining the distinction between poetic language and prose in terms of the Jakobsonian dichotomy metaphor/metonymy, Johnson's analysis also shows that the demystification of the poetic is as much an effect of semantics, or theme, as of relationships among terms. If the banalization, devalorization, or *devenir-cliché* of certain "poetic" expressions is the result of their juxtaposition with terms perceived as prosaic by readers of the day, those prosaic expressions, because they constitute the unmarked term of the opposition poetry/prose, are perceived as "absolutely" prosaic—that is, their banality is a function of their meaning rather than of their linguistic environment. The "langage du comptoir," or "language of the counter" (see *DLP,* 130–33) of "L'Invitation au voyage" in prose, which brings the erstwhile high-flown rhetoric of gold, jewels, or treasures down to a pedestrian level, is one manifestation of a thematics of commerce or exchange that runs *throughout* Baudelaire's work, where it is juxtaposed and intermingled with the entire gamut of supposedly noneconomic Platonic-Christian values. The interplay between the themes of material or monetary wealth and of immaterial or intrinsic values tends to undercut not only the distinction between literal and figurative significations, but also the difference between the natural and the artificial, sincerity and deceit.

This subversion of traditional hierarchies is more a matter of thematics than of textual practice (for example, the choice of prose over verse, or realist technique as opposed to irrealism), a fact that is indicative of the poet's particular historical situation. Baudelaire was writing during the phenomenal rise of bourgeois, capitalist society, at a time when the questioning of traditional values "literally" took the form of an economic discourse, that is, when the notion of intrinsic value was being superseded by that of exchange value. The traces of that social evolution are everywhere apparent in Baudelaire's writings, in the motifs associated with city life—commercialism, prostitution, crowds, gambling.[32] Thus applying an economic discourse to Baudelaire no more entails imposing on his text an interpretive language that is foreign to it than does reading it in terms of romantic dualisms. The result of the copresence of romantic idealist and bourgeois materialist themes in the Baudelairean text is a conflict of codes from which emerges a sole truth: the fact of their mutual interdependence. Now this is precisely what Johnson demonstrates in regard to the relationship between "figurative" and "literal" language, poetry and prose. However, insofar as the applicability of post-Saussurean linguistics is assured via the intermediary of economic discourse, I would argue that that conflict of cultural codes is as omnipresent as is the analogous interaction between idealist and materialist language. If the work of demystifying romantic language seems to have fallen more heavily on the *Petits Poèmes en prose* than on *Les Fleurs du mal,* this is largely because the former are billed as vignettes of Parisian life. Similarly, the *Tableaux parisiens* may appear more "disillusioned" than the poems of *Spleen et idéal.* The fact remains, however, that from "Au lecteur" ("To the Reader") and "Bénédiction" on, the rhetoric of good and evil is bound up with a "langage du comptoir" in such a manner that it becomes impossible to determine whether the poet identifies with Jesus or with the merchants in the temple.

Les Fleurs du mal has two beginnings, "Au lecteur" and "Bénédiction"; each proposes a program for reading Baudelaire. If, on the one hand, these two programs correspond to the two postulations, *Satan/ Dieu,* they also correspond to the opposition *vaporisation/concentration.* "Au lecteur" places the text under the sign of *Satan Trismégiste:*

Sur l'oreiller du mal c'est Satan Trismégiste
Qui berce longuement notre esprit enchanté
Et le riche métal de notre volonté
Est tout vaporisé par ce savant chimiste. (*OC,* 5)

On the pillow of evil, it is Satan Trismegistus who slowly rocks our
enchanted minds, and the rich metal of our will is vaporized by that
cunning chemist.

The Satan thus invoked is not simply the counterpart to the Christian god; the qualification *Trismégiste* transforms him into a representative of pagan mythology. The allusion is to Hermes Trismegistos, the
Greek appellation for the Egyptian god Thoth, the inventor of writing, scribe and interpreter to the gods; Hermes Trismegistos is credited
with a number of mystical, philosophical, and alchemistic writings.
The Greeks identified him with Hermes, god of eloquence, commerce,
and theft. Hence of course the reference here to the "rich metal of our
will," as well as a number of allusions, throughout Baudelaire's works,
to the verbal alchemy of the writer, who changes things into their
opposites—be he an "unknown Hermes" who transforms "gold into
iron and heaven into hell" (*OC,* 73), or the "perfect chemist and blessed
soul" who proclaims to the city of Paris: "You gave me mud and I have
made it into gold" (180). It is no coincidence if the city of Paris, donor
of all that mud, is referred to as an "énorme catin" ("huge whore")—not
only are prostitution and mud frequently associated with Paris, but in
"Au lecteur," an "antique catin" is representative of clandestine pleasures. Now the prostitute, that "hired body" (32), is a sort of pay-as-
you-go muse, a parodic version of her idealist counterpart; her tutelage
invites the reader to literalize the allusions to gold, which is either
vaporized or produced with her help. It should be remarked, however,
that when the poet is *producing* gold, he becomes a "blessed soul"
("âme sainte"): thus the sanctity of the poet is connected with the production of wealth in a context that causes the term *or* ("gold") to vacil-
late between the literal and the figurative.

In "Bénédiction" (*OC,* 7–9), the poet is patently assimilated to the
Christ child in a display of romantic *dolorisme* so blatant that it has
alternatively been dismissed by critics or taken as a sign of Baudelaire's
most unutterable suffering.[33] Now "under the invisible protection of
an Angel," the poet-Christ—although he subsists on a suspiciously
pagan diet of ambrosia and nectar—is being purified in preparation for
the "holy ecstasies" ("saintes voluptés") of eternal incorporeal existence.
The symbol of his nobility ("noblesse") will, appropriately, be a "mystical crown" made of "pure light"—that is, a halo beyond price, since
the poet specifies that even the rarest metals and gems, assembled by

the hand of God, are unsuitable components for it. His pretensions to nobility notwithstanding, the Poet (capitalized in the text) is expressing himself through an impressive collection of romantic commonplaces—though the contradiction is not as great as it might appear, since *noble* comes from the Latin *nobilis,* for *knowable, well known, famous,* and of course a nobility not recognized as such would be of little value. Furthermore, the rhetoric of "Bénédiction" was well known in Baudelaire's day, so that one may wonder if the benediction (from the Latin *bene,* "well" and *dicere,* "speak") is not a fine speech for the benefit of a public that frowns upon impenitents. One might argue that the rhetoric of evil was familiar to the poet's contemporaries, as well, and is equally insincere,[34] but then I am not proposing that there is a choice to be made between a good and an evil Baudelaire, since they are integral parts of the same configuration. As I suggested earlier, the opposition between "Au lecteur" and "Bénédiction" is not exhausted by the simple dichotomy God/Satan (and all the romantic-ironic dualisms that it implies: good/evil, essence/appearance, meaning/expression, high/low, eternity/temporality, work/play, sincerity/deceit, etc.). The vaporization-Hermes-alchemy-prostitution themes adumbrated in "Au lecteur" infiltrate Baudelaire's text in a subversive manner that destabilizes those seemingly clear-cut oppositions; the Hermes-alchemy "program" for reading Baudelaire brings out an implicit commentary on the transmutability of meanings and the relativity of values.

The article "L'Ecole païenne" ("The Pagan School") constitutes one of a number of nodal points in the network that Baudelaire's text weaves out of the motifs of Christianism versus paganism, idealism versus materialism. Anterior to *Les Fleurs du mal,* the article appears to be a vehement defense of the idealist position represented by the *Poëte* of "Bénédiction." The critic ironically presents the pagan position—which he attributes to the noxious influence of a "Literature corrupted by materialistic sentimentality" (*OC,* 624/73)—by ascribing it to an*other,* in what is ostensibly a citation: "We must return to the true doctrines, *momentarily* obscured by the vile Galilean" (623/73). The narrator (whose moralistic tone and indignant rejection of the artist-as-opium-eater image propagated by the Pagan School [626/75] recall the narrator of *Les Paradis artificiels*) assumes the voice of reason, extolling "the pure delights of honest activity," while condemning the "pagan" for his disdain for "the useful, the true, the good, the truly admirable," nourished by an "immoderate love of form" (627/76–77). He berates the "pagan" poets for practicing a soulless, unoriginal, mercenary formalism:

Pastiche! pastiche! Vous avez sans doute perdu votre âme quelque part, dans quelque mauvais endroit, pour que vous couriez ainsi à travers le passé comme des corps vides . . . ? Qu'attendez-vous du ciel ou de la sottise du public? Une fortune suffisante pour élever dans vos mansardes des autels à Priape ou à Bacchus? . . .

Est-ce Vénus Aphrodite ou Vénus Mercenaire qui soulagera les maux qu'elle vous aura causés? Toutes ces statues de marbre seront-elles des femmes dévouées au jour de l'agonie, au jour du remords, au jour de l'impuissance? Buvez-vous des bouillons d'ambroisie? Mangez-vous des côtelettes de Paros? Combien prête-t-on sur une lyre au Mont-de-Piété? (626/75)

Pastiche, Pastiche! Apparently you have lost your soul somewhere, in some bad spot, since you seem to be running through the past like empty bodies . . . ? What do you expect from heaven or the stupidity of the public? Enough money to raise altars in your attics to Priapus and to Bacchus? . . . Will Venus Aphrodite or the Mercenary Venus assuage the griefs she will have caused you? Will all those marble statues be devoted wives on the day of death, the day of remorse, the day of helplessness? Do you drink broths made of ambrosia? Do you eat cutlets from Paros? How much can you get on a lyre at the pawnshop?

The ambrosia that the narrator sarcastically suggests will feed the *païens* here presumably represents the vacuity of art without substance, the empty rewards of art for art's sake, a mere pastiche of real art ("you can't eat appearances"); as such, it is a parodic version of the "real" ambrosia, that other-worldly nourishment for the pure, incorporeal being of the true Poet. But, to follow the same logic, you can't eat essences, either: it is very hard to distinguish between the vacuity of pure form and the immateriality of pure essence, or soul. The problem is complicated by the fact that the narrator must have recourse to the signs of material wealth in order to explain the difference in value between empty formalist art and art that represents the "just" and the "true." Woe to the child nourished on mere appearances:

Si la puissance dans le crime ou dans l'art ne l'élève pas au-dessus des fortunes vulgaires, à trente ans il crèvera à l'hôpital. Son âme, sans cesse irritée et inassouvie, s'en va à travers le monde, le monde occupé et laborieux . . . comme une prostituée, criant: Plastique! plastique! (*OC*, 627/76)

If power in crime or in art do not raise him above the average lot, at thirty he will die like a dog in the poorhouse. His soul, constantly excited and unappeased, goes about the world, the busy, toiling world . . . like a prostitute, crying: Plastic! plastic!

The prostituted pagan out hawking his virtues here represents a parodic version of the pure Christian soul—parodic because it literalizes or concretizes the ideal or immaterial, thus devalorizing the supposedly priceless (paradoxically by valorizing it, by attributing to it a monetary value). However, the inescapable implication is that true art, art that represents the True, should be rewarded by material wealth; the distinction between artist and prostitute fades. The narrator has already lamented the fact that "many people have encouraged with their money and their applause this deplorable craze" (*OC,* 626/75); in his conclusion he recounts an anecdote implying that formalist art is a kind of counterfeit currency used to buy recognition (i.e., nobility):

> Je me rappelle avoir entendu dire à un artiste farceur qui avait reçu une pièce de monnaie fausse: Je la garde pour un pauvre. Le misérable prenait un infernal plaisir à voler le pauvre et à jouir en même temps des bénéfices d'une réputation de charité. (628/77)

> I recall having heard an artist, who was a practical joker and who had received a false coin, say on one occasion: I shall keep it for some poor person. The wretch took an infernal pleasure in robbing the poor and in enjoying at the same time the benefit of a reputation for charity.

Virtually the same anecdote provides the pretext for the prose poem "La Fausse monnaie," in which the principal "profit" that the joker-thief hopes to reap from his charity is explicitly designated as salvation, or that true nobility enjoyed by the Poet of "Bénédiction":

> Il avait voulu faire à la fois la charité et une bonne affaire, gagner quarante sols et le coeur de Dieu; emporter le paradis économiquement, enfin attraper gratis un brevet d'homme charitable. (*OC,* 274)

> He had wanted to perform an act of charity and make a good deal at the same time, earn a little money and God's love, to get to heaven economically; in short, to pick up the credentials of a charitable man for nothing.

The narrator's reproach bears not on the fact that his companion presumes to buy salvation, but that he is attempting to do so with *counterfeit money;* indeed, a particularity of the virtue of charity is that it always implies a monetary transaction, as the etymology suggests (*caritas:* Christian love, costliness, high regard, love—from *carus,* dear, costly, loved). Paradoxically, if the essence of charity is Christian love, this essence cannot manifest itself except through the formal act of donation; good intentions of themselves are worthless, because unknowable if not displayed.[35] There is a clear analogy here with the phenomenon of prostitution,[36] which also served as an emblem of soulless art: presumably the prostitute is debased because she sells her body, all the exterior manifestations of love, without the soul, or sentiment (prostitute is from *prostituere*, to expose publicly); but as is the case with charity, the *caritas* or *venus* is nothing if not displayed in the proper forms—so how is it possible to distinguish between the real and the counterfeit? And what difference does it make, since the contract only specifies the form? The narrator of "La Fausse monnaie" indirectly raises just such a question, for although he concludes by condemning his companion for "the ineptitude of his calculation," thereby implying that the practical joker was foolish to think he could pass off his charity for real, this is only after he has first mistakenly assumed that the purpose of the joke was to inspire an amusing speculation on the possible consequences of the act. One possibility that occurs to him—"Might it not proliferate into real coins?"—is apparently that the coin *could* pass for real, in which case the act of charity would be realized, as well. Thus, as Suzanne Guerlac has argued, the prose poem constitutes a meditation on the act of interpretation: "there is no way of telling" within the context of the poem whether the coin is false or real, since its value (like the meaning of a text) would depend on its exchange value (or interpretation)—that is, the value given it by *another*.[37] I would qualify her conclusion with a single nuance: the point to be taken from this is not that there is "no way of telling" if the coin is real or false (which suggests that it *does* have an intrinsic value, even if unknown), but rather that the reader should assume that it *is* false, according to the donor's standards. The narrator's insight (which he later seems to deny) is that *true* and *false* are meaningless outside of a system of exchange determined by convention; the same perspicacity is apparent in his cynical allusion to the "brevet d'homme charitable," for *brevet* (a kind of certificate) signifies "title or diploma issued by the state, permitting the holder to exercise certain functions and certain rights." A *brevet* is a paper-money version or textual equivalent of the coin.

Needless to say, then, if the allegory of the false coin was intended to denounce the bad faith of the *école païenne* and the *école plastique*, it casts more than a little doubt upon the credibility of Baudelaire's own self-announced "good faith" in exposing this "dangerous comedy" (*OC*, 628/77). In pronouncing a *malédiction* on paganism, frivolity, artificiality, and deceit in the name of Christianism, labor, authenticity, and sincerity, is he bargaining for "the credentials of a charitable man"? But what then of Baudelaire's praise, elsewhere, for Banville, and his eloquent defense of art for art's sake in the Gautier article ("Poetry . . . does not have Truth for its object, it has only Itself" [685])? Do any of these represent the authentic word of Baudelaire? Is that word "worth" anything? The lesson of "La Fausse monnaie" is of course that it all depends upon what the reader will buy.

There was really no need, in fact, to speculate that "Bénédiction" was all a matter of *bien dire* and *bénéfices;* Baudelaire has done it for us. In "Perte d'auréole" ("The Lost Halo" [*OC,* 299–300]), the romantic-idealist poet is presented in a situation analogous to that of the trick-ster in "La Fausse monnaie" (or in "L'Ecole païenne"). He is recognized at the outset by his interlocutor (both speak in the first person, so neither can be considered the narrator), who ironically expresses his astonishment at finding "the drinker of quintessences . . . the ambrosia-eater" in "a place of ill repute [*mauvais lieu*]!" The explanation is that the poet—like the pagan who has "lost [his] soul in some bad spot [*mauvais endroit*]" (626/75)—has lost his halo in the mud of a Parisian street. The soul-halo of this poet is not a "diadem . . . of pure light" (9), a symbol of intrinsic and quintessential *nobility;* it is a golden ring (*auréole*) which, like the *brevet* of "La Fausse monnaie," is simply a sign, or as the poet puts it, an insignia (*insigne*), that is, a "badge, em-blem, or other distinguishing mark of office or honor." Without it, its owner can "go about incognito . . . like simple mortals," a welcome prospect for one weary of "dignity." Moreover, the poet—uniting the roles of both the practical joker and the speculative narrator of "La Fausse monnaie"—gleefully anticipates the consequences of his halo's falling into other hands: "Ensuite je pense avec joie que quelque mau-vais poëte la ramassera et s'en coiffera impudemment. Faire un heureux, quelle jouissance! et surtout un heureux qui me fera rire! Pensez à X, ou à Z! Hein! comme ce sera drôle!" ("And then I think with delight that some bad poet will pick it up and brazenly put it on. What a joy to make someone happy! especially someone who will make me laugh! Think of X, or of Z! How funny that would be!"). But the ironic poet may not have the last laugh, because the malicious act of "charity" ("making someone happy") he imagines could turn out to be real; like the fake coin, the newly acquired insignia could generate some *béné-fices* (profits, benefits). The *brevet* of the "noble" (ambrosia-eating, etc.) poet is a romantic-idealist rhetoric recognizable by the commonplaces (*lieux communs*) that anyone *can* pick up, and which do not constitute a guarantee of authenticity. Like the prostitute, they are public prop-erty. The question is, will the bad poet know how to turn them to his advantage? Due to the silence of the narrative voice in "Perte d'auréole," the reader is left to speculate.

The place of ill repute (*mauvais lieu*) in Baudelaire is a place where people lose their souls or sell them: where the *propre* (in every sense: the clean, the proper, that which is proper or distinctive to something, that which is appropriate or suitable) becomes *impropre* (etymologically, the converse of the *propre*), where essence becomes property, where the immaterial is materialized and the absolute is relativized. It is a hell, but a peculiar one: not simply the opposite of heaven, the realm of the ideal and the immutable, but a parody of it, where eloquence and commerce transform the ideal into the commonplace, the priceless into common tender. Such is the gambling-hall hell of "Le Joueur généreux" ("The Generous Gambler"),[38] a playful Satan Trismegistus figure who seduces the narrator with his "suavity of diction" and reimburses him for his soul with material wealth. The brothel is the place of ill repute *par excellence* because the institution of prostitution is emblematic of the law of inherent otherness, according to which *tout passe par l'autre*: the *moi* is always *tous*, interior is exterior, intrinsic value is always already extrinsic, or exchange value. If poetry is a "holy prostitution of the soul" in that it entails opening the self to otherness, it is so in the most literal sense, too, as the cynical narrator of "Conseils aux jeunes littérateurs" ("Advice to Young Men of Letters") insists: "Literature, which is the most invaluable material, is first of all the filling up of columns; and the literary architect, whose name alone does not assure a profit [*bénéfice*], must sell at any price" (*OC*, 478–79).

"La Muse vénale" thematizes the poet's situation in more romantic terms:

O muse de mon coeur, amante des palais,
Auras-tu, quand Janvier lâchera ses Borées,
Durant les noirs ennuis des neigeuses soirées,
Un tison pour chauffer tes deux pieds violets?

Ranimeras-tu donc tes épaules marbrées
Aux nocturnes rayons qui percent les volets?
Sentant ta bourse à sec autant que ton palais,
Récolteras-tu l'or des voûtes azurées?

Il te faut, pour gagner ton pain de chaque soir,
Comme un enfant de choeur, jouer de l'encensoir,
Chanter des *Te Deum* auxquels tu ne crois guère

Ou, saltimbanque à jeun, étaler tes appas
Et ton rire trempé de pleurs qu'on ne voit pas,
Pour faire épanouir la rate du vulgaire. (*OC*, 14–15)

O muse of my heart, lover of palaces, will you have, when January unleashes its north winds, during the dark desolation of snowy evenings, a coal to warm your blue feet? Will the nocturnal rays that filter through your shutters warm your mottled shoulders? When your purse is as dry as your palate, will you harvest the gold of the azure-vaulted skies? To earn your bread each night, you must, like a choir boy, swing the censer [idiomatically, "pour out flattery"], sing *Te Deums* in which you don't believe, or, like a hungry acrobat, display your charms and your laugh bathed in unseen tears, to make the vulgar herd shake with laughter.

The oxymoronic incarnation of the muse in the person of a prostitute sets up a play between material and immaterial, prosaic and poetic, literal and figural, which marks the entire poem.

For if the *venal* (which is derived from *venum*, "sale," as is *vil*) debases the figure of the muse, the poetic allusion simultaneously dignifies the prostitute. The same language that banalizes the noble also "ennobles the lot of the basest things" (*OC*, 79). Similarly, the play on palace/palate (*palais/palais*) creates an anomalous link between the romantic magnificence of palatial elegance and the sordid banality of starvation. The "gold of the azure-vaulted skies" (*azur* of course always evokes the ideal or the infinite) is devalorized by the context into simple currency—and vice versa: money is endowed with a romantic aura. Thus the poem contains an implicit commentary on the alchemic powers of language, in which the literal and figurative senses of gold are indissociable. It is both an exercise in "extracting beauty from evil" with fine language, and a blunt statement on the material benefits that can be derived from reciting *Te Deums*—or benedictions—"en parfait comédien." Thus the theme of prostitution articulates the problematic of referentiality (content versus form) with that of sincerity (good faith versus bad faith). For by pointing to the indifference of the referent, the poet is asserting the priority of signifier over signified, thus affirming that the "essence" or "soul" of art is in its appearance; the intrinsic value of art lies paradoxically in what is apparently most extrinsic: mere words, artifice. If this is the case, art has nothing to do with "expression," and the very question of the sincerity of a work of art is meaningless.

Defenders of the "good-hearted" Baudelaire have made much of the sympathy for the poor and the oppressed supposedly expressed in his numerous poems on beggars, prostitutes, and the like. But those poems—sincere or insincere—are also about the illusions conjured up by poetic language. "A une mendiante rousse" ("To a Red-Haired Beggar Girl" [*OC*, 79–81]) is a case in point: the poet begins by claiming that despite her rags, he recognizes the beggar-girl's "natural" beauty, but then proceeds to "dress" her in the finery and jewels that would make her beauty manifest, thus inspiring suitors to shower her with gifts and poets to glorify her in verse:

Perles de la plus belle eau
Sonnets de maître Belleau
Par tes galants mis aux fers
Sans cesse offerts

Pearls of the finest water, sonnets by Master Belleau, constantly offered by your suitors, enchained by love. . . .

Although the conclusion asserts once again that her beauty is inherent, independent of any supplement contributed by ornamentation— "Va donc, sans autre ornement, / Parfum, perles, diamant, / Que ta maigre nudité, / O ma beauté!" ("Go then, with no other ornament— perfume, pearls, diamonds—than your thin nudity, O my beauty")— the very existence of the poem undercuts that assertion, since that "beauty" is a product of the poet's eloquence. Moreover, the poem thematizes its own subterfuge by implying an equivalence between material adornment and poetry (pearls and sonnets): just as the girl's "natural" beauty is unrecognizable without the conventional accoutrements of beauty, so the poet can only affirm the aesthetic value of the unconventional poetic object by clothing it in conventional formulas. The mechanism of poetic artifice is particularly apparent in this poem because it thematizes the problem of inherent versus superficial beauty in terms of content versus form. But it is nonetheless evident in those poems in which the indifference of the referent is only implied, as is the case with "La Chevelure" or "L'Invitation au voyage" and the other poems of suprasensuality. Indeed, if we reread "La Chevelure" in a somewhat more literal frame of mind, it becomes apparent that the final stanza contains a semi-explicit allusion to its own rhetorical ruses: the narrator steps back at the end to point out that the voyage has been an exercise in the creative power of the poetic imagination (hence the oxymoron—"O fertile lethargy"—since he has produced only an illusion), and that he intends to repeat the experience:

Longtemps! toujours! ma main dans ta crinière lourde
Sèmera le rubis, la perle et le saphir,
Afin qu'à mon désir tu ne sois jamais sourde!
N'est-tu pas l'oasis où je rêve, et la gourde
Où je hume à longs traits le vin du souvenir? (*OC,* 26)

For a long time, forever! my hand in your heavy mane will strew rubies, pearls, and sapphires, so that you will never be deaf unto my desire! Are you not the oasis where I dream, and the gourd from which I drink deeply of the wine of memory?

While it can be argued that the metaphoricity of the language in the final stanza maintains the illusion of unity and totality—the sense of "universal analogy" of the type made famous in the poem "Correspondances"—I would contend that the concluding question reasserts the distance that separates "je" from "tu," the narrator from the Other, and breaks the spell of the symbolic language by alerting the reader to the *sorcellerie évocatoire* that Baudelaire has been practicing here. The question "are you not the oasis?" calls attention to a metaphoricity that would have passed unnoticed in the affirmative; of course "tu" *is* not the oasis, etc., but rather has been serving that function, standing for the muse in her capacity as pretext for erotic fantasies. I refer the reader to Barbara Johnson's discussion of the dilemma that this question poses for the reader (is it a "rhetorical" question or a "real" question?), in which she demonstrates that either reading calls into question the functioning of the metaphor (*DLP,* 51). I would disagree with Johnson's conclusions only in maintaining that this ambiguous ending must have a more radical effect on our reading of the entire poem than it does for her analysis. I would argue that the final verse of "La Chevelure" offers an example of what de Man, in "The Rhetoric of Temporality," terms an ironic or demystified language—that is, a language that asserts its own artificiality (its inadequacy in suppressing the difference between sign and meaning)[39]—because these concluding lines affirm that poetry is not (about) possession, but dispossession, i.e. (about) desire. In this respect I concur with Leo Bersani's reading of the poem, which shows how it exemplifies the Freudian notion that "desire is always a lack" (see *BF,* 35–45). For Johnson, there is indeed a moment of disillusionment, but not within "La Chevelure" in verse; it is rather the prose version of the poem, "Un Hémisphère dans une chevelure" ("A Hemisphere in a Head of Hair"), which, via a "barely perceptible ironization of its own illusion" (*DLP,* 40), constitutes "a deconstructive reading of the verse poem" (48). Furthermore, Johnson's demonstration of how this deconstructive reading functions is a very convincing one. However, because the subject of her book is the difference between the verse and the prose poems (insofar as that difference forces us to rethink the nature of figurative language in general), the exigencies of her argument lead her to establish an overly rigid opposition between *Les Fleurs du mal* and the *Petits Poèmes en prose,* thereby ignoring some of the irony of the *Fleurs.*

To return to the final stanza of "La Chevelure," the suggestion, in the last two lines, of a kind of convention or contractual agreement uniting poet and mistress-muse reflects back on the preceding lines, which we were straining to read metaphorically (but how? as "the metaphorical evocation of the sexual act," as Johnson suggests? [*DLP,* 45]), giving them a decidedly more mundane cast. The pearls, rubies, and sapphires that the poet will strew in the woman's hair so that she will always respond to his desire in fact imply a contractual relationship between the two "lovers" far more explicitly than does the final question—more explicitly, but none the less figuratively, since the precious stones are but emblems of an exchange value—but then they are that "literally," as well. Once again, the distinction between the figural and literal blurs . . . and once again that blurring is implicitly linked with the prostitution motif.

Such poems as "A une mendiante rousse," and less obviously, many other *Fleurs du mal*, implicitly pose the question "Laquelle est la vraie?" ("Which Is the Real One?") [*OC,* 290–91]), which is raised in the prose poem by that name. As long as she is *Bien dite* ("well said"), it matters not whether Bénédicta—and the allusion to "Bénédiction" is certainly not gratuitous—is "really" *idéal* or *canaille* (*DLP,* 76), just as the question of what Baudelaire "really" thought is irrelevant. Much Baudelaire criticism has turned on the question of good faith versus bad faith—or sentiment versus artifice. But the implicit "message" of *Les Fleurs du mal* is that this is an illusory opposition—a message to which the more explicit, allegorical commentaries on the question in such texts as the *Petits Poèmes en prose* should not deafen us.[40] The verse and the prose poems, as well as the critical articles, pose the same questions in a variety of languages—the nostalgic romantic-ironic rhetoric of the *Fleurs,* the cynical allegorical language of the prose poems, or the overbearing discourse of knowledge in the criticism. It is easy to be seduced by the lyricism of the *Fleurs* into taking them too "literally," or seriously, precisely because we take them too "figuratively," by reading them "straight," as the metaphorical, purely (or primarily) connotative texts they ostensibly are. Yet when literalized, the language of the *Fleurs* takes on all the grotesqueness of a self-parody—and the process of literalization can be conducted with or without reference to the *Petits Poèmes en prose,* although those texts, as we have seen, corroborate the conclusions of an irreverent reading of *Les Fleurs du mal.*

The danger of designating the ironic-allegorical prose poems as deconstructive readings of a poetic language characterized by its "fundamental ignorance [*méconnaissance*] of its relationship to other codes" (*DLP,* 139) is that such an assertion—even though it assiduously avoids any suggestion of authorial intent—comes perilously close to implying that the author of the verse poems was a victim of the same *méconnaissance* that characterizes the poetic language, whereas the author of the prose poems was disillusioned. However, the studied unsentimentality[41]—or resigned cynicism—of a text such as "La Fausse monnaie" is as coded as the lyricism of the *Fleurs;* to paraphrase de Man, to use a demystified language is not the same as to be demystified. The same

may be said, of course, for mystified language. The cynical narrator of
many of the prose poems might well be a romantic idealist traveling
incognito; inversely, a cynical poet could just as well don the insignia
of noble, romantic rhetoric. We tend to forget this, particularly in the
latter case, because a "sincerity-effect," or air of mystification, is coded
into the rhetoric of lyricism. But the incognito metaphor is not intended to suggest that the poet can be distinguished from the mask,
the speaker from the voice; as Vincent Descombes has remarked in a
paraphrase of Derrida, "the only way to pretend to speak Chinese
when one is speaking to a Chinese citizen, is to address him *in
Chinese.*"[42]

In a proposed preface for a third edition of *Les Fleurs du mal*, Baudelaire declines to "expliquer pourquoi et comment j'ai fait ce livre":

> Mène-t-on la foule . . . dans la loge de la comédienne? Montre-t-on
> au public . . . le mécanisme des trucs? Lui explique-t-on . . . jusqu'à
> quelle dose l'instinct et la sincérité sont mêlés aux rubriques et au
> charlatanisme indispensable dans l'amalgame de l'oeuvre? (*OC*, 188)

> Do you take the throngs . . . into the actress's dressing room? Do
> you show the public . . . how special effects are produced? Do you
> explain to them . . . what dosage of instinct and sincerity are mixed
> with the rubrics and the charlatanism that is indispensable in the
> amalgam of the work?

That refusal—some would say failure—to "close off the plurality of
codes" (*SZ*, 212/206), however limited that plurality might be, either by
explaining his work from without or by rigidly hierarchizing the
codes within it, was Baudelaire's legacy to postmodernity. If there is a
figure of the "humoristic" artist in the Baudelairean text, it is perhaps
the *comédien* Fancioulle, the mime who is indistinguishable from his
role, and whose only insignia—an "invisible halo . . . in which were
mingled, in a strange amalgam, the rays of Art and the glory of Martyr-
dom" (*OC*, 271)—represents an eccentric alloy of artifice and sentiment, of *feu d'artifice* and *dolorisme*. It is no coincidence if, in "De l'essence du rire," the Hoffmannian mime, creator of *le comique absolu*,
incarnates the nonironic artist who cedes the perilous pleasure of having the last laugh to his audience.[43] Perhaps the reader should sense a
warning in this characterization of his art: "The essence of this comic
is to appear unself-conscious and to develop in the spectator, or rather
in the reader, a joyful sense of his own superiority" (993).

It is difficult to conclude with these words in mind. Can there be a
last word on Baudelaire? Is it possible to respond with any certitude to
the question "lequel est le vrai?" by choosing between the ironic, dualistic, Melmoth-like poet and the humoristic pluralistic trickster? In the

light of the preceding, it is predictable that I will answer in the negative; but I will not say that there is no difference between the two, nor
that that difference is "indifferent." The romantic-ironic version of
Baudelaire is, in Barthesian terms, "readable" in his works; it is a product of his society and his time, together with a philosophical tradition
that assures the continuity of his categories and those of the contemporary reader. The humorous Baudelaire is "writable," a figure or
configuration that emerges from the text only through a process of
rewriting. It is not solely, however, a product of contemporary intellectual history; what makes it possible are the traces, in Baudelaire, of an
emergent postmodern mentality. But that nascent postmodernity
which will mature into the contestation of consecrated forms here
manifests itself principally through theme, so that Baudelaire remains
a modern at least in this respect: he has yet to relinquish "the solace of
good forms."

5 : Proust
Forgetting Things Past

Mais le démon socratique, l'ironie, consiste à devancer les rencontres. Chez Socrate, l'intelligence précède encore les rencontres; elle les provoque, elle les suscite et les organise. L'humour de Proust est d'une autre nature: l'humour juif contre l'ironie grecque. Il faut être doué pour les signes, s'ouvrir à leur rencontre, s'ouvrir à leur violence. L'intelligence vient toujours après.[1]

But the Socratic demon, irony, consists in anticipating the encounters. In Socrates, the intelligence still comes before the encounters; it provokes them, it instigates and organizes them. Proust's humor is of another nature: Jewish humor as opposed to Greek irony. One must be endowed for the signs, ready to encounter them, one must open oneself to their violence. The intelligence always comes after.

L'impression est pour l'écrivain ce qu'est l'expérimentation pour le savant, avec cette différence que chez le savant le travail de l'intelligence précède et chez l'écrivain vient après. Ce que nous n'avons pas eu à déchiffrer, à éclaircir par notre effort personnel, ce qui était clair avant nous, n'est pas à nous. Ne vient de nous-même que ce que nous tirons de l'obscurité qui est en nous et que ne connaissent pas les autres.[2]

The impression is for the writer what experiment is for the scientist, with the difference that in the scientist the work of the intelligence precedes the experiment and in the writer it comes after the impression. What we have not had to decipher, to elucidate by our own efforts, what was clear before we looked at it, is not ours. From ourselves comes only that which we drag forth from the obscurity which lies within us, that which to others is unknown.

Deleuze's comment, which essentially makes Proust a postmodern, echoes a passage of *Le Temps retrouvé* that is redolent of romanticism: those pages in which the author of *A la recherche du temps perdu* expounds on the "lesson of idealism" (3: 910/3: 948) given him by fate one afternoon at the Guermantes', exalting "inner reality" as "the supreme truth" (3: 882, 902/3: 917, 939) to be communicated through the signs of art. But Deleuze has seized upon the fundamental distinction between the Proustian conception of art and a truly romantic one: the former accords a constitutive—rather than a "reconstitutive," or representational—value to language. When Proust writes that "the world . . . was not created once and for all, but is created afresh as often as an original artist is born" (2: 327/2: 338), he is asserting, not that art "distorts" life, but that art is the production of "reality"; truth is not discovered, but invented. Thus he constantly alludes to the difference between scientific discourse and art: the scientist presupposes the existence of a single totalizable universe regulated by immutable laws; the artist knows that those laws do not preexist, but that every original work of art reinvents them. For the author of the *Recherche*, "the universe is true for us all and dissimilar to each of us" (3: 191/3: 189).

Hence his disdain for "art that calls itself 'realist,'" a sort of "procession of things upon the screen of a cinematograph" which, far from representing reality as it is, merely accumulates those commonplaces— "hackneyed phrases" (3: 881–82/3: 917)—that convention and habit have led us to take for reality: "a sort of waste product of experience, more or less identical for each one of us, since when we speak of bad weather, a war, a taxi stand, a brightly lit restaurant, a garden in bloom, everybody knows what we mean" (3: 890/3: 925). Unlike the romantics, Proust does not bemoan the *inadequacy* of language for self-expression; he only abhors the parroting of clichés—what Barthes will call *la doxa,* or *la bêtise.*[3] True art, according to Proust, effects what the Russian formalists will call a "defamiliarization" of its object; in this respect, the style of *A la recherche du temps perdu* is closer to that of a Robbe-Grillet novel than to Balzacian realism.[4] The writer's task consists of unsettling the reader's habits of perception and of naming, producing a bewildering yet joyful sense of disorientation akin to the *jouissance* that the author of *Le Plaisir du texte* will later associate with the experience of reading the *nouveau roman.* Of course each new "representation" of the world will in turn be taken for a "natural" image of reality, as soon as it has grown familiar, and the task of re-creating the world will fall to another artist. Thus the referent of the literary text is of the utmost unimportance; the specificity of a text lies in the *relationships* that it institutes among things.[5] Hence the primacy that Proust accords to the analogies created through "metaphor":

> On peut faire succéder indéfiniment dans une description les objets qui figuraient dans le lieu décrit, la vérité ne commencera qu'au moment où l'écrivain prendra deux objets différents, posera leur rapport, analogue dans le monde de l'art à celui qu'est le rapport unique de la loi causale dans le monde de la science, et les enfermera dans les anneaux nécessaires d'un beau style; même, ainsi que la vie, quand, en rapprochant une qualité commune à deux sensations, il dégagera leur essence commune en les réunissant l'une et l'autre

pour les soustraire aux contingences du temps, dans une métaphore.
(3: 889/3: 924–25)

[The writer] can describe a scene by describing one after another the
innumerable objects which at a given moment were present at a particular place, but truth will be attained by him only when he takes
two different objects, states the connexion between them—a connexion analogous in the world of art to the unique connexion
which in the world of science is provided by the law of causality—
and encloses them in the necessary links of a well-wrought style;
truth—and life too—can be attained by us only when, by comparing
a quality common to two sensations, we succeed in extracting their
common essence and in reuniting them to each other, liberated
from the contingencies of time, within a metaphor.

Proustian "truths" or "essences," despite their Platonic lineage, do
not belong to an eternal, transcendent world reflected in the temporal
and material world, for they are not "expressed" through language, but
produced by it. To deny the existence of "objective" truth is not, however, to simply supplant it with "subjective" truth in the traditional
sense, for the Proustian self—one of "those worlds which we call individuals" (3: 258/3: 259)—is not so much a subject, or Cartesian *cogito*, as
a viewpoint on the world, a source of vision, a manner of organizing
and totalizing reality through the signs of art. The Proustian subject is
already a postmodern subject insofar as it produces itself through writing; the "inner book" (3: 879/3: 913) is just that: a text, a constellation
of metaphors. Furthermore, the author of the *Recherche* elaborates a
theory of reading in keeping with a postmodern conception of subjectivity, describing the reading process as a confrontation of two texts. In
effect he asserts that every reader can—and should—"rewrite" the text
before him:

En réalité, chaque lecteur est, quand il lit, le propre lecteur de soi-
même. L'ouvrage de l'écrivain n'est qu'une espèce d'instrument
optique qu'il offre au lecteur afin de lui permettre de discerner ce
que, sans ce livre, il n'eût peut-être pas vu en soi-même. La reconnais-
sance en soi-même, par le lecteur, de ce que dit le livre, est la preuve
de la vérité de celui-ci, et *vice versa*, au moins dans une certaine
mesure, la différence entre les deux textes pouvant être souvent im-
putée non à l'auteur mais au lecteur. De plus, le livre peut être trop
savant, trop obscur pour le lecteur naïf, et ne lui présenter ainsi
qu'un verre trouble avec lequel il ne pourra pas lire. Mais d'autres
particularités (comme l'inversion) peuvent faire que le lecteur a
besoin de lire d'une certaine façon pour bien lire; l'auteur n'a pas à
s'en offenser, mais au contraire à laisser la plus grande liberté au
lecteur en lui disant: "Regardez vous-même si vous voyez mieux avec

ce verre-ci, avec celui-là, avec cet autre." (3: 911/3: 949; see also 3: 1033/3: 1089)

In reality every reader is, while he is reading, the reader of his own self. The writer's work is merely a kind of optical instrument which he offers to the reader to enable him to discern what, without this book, he would perhaps never have perceived in himself. And the recognition by the reader in his own self of what the book says is the proof of its veracity, the contrary also being true, at least to a certain extent, for the difference between the two texts may sometimes be imputed less to the author than to the reader. Besides, the book may be too learned, too obscure for a simple reader, and may therefore present to him a clouded glass through which he cannot read. But other peculiarities, such as inversion, may make it necessary for the reader to read in his own particular fashion in order to read with understanding, and the author must not be indignant at this; on the contrary, he must leave the reader all possible liberty, saying to him: "Look for yourself, and try whether you see best with this lens or that one or this other one."

Because they situate truth neither in a transcendent, objective reality exterior to the knowing subject, nor in a purely subjective, prelinguistic interiority, Proust's theories of art reflect a breakdown of the subject/object dichotomy, which marks the demise of what I would term, at the risk of overgeneralization, "nineteenth-century" ontology. I refer thus to a still-prevalent, even if subconscious, belief in the transcendence of the real, which in turn implies a Cartesian *cogito*— presuppositions fundamental to modernist theories of literature and conceptions of genre. This conceptual framework grounds not only a referential model of fiction, but also a referential model of autobiography (the presupposition that the ego is a distinct entity susceptible to totalization and representation). The traditional opposition between novel (a fictional narrative about the Other) and autobiography (a true narrative about the self) was founded upon the relative autonomy of the terms *self/other, knower/known;* it was precisely the unproblematic nature of this distinction that made possible such notions as the "fictionalized autobiography" or the "autobiographical fiction," the one consisting in disguising the self behind a veil of fictional names and situations, the other of injecting bits of subjective reality into a fictional narrative. Since both novel and autobiography presupposed the intelligibility of the real and the coherence of the subject, they shared a set of literary conventions governing narrative structure, psychological motivation, causality, verisimilitude, and so on. The question of the relationship between fiction and autobiography is a crucial one for the reader of Proust, both because critics have so often emphasized the autobiographical elements of his work, and because the relationship of an author's life to his art is a recurrent theme throughout Proust's own writings.

Yet if Proust is in any sense a postmodern author, it is because in the *Recherche* his theories—and, as we shall see, his practice—undermine the distinctions that grounded traditional notions of genre, so that "the" Proustian novel is neither a novel nor an autobiography in the traditional sense, but a theoretical fiction destined to demonstrate the irrelevance of those categories to works of literature. But *A la recherche du temps perdu* is the product of a long apprenticeship, which is not only recounted in fictionalized form in that work, but which can be traced in the evolution of Proust's style from the ironic, "decadent," Oscar-Wildean texts of *Les Plaisirs et les jours* to the fragmented, self-consciously autobiographical fiction of *Jean Santeuil,* to the humorous, labyrinthine narrative of the *Recherche.* For if Proust's works do not belie the narrator's assertion that "the great men of letters have never created more than a single work" (3:375/3: 382), their continuity is purely thematic, and tenuously so, at that. A number of motifs—all variations on the theme of desire—recur throughout the Proustian text, but the changes in their treatment manifest a radical shift in aesthetic that can only be the effect of an ontological revolution. The style and narrative techniques characteristic of the earlier Proust attest to a belief in a transcendent reality that an autonomous subject strives to know and master through representation. The referent-bound narratives of *Les Plaisirs et les jours* and *Jean Santeuil* are generally confided to worldly-wise and even supercilious narrators; in *A la recherche du temps perdu,* the decline in the importance of the referent, as evidenced by the proliferation of "metaphor," is concomitant with the appearance of the Proustian narrator, who abandons all pretense of capturing, controlling, and totalizing reality from a position above and beyond it, situating himself within the narrative—and within the world of signs. Indeed the narrator has ceased to "believe" in Reality; he knows that there are only signs, whose meanings can never be stabilized or finalized, for they belong to different (and mutually exclusive) worlds, selves, and moments in Time.

Les Plaisirs et les jours is a collection of short texts—vignettes, portraits, short stories, poems in alexandrine verse, prose poems—that echo and even imitate Proust's literary antecedents more than they herald the work to come. La Bruyère and La Rochefoucauld, Stendhal and Flaubert haunt these pages; however, the works are most strongly reminiscent of Chateaubriand and Baudelaire, for they exude nostalgia for the lost plenitude of a paradisiacal past and longing for an ideal state of unity and harmony. In *Les Regrets rêveries, couleur du temps*, ennui-stricken characters seek refuge and solace in nature: "Then we knew that the moon was weeping and that her sadness was in tune with ours. . . . She had inspired with her own sweet and irresistible despair woods, fields, and sky, which were now once more reflected in the sea, as well as in my heart that saw clearly into her heart at last."[6] The nature of these texts is a quintessentially romantic one, the antithesis of culture, and the symbol of the lost innocence of an edenic past. "La mer"—which recalls the title's ironic allusion to Hesiod's *Works and Days*—offers an exemplary image of the unity, harmony, and purity of an idealized past:

> La mer fascinera toujours ceux chez qui le dégoût de la vie et l'attrait du mystère ont devancé les premiers chagrins, comme un pressentiment de l'insuffisance de la réalité à les satisfaire. Ceux-là qui ont besoin de repos avant d'avoir éprouvé encore aucune fatigue, la mer les consolera, les exaltera vaguement. Elle ne porte pas comme la terre les traces des travaux des hommes et de la vie humaine. . . . De là cette grande pureté de la mer que n'ont pas les choses terrestres. Et cette eau vierge est bien plus délicate que la terre endurcie qu'il faut une pioche pour entamer. (*PJ*, 143/167–68)

> The sea will always fascinate those who have known the disgust of life and the lure of mystery even before their first sorrows, like a presentiment of the inadequacy of reality to satisfy them. Those who feel the need of rest, even before they have experienced fatigue, the sea will console and vaguely exhilarate. Unlike the earth, it bears no traces of men's toil and of their lives. . . . Hence that perfect purity of the sea unknown to the things of the earth. And this virgin water is much more delicate than the hardened earth, which it takes a pick to dent.

Virtually all the characters of *Les Plaisirs et les jours* languish, whether from unrequited love or fatal illness—the latter being but a symptom of terminal desire. The recurrent motif of the bedtime kiss reveals that infinite longing is ultimately a desire for reunion with the mother, who incarnates the Origin (nature, paradise lost). In "The End of Jealousy," for instance, a moribund Honoré, jealously imagining his fiancée's future spouse, is reminded of "one of his little-boy exigencies [*désirs*]"—that on those evenings when his mother was to go out, she kiss him and depart immediately at his bedtime, to spare him the anxiety of knowing she was to leave while he slept (*PJ*, 161/214). Hence his insistence that Françoise marry before his death. In "The Death of Baldassare Silvande," the elements of a romantic landscape are explicitly associated with the mother's kiss, as "the sound of distant bells" conjures up the image of the dying protagonist's childhood château and "his mother when she kissed him upon coming home, then when she tucked him in bed in the evening, warming his feet in her hands, staying with him if he could not sleep" (*PJ*, 27/29–30). The narrator of "The Confessions of a Young Girl," having defiled herself in her mother's eyes, commits expiatory suicide, fortunately bungling the job just enough to have time to confess her sins to the reader—and to reminisce about her mother's nightly embrace—before expiring. Thus *Les Plaisirs et les jours* seems to rehearse obsessively the opening scene of *A la recherche du temps perdu* in the form of a lament over a lost object. Indeed, several other of the principal themes of the *Recherche* figure prominently in *Les Plaisirs*, where all are variants or ramifications of the paradise lost motif. Jealousy, or the despairing anger over the impossibility of ever fully knowing, and thereby possessing the Other, is of course a fundamental component of the prototypical desire for the mother. A perpetual dissatisfaction with lived reality, or accessible objects—"Life is like this sweetheart. We dream of it and we love it in dreaming of it. But we must not try to live it" (*PJ*, 112/125)—is another common aspect of romantic melancholia that will leave traces in the theories of the *Recherche*, as is the concomitant theme of the alienation of self through social exchange ("The Stranger"). And finally Time, the essential evil of the postlapsarian condition, is well in evidence, particularly in *Les Regrets*, accomplishing the work of difference through change and death. Just as in the *Recherche*, our different selves or egos [*moi*] are born and die—although the language of the earlier work is less Freudian: "We know that one day, the woman by the thought of whom we live will be as indifferent to us as are now all those others except herself" (*PJ*, 119/135).[7]

But in *Les Plaisirs et les jours*, those themes are not incorporated into a theory of writing as they will be in *A la recherche du temps perdu*. The pages of *Les Plaisirs* alternately mourn and phantasize the recovery of a shattered unity, whereas the entire text of the *Recherche* is an elaboration of the premise that "the only true paradises are the paradises that we have lost" (3: 870/3: 903)—lost, without having ever possessed them.[8] For the real lesson of the madeleine (though the narrator will not grasp it until *Le Temps retrouvé*) is that there never was a "paradise present." The madeleine epiphany, like the Proustian privileged moments, is a sign to the writer that the goal of art is not to recapture a transcendent signified. As Deleuze points out, in *Proust et les signes*, memory plays no part in the "steeples of Martinville" episode.[9] The magic of the steeples is not to be found in a forgotten past—nor even in a hidden present, a secret concealed beneath their appearance, a fact that Marcel perceives only dimly at this stage of the *Recherche*:

Sans me dire que ce qui était caché derrière les clochers de Martinville devait être quelque chose d'analogue à une jolie phrase, puisque
c'était sous la forme de mots qui me faisaient plaisir que cela m'était
apparu, demandant un crayon et du papier au docteur, je compo-
sai . . . le petit morceau suivant. (1: 181/1: 197)

Without admitting to myself that what lay hidden behind the steeples of Martinville must be something analogous to a pretty phrase,
since it was in the form of words which gave me pleasure that it had
appeared to me, I borrowed a pencil and some paper from the doctor, and . . . composed the following little fragment.

Although he feels compelled to write about the *clochers,* and having
done so experiences a joyful sense of relief, Marcel is not yet free of the
delusion that the source of his elation is something inherent in the referent of his text rather than the act of artistic creation itself. Only as
he nears the end of his quest will he come to reject any "material explanation" (3: 375/3: 382) for the joy of such moments, and not until *Le
Temps retrouvé* will he develop his notion of metaphor as the production of truth. Indeed, Marcel's first literary effort is only timidly metaphorical in comparison with much of its context; it is illustrative of a
phrase in the narrator's apprenticeship that corresponds to the world
view implied by the style of *Les Plaisirs et les jours,* in which metaphor
is used sparingly. The passage from "La Mer" cited earlier is not atypical
in its linearity and its allusive, yet minimally metaphorical language,
not to mention the romantic banality of the sentiments expressed in it.
The mark of "Proustian" metaphor (that of the *Recherche*) is the dissimilarity or seeming irreconcilability of the terms united in the "necessary
links" of language; the greater the apparent difference between terms,
the greater the work of writing, the more manifest is the humor of
Proust's style. There are glimmers of Proustian humor in *Les Plaisirs,* as
in the portrait of Honoré preparing to bid his mistress farewell for the
evening:

Tout en s'habillant pour aller dîner, sa pensée était suspendue sans
effort au moment où il allait la revoir comme un gymnaste touche
déjà le trapèze encore éloigné vers lequel il vole, ou comme une
phrase musicale semble atteindre l'accord qui la résoudra et la rap-
proche de lui, de toute la distance qui l'en sépare, par la force même
du désir qui la promet et l'appelle. (*PJ,* 147/193–94)

While dressing for dinner his thoughts were unconsciously hanging
on the moment when he would see her again, just as an acrobat already touches the distant trapeze as he flies toward it, or as a musical
phrase seems to reach the chord that will resolve it, drawing it across

the distance separating them by the very force of the desire that presages and summons it.

Such metaphors are relatively infrequent, however, and generally have not the amplitude of those in Proust's later work. *Les Plaisirs et les jours* remains fundamentally romantic-ironic in style insofar as it does not seriously challenge the primacy of the signifier.

Nor does it challenge the ipseity of the speaking subject. The prevalence of an autonomous and authoritative narrative voice reinforces the ironic tenor of the work. A number of the texts are written in the third person, and are endowed with a classic "omniscient narrator," who refrains from direct interventions. Elsewhere—notably in several of the "Fragments de comédie italienne" (e.g., "A une snob," "Oranthe," "Eventail," "Olivian") a first-person narrator addresses his characters directly, ironically chiding them for their affectations. "So you didn't go to bed last night and you haven't washed this morning?" begins the study of Oranthe, the young artist wallowing in his role of misunderstood, harried, suffering romantic. "Brilliantly gifted as you are," continues the ironic voice, "do you think that isn't enough to distinguish you from common mortals, and that you have to act such a pitiful role besides?" The text concludes upon a lucid critique of romantic-ironic comportment: "The trouble with you is that to the soul of the artist you have added all the prejudices of a bourgeois, only showing the reverse side and without deceiving us" (*PJ*, 45–46/70–71). By taking biographical material—i.e., the resemblances between the young Proust and Oranthe—into consideration, one might argue that such passages (and they are numerous in *Les Plaisirs*) entail a considerable amount of self-irony on Proust's part. Strictly speaking, however, it is not necessary to have recourse to a referent to characterize the tone of the passage as ironic; it is quite possible to do so on the basis of the relationship established between narrator and character. Whether we take the diegetic material to be autobiographical or not, the narrator's status is, to use Genettian terminology, extradiegetic-heterodiegetic: the narrator recounts from the "outside" a narrative in which he does not figure.[10] Extra-heterodiegetic narration is conducive to irony, if neither a necessary nor sufficient condition for it, since the distance and absolute difference between the narrative voice and narrated characters is so clearly marked.[11] In the "Oranthe" passage quoted above (partly because of its openly sarcastic tone), the spiraling movement of irony described by de Man is easily discernible: the romantic-ironic personage, in an attempt to step outside bourgeois mores, in fact only succeeds in exemplifying them all the more fully, through an exaggerated inversion of bourgeois codes. The ostensibly demystified narrator then repeats the process, assuming a position of exteriority and superiority, only to incarnate in turn the supercilious bourgeois accusing the Other of being a mystified bourgeois. In this respect, the numerous indictments of snobism and *mondanité* in general that appear in *Les Plaisirs* are all pointedly ironic. In any case of extra-heterodiegetic narration, however, the narrator's stance is ironic in the broader sense in which I have been using the term, in that it constitutes the speaker's claim to occupy a metadiscursive position and presupposes a clear-cut distinction between the real and the fictional (i.e., between the extradiegetic space occupied by the speaker and the fictional realm of the diegesis, or, as in the case of *Brulard* and traditional autobiography in general: an absolute distinction between subject and discourse, what I am and what I say). Even in the autodiegetic narrative of "Confession d'une jeune fille," which of all the texts of *Les Plaisirs* most closely approximates the narrative technique of the *Recherche* (as far as voice is concerned), the narrator speaks from a position of wisdom in relation to a former, fallen self. Finally, the author himself is inevitably implicated in the irony by his choice of a narrative technique that presupposes the authority of metalanguage.

The narrator who says "je" in *Les Plaisirs et les jours* cannot, therefore, be assimilated to the autodiegetic "je" of *A la recherche du temps perdu*, in which the narrator, even while alluding at times to the temporal distance separating him from the protagonist "Marcel" nonetheless tends to minimize that distance, or the disparity in knowledge it implies. He does so (or Proust has him do so) chiefly, of course, in order to avoid giving away the "surprise ending"–the "revelation" in *Le Temps retrouvé*, but the result is a collapsing of the extradiegetic realm into the diegetic, since the narrator "fictionalizes" himself by aligning himself with the character he is narrating. By a sort of contagion inversely analogous to that which results from the outward spiraling of irony (for it occurs here through a further collapsing of discursive levels), the "fictionality" of the narrator tends to affect the status of the author as well, undermining his exteriority and therefore his authority. Although editor Yves Sandre holds that Proust's use of the first person in *Les Regrets* introduces "the famous 'I' which, as he said, is less himself than an ideal narrator" (*JS*, 954), the ego it implies here is less Proustian than Baudelairean in that it functions as a unified subject engaged both in the expression of an interior self and the depiction of a universe whose charms, however anthropomorphic, are described as though they were inherent in the domain of reality.

The occasional use of "nous" in *Les Plaisirs*, particularly in *Les Regrets* ("We know that . . . the woman by the thought of whom we live will be as indifferent to us," etc.) is perhaps more prophetic of the work to come than that of the first person singular. For the "nous" subsumes narrator (*je*), character (*Marcel-je*), and narratee (*vous*) in the formulation of Proustian "laws," thereby contributing to the telescoping of narrative strata that characterizes the *Recherche*. Furthermore, the appearance of the ubiquitous "nous" will be one of the primary marks of a shift away from a purely episodic and anecdotal narrative fiction conceived as the expression of a single speaking subject, toward a theoretical fiction the primary purpose of which is neither (self-)expression nor (self-)representation, but the elaboration of laws that negate the individuality and autonomy of the ego. The Proustian law is a correlative of Proustian metaphor, since both involve the establishment of relationships among elements that are indifferent in themselves, and thus entail the privileging of signifier over signified.

Not until Proust abandons an "expressive" notion of literature will he be able to write *A la recherche du temps perdu*. The chief interest of his *Jean Santeuil*, in many respects the prototype of the *Recherche*, lies in the manner in which the narrative constantly questions the validity of the lyrical type of art that it nonetheless continues to exemplify. In one memorable scene from the protagonist's school days, Jean is plunged deep into Hugo, in search of "the secret of life, death, and his own soul" (*JS*, 238/75), when his iconoclastic schoolmaster, M. Rustinlor, precipitates a cataclysm in his aesthetic universe by dismissing *Les Contemplations* as inferior verse, "surchargé . . . de métaphysique embêtante" ("overburdened with tiresome metaphysical considerations"). Having affirmed that "[les] vers plastiques et purement extérieurs . . . sont par cela même infiniment supérieurs aux vers qui signifient quelque chose" ("plastic and wholly abstract compositions are always infinitely superior to poetry which sets out to mean something"), Rustinlor further disconcerts his pupil by characterizing Racine as "un assez vilain coco" ("a pretty nasty bit of goods") and cheerfully seconding Gautier's judgment that the great tragedian left but one beautiful line, "La fille de Minos et de Pasiphaé" (*JS*, 239–40/70–76). Such is Jean's consternation that he will spend a sleepless night questioning his faith in literature as the medium destined to reveal the essences of reality:

> Si la plus haute poésie n'était pas celle que remplissaient les grandes réalités en présence de qui il vivait, qui restaient à le regarder pendant ses promenades, pendant son travail, lui disant: regarde-nous, élucide-nous, pénètre-nous, la poésie n'était rien. Ou plutôt comme le disait M. Rustinlor n'étaient-ce pas ces réalités qui n'étaient rien? Oubliait-il un moment ses tourments, "la fille de Minos et de Pasiphaé" venait les réveiller avec une cruauté bien digne de cette origine monstrueuse. Et pourtant ce n'était pas sans plaisir qu'il se

répétait cette boutade de Gautier. . . . Habitué jusqu'ici à estimer les vers d'après la richesse de leurs sens non moins que l'éclat de leurs images, il éprouvait, à entendre célébrer par-dessus tous celui-ci où il n'y avait ni idée ni image, cette surprise joyeuse que nous éprouvons chaque fois qu'une parole neuve vient changer pour nous la face du monde ou les termes du problème de la pensée. (*JS,* 240/76–77)

If the noblest poetry was not that of which the subject-matter consisted of the great realities which surrounded him, which gazed upon him when he went walking, or sat working, saying: "Look at us, explain us, get to our very heart"—then poetry was nothing. Could it be, on the contrary, that it was Monsieur Rustinlor who was right, and that it was these realities that were nothing? If, for a moment, he escaped from the torment of his thoughts, *La fille de Minos et de Pasiphaé* brought them back into his mind with a cruelty worthy of such a monstrous origin. Nevertheless, it was not without a certain feeling of pleasure that he repeated Gautier's sally to himself. . . . Having, so far, been in the habit of valuing poetry as much for the richness of its meaning as for the brilliance of its imagery, he was conscious now, hearing somebody give supreme importance to a line which contained neither thought nor imagery, of that feeling of surprised delight which seizes upon us whenever an uttered word sets our world in a new light or changes, for us, the terms of an intellectual problem.

The passage prefigures some of the fundamental themes of the *Recherche:* that reality "is nothing," that the referent of a work of art is indifferent, that a shift in aesthetic constitutes a "new creation of the world" (1: 834/1: 892). Yet the reader of *Jean Santeuil* senses that the author, like the protagonist, never resolves the conflicts of that sleepless night, and continues to cling to his belief that the objective world exists independently of the subjective, and harbors secrets that it is the artist's task to bring to light. The incorporation into the early novel of numerous "theoretical" passages that raise the questions of the nature and purpose of art, the relation of art to life, and similar aesthetic questions makes *Jean Santeuil* seem infinitely more "Proustian" than did *Les Plaisirs et les jours,* an impression that is reinforced by the appearance of the prototypes of various characters of *A la recherche du temps perdu,* not the least of which is the protagonist himself, who has a great deal in common with Marcel. Like *A la recherche du temps perdu, Jean Santeuil* is the story of a quest—for truth and for a vocation—but that quest is an endless, aimless wandering in search of an unknown object. More precisely, *Jean Santeuil* is the quest, or a stage in the quest, of which the *Recherche* is the theoretical fiction. The former is, simply, a search for something to write *about;* the latter, the gradual revelation that writing, if it is to be art, cannot ultimately be "about" anything—except writing itself.

But *Jean Santeuil* continues to adhere to a referential model of literature, and conforms to the traditional narrative conventions associated with it. The result is a self-conscious hybrid of novel and autobiography, in which Proust himself seems uncertain as to which genre he should pursue. "Puis-je appeler ce livre un roman?" he writes in an unfinished preface, "c'est moins peut-être et bien plus, l'essence même de ma vie, recueillie sans y rien mêler, dans ces heures de déchirure où elle découle. Ce livre n'a jamais été fait, il a été récolté" ("Should I call this book a novel? It is something less, perhaps, and yet much more, the very essence of my life, with nothing extraneous added, as it developed through a long period of wretchedness. This book of mine has not been manufactured: it has been garnered" [*JS*, 181/1]). While—as biographers have noted[12]—the diegetic material of the work is more directly autobiographical than that of the *Recherche*, Proust adopts a narrative strategy more in keeping with an eighteenth-century novelistic convention that situates the narrator at two removes from the protagonist than that of traditional autobiographical narrative. A primary (extradiegetic) narrator explains in the preface how he has come to possess a manuscript by the novelist C., whom he had befriended at Beg-Meil; the secondary (or intradiegetic) narrator (supposedly the novelist C.—or rather, a narrator of C's invention!—but indistinguishable, stylistically, from the narrator of the preface) then recounts Jean's story in such a manner as to maintain his distance from and authority over his protagonist. He solicits the reader's complicity by periodically addressing him as *tu* (or *vous*), while dissociating himself completely from the spatio-temporal sphere of the diegesis, or fictional realm of the story: "In those far distant days of which I am now speaking, dear reader, when Monsieur Santeuil was a gentleman with a black beard, and Madame Santeuil a young smiling fair-haired woman in a fantastic velvet dress, whom you might have seen, while Jean was still alive, in his photograph album . . . " (*JS*, 579/283). Dead and buried, the characters of *Jean Santeuil* subsist only in the photographs of an old album or in the pages of a novel which at times seems itself to be a collection of images—or a procession of them on a screen:

> Regardez-les répandus aux divers coins de la pièce. . . . L'un, étendu dans la position de ceux qui font venir auprès d'eux leurs animaux favoris, ayant commodément logé au coin de sa bouche sa pipe bien-aimée, fumeuse et flamme et fumée pour les autres, pour lui si douce, se fait caresser par elle d'une haleine suffisamment attiédie son gosier saturé de viandes et de boissons. . . . Un petit verre de cognac est près de lui, sur une petite table approchée suffisamment

pour qu'il puisse le boire . . . sans avoir à se déranger. Un autre,
étendu dans la même position devant la grande baie vitrée . . . (*JS*,
287/98)

Look at them then, scattered about the room. . . . One may be re-
clining in the posture of those who summon to their side their favourite animals, his much-loved pipe settled comfortably in the
corner of his mouth, a thing of smoke and flame and stench for
others, for him so sweet because it soothes with its warm, but not
too warm, breath a palate rich with the fumes of food and drink.
. . . A glass of cognac stands beside him, near enough for him to
sip . . . without his having to move. Another, similarly stretched at
length close to the great bay-window . . .

Similarly, because the narrator of *Jean Santeuil* observes the protagonist from the outside—or from the outside in, since he bears witness to his thoughts as well as his actions—the narration takes on the
character of a series of vignettes of Jean, with explicatory captions:
"'Yes,' answered Jean, 'aren't you going out, chum?' He liked saying
'chum,' it gave him a feeling that he was one of them" (*JS*, 569/471).
There is even a detailed description of a portrait of Jean that appeared
in a public exhibition (675/715), an objectification unthinkable for the
protagonist "je" of the *Recherche*.

Yet despite the ironic distance that the stratified narrative instates
between the protagonist and the narrator—who occasionally refers to
Jean as "notre héros"—the novel nonetheless has the somewhat discomfiting tone of a confession in the third person. This is partly because
of the content of certain passages, to which we shall return later. But
it is also due in large part to the sudden intrusion of "je" in several
passages—not to introduce a narratorial commentary regarding Jean's
behavior, but to assume an utterance that would normally be attributed to the character. For instance, having described how Jean's love
for Marie Kossichef (a Gilberte prototype) has gradually faded into
such indifference that he ignores an opportunity to see her again after
a long separation, the narrator—primary or secondary?—remarks: "I
would have thought that I would have wanted more than anything else
to see Mademoiselle Kossichef again, and that curiosity at least would
have survived my passion" (*JS*, 386). Genette is doubtless partly correct
in ascribing such unwarranted eruptions of the first person to Proust's
impatience, not to better "express himself," but to dispense with the
complexities of introducing a running commentary into a stratified
narrative. The identification of narrator and protagonist in the *Recherche* will obviate the necessity of constantly changing voices in
order to accompany the narrative with a theoretical discourse that
constitutes the novel's primary raison d'être. However, while the

abrupt lapses into the first person in *Jean Santeuil*, like the frequent
occurrences of the Proustian "nous" ("Fortunately for our continually
changing existence . . . our potentialities of affection do not stay con-
centrated on what we have left behind us" [*JS*, 385/394]), do anticipate
the later privileging of the narrator's "ideological function"–i.e., his
didactic or commentatorial role[13]–that function has not yet attained
the prominence in *Jean Santeuil* that it will have in the *Recherche*, and
this not merely because the third-person narrative is ill-suited to accommodate it. One may infer from many other pages of *Jean Santeuil*
that Proust is still in the thrall of traditional notions of self-expression
and representation, and is attempting to demonstrate his own originality within the confines of the genres to which they gave rise. Thus
when not only "je," but the name "Marcel" appears in the place of "il"
or "Jean" ("It would be better for me to call you Marcel and you to call
me Charlotte," proposes an earlier incarnation of Albertine [*JS*, 831/
182]),[14] it seems more symptomatic of the author's ambivalence as to
the nature of his work than of the technical difficulties pursuant to a
definitive choice of narrative voice. In the *Recherche*, "Marcel" is a
proper name occurring in a context in which a pronoun would be
awkward; in *Jean Santeuil*, it is the name of the author supplanting
that of his fictional character.

The dilemma implied by this vacillation is thematized in *Santeuil*:
given that art is the only means of salvation, is that salvation achieved
by writing *about* oneself, or about the non-self–that is, through objectification of the ego or appropriation of the Other–two means of re-
covering a lost unity? "Given by Nature the duty of preserving some
god dwelling in the marshy places of the spirit and on their borders,"
Jean feels compelled to write, but instinct warns him that self-preserva-
tion is not self-representation: "Those who had known him could to
some extent when reading him say: 'That's certainly him,' though to tell
the truth, he couldn't write about himself, for whenever what he was
writing had to do with him, his pleasure ceased, and he heard a warning
voice telling him that he was no longer writing what he ought to write"
(*JS*, 703–4/719). The idea that pleasure–"that peculiar feeling of delight
which for him was the true sign of value in ideas" (*JS*, 703/719)–is the
criterion of true art, brings into play the emergent theme of the
privileged moment. The motif recurs several times in *Jean Santeuil* in
the form of an experience of involuntary memory, which the protagonist is attempting to integrate into a theory of literature. Thus the passage in which Jean relives a tempest at Penmarch through a winter
storm at the Château de Réveillon incorporates a long meditation on
the difference between vacuous, superficial literature and the authentic,
profound art whose secret seems to be born on the tempestial winds:

La poésie, l'inspiration, ce vent semblait la réveiller en Jean . . . il pensait de plus en plus à découvrir de nouvelles idées qui en faisaient naître d'autres, non point de ces folles idées qui se rapportent à nous et que les enfants d'imagination (et plusieurs restent toujours enfants pour cela) ont indéfiniment en se déshabillant, en se promenant, qui se rapportent à nous et nous imaginent ce que nous désirons: "Je vais trouver en rentrant une lettre de celle que j'aime et pourtant que je ne connais pas, et qui va m'avouer son amour. Voici ce que je répondrai. Et nous irons dans un salon où le monsieur que je n'aime pas sera, et voici les discours impertinents pour lui qu'on tiendra, et voici ce que je dirai." Mais de telles idées sont des idées creuses, qui en appellent d'autres, mais creuses aussi. Elles imitent la réalité en s'y substituant, mais sans la dépasser. . . . Et puis après nous ne nous sentons pas contents, tout cela est inutile, c'est comme les romans impressionnistes et naturalistes. . . . C'est une concurrence inutile à l'inépuisable et insatisfaisante réalité. . . .

Mais ces idées qui venaient à Jean en écoutant le vent étaient des idées autres qui semblaient non pas creuses mais pleines, à la fois dans le passé, son passé à Penmarch, et le présent, et plus profondes, les reliant, plus réelles, montrant par là le prix de la minute passée et de la minute présente, quelque chose qui, lui, existait vraiment et ne finirait pas à la minute même. De sorte qu'il ne se disait pas: "Encore un rêve insensé, je n'irai pas plus cette année que l'année précédente à Penmarch," mais qu'y aller ne lui paraissait presque pas nécessaire. (*JS*, 535–36/487–88)

Poetry and inspiration, these it was that the wind seemed to wake in Jean . . . he thought he would discover new ideas, which in their turn would give birth to others—not those mad ideas which turn inwards on ourselves, such as imaginative children have (and in this respect, there are many who remain children all their lives) as they undress for bed, or go walking, ideas which have to do only with ourselves and body forth the things we most desire: "When I get back I shall find a letter from the girl I love, though as yet I do not know her, and she will tell me of her love, and this is what I shall reply. And we shall go into a room where a man I do not like is sitting, and these are the insulting things that we shall say . . . and I shall say this or that." Ideas of this kind are insubstantial things, and call up others no more substantial than themselves. For they imitate reality, and substitute themselves for it. . . . But later we feel discontented. It is all so useless, all so like what we find in impressionist and naturalistic novels. . . . Such ideas are in mere competition, and vain at that, with an inexhaustible and unsatisfying reality. . . .

But the ideas that came to Jean as he listened to the wind were of another kind. They seemed not empty, but packed full, not only of the past—his own past at Penmarch—but of the present, too; ideas that went deeper, and, linking the present and the past, were more real, for they showed the value of the moment past and of the moment present and held a something that in very truth existed, and would not end in the here and now. What he told himself was not, "This is just another silly dream; I shall no more go back to Penmarch this year than I did last." No, what he felt was that to go there was no longer necessary.

In rejecting a mimetic conception of art, Jean attains a level of "enlightenment" comparable to that of the narrator who, early in *Le Temps retrouvé*, analyzes his disenchantment with the type of writing practiced by the Goncourt brothers, concluding that great art, as he conceives of it, is not a product of observation and imitation. Reading the Goncourts' journal, the narrator is seized by the desire to see the referent, to return to the Verdurins' to see all the wonders he had himself failed to observe there, yet he realizes at the same time that he has a different way of seeing: "I did not see the guests, because, when I thought I was looking at them, I was X-raying them." Ignoring individual characteristics, his eye perceives only "a collection of psychological laws" (3: 719/3: 738). Like Marcel, Jean is discovering that his own work must be composed of essences rather than appearances. But unlike the *Recherche, Jean Santeuil* does not extend the notion of essences to include the similarities revealed by psychological "laws" and, finally, all the analogies established by metaphor. Thus Jean—and presumably, his creator—entertains the idea that his work should consist solely of the revelations of involuntary memory; describing Jean's joy when a view of the Lake of Geneva revives the sensations associated with a seascape at Réveillon, Proust lapses into the first person to comment, "I have always put sufficient trust [in this pleasure] not to write anything of what I saw, of what I thought, of what I arrived at by reasoning, of what I recalled, so as to write only when a past moment suddenly came to life again in a smell, in a sight" (*JS*, 401/410). Needless to say, this principle is not applied in *Jean Santeuil*, in which the vast majority of the episodes are unrelated to such epiphanies—of necessity, of course, since, as the narrator of *Le Temps retrouvé* will acknowledge in the course of the final theoretical fanfare, "those . . . impressions . . . are . . . too rare for a work of art to be constructed exclusively from them" (3: 898/3: 935). Nonetheless, he realizes—and this is the discovery that made *A la recherche du temps perdu* possible—that nature, through involuntary memory, "had . . . placed me . . . on the path of art" (3: 889/3: 925), by allowing him to perceive beauty in relationships, rather than in individual persons or things. The involuntary memory plays a crucial role in the *Recherche* because it provides, not subject matter, but a stylistic model for the author to follow. It is precisely at this point in the *Recherche* that Proust formulates the famous theory of metaphor cited earlier: "Truth will be attained . . . only when the writer takes two different objects, states the connexion between them . . . and encloses them in the necessary links of a well-wrought style" (3: 889/3: 924–25). Thus when the narrator discovers that "these materials for a work of literature were simply my past life" (3: 899/3: 935), he has long since been disabused of the belief that "the things of the past have a charm in themselves," so that the artist should "transfe[r] them bodily into his work" (2: 551/2: 572).

Jean Santeuil, however, ultimately fails to transcend mimesis. If Proust does not adopt the autodiegetic technique experimented with earlier in "La Confession d'une jeune fille," it is no doubt to avoid "talking about himself"; yet in the radically heterodiegetic narrative form he does choose, "Jean" merely becomes a reified "je" (is the near-homonymy of *je/Jean* a coincidence?), and the various episodes of his existence, so many substitutes, or attempts to compensate, for "unsatisfying reality." As in *Les Plaisirs et les jours*, the theme of the mother's kiss has a privileged status, for the protagonist's relationship to the mother is the archetype for all his relationships with the Other—as well as a figure for the artist's attitude toward the real, or the referent.

Rather than recurring obsessively throughout the text as it does in *Les Plaisirs*, though, the *baiser du soir* episode opens *Jean Santeuil*—that is, following the preface establishing the various levels of the narrative.[15] It is dispatched in ten pages (of the Pléiade edition) of virtually digression-free narrative. The scene is set in two pages consisting primarily of dialogue between Mme Santeuil and a Swann prototype, M. Surlande, interrupted by Jean's appearance at his bedroom window, bidding his mother to come to him; she obligingly complies, and following a two-page commentary-flashback in which the narrator explains Jean's horror of bedtime and the events immediately leading up to his audacious decision to cede to his "guilty desire" (*JS*, 207/30) to call out the window, including a feeble attempt to enlist the aid of Augustin (future Françoise), the mother arrives to comfort Jean briefly, but as she is leaving again, Jean goes into hysterics, so that she consents to stay until her son falls asleep; the two concluding pages are devoted to the narrator's reflections on the significance of the incident. The narrator, who enjoys a certain omniscience, reads the thoughts of Mme Santeuil and Augustin and, adopting a lordly "we"—which is not the "we" of Proustian "laws"—affects an impassive detachment from his protagonist. Nevertheless, his commentary is marked by a note of pathos that both underscores the artificiality of the ironic narrative stance and heightens the romantic overtones of the lonely protagonist's plight:

Enfin nous avons une dernière raison pour avoir, comme Jean lui-
même, pris au sérieux ces chagrins d'enfant, c'est que, malgré le sourire du docteur ou de son père, il n'en éprouva peut-être jamais de plus
cruels. Plus tard . . . quand il était triste . . . il pouvait . . . s'évader.
. . . Mais son enfance s'agita misérablement au fond d'un puits de
tristesse dont rien ne pouvait encore l'aider à sortir. . . . Alors la
tristesse seule régnait sur sa sombre enfance. (*JS*, 210–11/33–34)

There is one last reason why we, no less than Jean himself, should
take seriously those griefs and torments of his childhood and that is,
that in spite of the doctor's smiles and his father's, he was never, in
the years to come, to know any that were more lacerating. Later . . .
whenever he felt depressed . . . he could . . . escape. . . . But his
childhood struggled desperately at the bottom of a well of wretchedness from which nothing could release him. . . . Sadness had reigned
in undisputed sovereignty over his shadowed childhood.

Metaphor is limited almost exclusively to these commentarial passages, where it serves an essentially "expressive" function, by dramatiz-
ing Jean's misery as, alone in bed in the dark, he is condemned to "lie
there . . . like a prey abandoned—mute, motionless, and blind—to the
horrible shapeless suffering which, little by little, would grow as vast
as solitude, as silence and as night"—at least until the mother's kiss
"calmed, like a magic spell, like oil on a stormy sea, his agitated spirit"
(*JS*, 205–206/28). The use of nature imagery to evoke the artist's state of
mind is a stroke of unoriginality reminiscent of *Les Plaisirs et les jours*,
particularly since the sense of restored plenitude resulting from the
reunion with the mother through her nightly kiss is metaphorically
associated with the return to a calm and peaceful state of nature.[16]
While the metaphors and similes of this version of the *drame du
coucher* are predominantly of the type commonly used in the depiction of the romantic personage, they are also subordinated to the narrative, or referential, function of the text, so that the passage produces
the effect of a "realistic," factual account of an event in the life of a
single individual. Indeed, George Painter finds it so "matter-of-fact"
that it "probably contains the literal truth," and therefore follows it in
his biography of Proust.[17]

More important, however, than the "literal truth" of the account is
the significance that the narrator attributes to the incident and its relation to subsequent episodes in the novel. Not only does the mother
capitulate to Jean's demand, she absolves him of responsibility for his
behavior, attributing it to "an involuntary nervous condition," words
that, the narrator informs us, "exercised a profound influence on his
life," for so exculpated by his mother, he is redeemed, saved from the
limbo of nonexistence and accorded the status of an individual: "That

new sense of irresponsibility which his mother had just publicly recognized in the presence of Augustin—as a nation recognizes a new government—taught him his rights, guaranteed his personal existence, and assured his future" (*JS*, 210/33).

Having reported the *drame du coucher*, the narrator pronounces the case closed: "In the course of this story we shall have no occasion to say more about Jean's anxiety at the moment of going to sleep. His life will lead us, as it led him, along more distant ways, and one cannot, alas, live one's childhood twice" (*JS*, 209/32). But the narrative of *Jean Santeuil* in fact never takes us far from this original scene in which Jean achieves recognition in his mother's eyes. It will be replayed throughout the novel on the stage of society; the actors in the role of the Other may change, but the plot remains the same: exonerated from an imaginary fault, Jean passes from the position of the accused to that of the Law. This scenario is epitomized in the fragment on the premiere of the opera *Frédégonde*, a rapid-fire, virtually metaphorless account of Jean's social apotheosis before the collected eyes of *le tout-Paris*. The episode opens as Monsieur and Madame Marmet, seeking an excuse to rescind their earlier invitation to Jean so that they may lure more prestigious guests to their loge for the premiere, start a one-sided quarrel by accusing him of a breach of *bienséance*. Thereupon Jean accepts an invitation to join his faithful friends the duke and duchess of Réveillon in their loge, along with the duchess of la Roche-foucauld, the king of Portugal, and the prince of Aquitaine, not to mention three minor nobles who decline Mme Marmet's invitation at the last minute in order to join the Réveillon contingent. When the Marmets (who have meanwhile resorted in desperation to inviting the pariah Schlechtemburg) spot Jean in so celestial a society, their mortification would seem to be complete. But at intermission, when the rancor-free protagonist sets out discreetly ("ashamed of his kindly impulse") to visit the Marmets' loge, he is forbidden by the duchess to so humiliate himself: "I am as fond of you as I am of my own son, and am entitled to speak to you as your mother would. . . . You really ought not to see any more of those people. You have plenty of friends without them, friends of ours, who all adore you" (*JS*, 681/538–39). To comply with the wishes of his adoptive mother, Jean must spend intermission parading about the theater on the arm of the king of Portugal, who (less unassuming than his young friend) announces maliciously: "Since I have a new friend, it is well that the people of Paris should know it by seeing him with me" (*JS*, 682/539). Thus, by metonymy, Jean himself fulfills the archetypal childhood fantasy of becoming king.

As if the symbolism of this scene were not apparent enough, how-ever, the script is rewritten for the protagonist and his mother in the final pages of the novel. Now Jean is twenty-two, his father is away, and his mother is "thinking only of her son" ("toute à son fils" [*JS*, 855/707]) at his bedside, to watch over him as he sleeps, to converse and to read with him when he awakens; the two are united as "spiritual lovers" (*JS*, 858). Jean assumes the position of the senior Santeuil, "seated [at lunch] opposite his mother, like the master of the house"; that afternoon he will literally exercise his father's legal rights by voting in his name, instead of casting his ballot for his own choice of candidate, "for I am his son even more than I am myself" (*JS*, 857/708-9). With an exemplary gesture of Deleuzean *ironie sadique*, Jean usurps the role of the Law, suppressing his own ego to identify with a "voracious superego." Through (re-)possession of the Lost Object, the subject accedes to the status of God the Father, the Selfhood of Being *en soi*.

This is the end of the novel, logically, if not in fact (since Proust never definitively assembled and ordered the fragments); there is nothing more to be said. *Jean Santeuil* is a classical family romance: the protagonist asserts his individuality and difference by denying his lineage (Jean is really a de Réveillon), but ultimately reaffirms the Law by becoming his own Father. It is a portrait of the artist as a singular individual, but not an "isolated individual" (*JS*, 857/709).[18] Similarly, the narrator's relationship to his character--that of a triumphant superego to a subdued ego—is homologous to the relationship between Proust and that reified *I* which he endows with all perfections, as father does son, yet maintaining a lordly detachment, as though to justify his existence by proxy. "True" or not, in this respect, *Jean Santeuil* typifies the traditional autobiographical project, à la Rousseau.

Yet Proust never completed *Jean Santeuil*. Apparently he senses that the work he was writing did not correspond to the one he was in effect writing about, in those passages of *Santeuil* dealing with the protagonist's artistic vocation. The author of *Jean Santeuil* never ceases trying to "go home again," to recover the past, to return to Penmarch, even while suggesting that true art would make that return unnecessary—or even undesirable, for it would thrive on absence and desire. Like the narrator of the opening pages of *A la recherche du temps perdu*, who, in repeated attempts to recall Combray, can only conjure up "the bare minimum of scenery necessary . . . to the drama of my undressing" (1: 44/1: 47), the Proust of *Santeuil* can only reproduce variations on the same scene. He exemplifies the traditional novelist, for as Barthes put it in *Le Plaisir du texte*, "Doesn't every narrative lead back to Oedipus? Isn't storytelling always a way of searching for one's origin, telling one's conflicts with the Law?" But what if there were no Law?—"why tell stories?" Such is the case for postmodernity: "Today we dismiss Oedipus and narrative at one and the same time: we no longer love, we no longer fear, we no longer narrate."[19] Already the nineteenth century had proclaimed the death of the Father in the "death of God," or the demise of Transcendence, ground of Meaning. Modernity mourned that death; postmodernity was to celebrate it. The traces of that shift in perspective are apparent in the transformation of the Proustian aesthetic between *Jean Santeuil* and *A la recherche du temps perdu*. When Proust abandoned *Jean Santeuil,* he abandoned the classic *récit,* and the aspirations to selfhood that it implies.

Nevertheless, Proust was not to begin the *Recherche* for several years. When, and how, did the *Recherche* become possible? Certainly, as many critics have insisted, an important biographical factor was the death of Proust's parents—his father in 1903 and his mother in 1905. But as a personal tragedy, the event is banal. It is only insofar as Proust was able to integrate it into his later work as the archetypal experience of that loss of Transcendence which was a fundamental preoccupation of nineteenth-century thought, and to make the assumption and affirmation of that loss a condition *sine qua non* for the genesis of the novel to come, that the biological death of the Other can be regarded as significant in the emergence of a postmodern theory of self in *A la recherche du temps perdu.*

In 1908 or 1909, he begins a work on Sainte-Beuve.[20] He is of two minds as to the form it should take: an academic essay or a conversation with his mother? An unlikely dilemma, it would seem, but the result will in fact be a hybrid of the two that will give rise to the uncertain genre[21] represented by *A la recherche du temps perdu. Contre Sainte-Beuve* is a theoretical polemic combined with, but not integrated into, a first-person narrative interspersed with "autobiographical" details. The polemic still centers on the person of the artist, and is therefore still essentially a self-justification, but in a manner that is curiously at odds with the text of *Jean Santeuil.* In *Contre Sainte-Beuve,* Proust sets out to prove that the personal life of the artist is entirely irrelevant to the appreciation of his works; art is not self-revelation: "A book is the product of another self [*moi*] than that which we reveal in our habits, in society, in our vices."[22] Art is not self-representation; art is not representation, period:

> Les livres sont l'oeuvre de la solitude et les *enfants du silence.* Les enfants du silence ne doivent rien avoir de commun avec les enfants de la parole, les pensées nées du désir de dire quelque chose. . . .
>   La matière de nos livres, la substance de nos phrases doit être immatérielle, non pas prise telle quelle dans la réalité. (*CSB,* 368)

> Books are the work of solitude and *children of silence.* The children
> of silence must have nothing in common with children of speech,
> the thoughts born of the desire to say something. . . .
>   The content of our books, the substance of our sentences should
> be immaterial, not taken, unaltered, from reality.

The two ideas are developed concomitantly in the pages of *Sainte-Beuve,* where the pleasure of writing is once again invoked as the sign of an authentic vocation: "Pleasure (for he who writes) is perhaps the criterion of true talent" (*CSB,* 368).

At the same time, Proust is beginning to compose the fragments of a novel that will become *A la recherche du temps perdu.* The two are not distinct in his mind, nor are they on paper, but the title *Contre Sainte-Beuve* will serve to designate that evolutionary "moment" in which theory and fiction have not merged in a fiction of the self (not a fiction about the self, but a theory of the fictionality of selfhood). The "I" of *Contre Sainte-Beuve* still aspires to some objective existence in the eyes of a "you"—a "tu"—the mother, whom the narrator resurrects to play the role of interlocutor. There is more than one allusion to the death of *"maman"* in *Contre Sainte-Beuve.* Most notable is a passage in which the narrator reminds her of the sufferings caused him by her absence on the evenings when "you were not coming to say goodnight to me in bed" (*CSB,* 354). But, responds the mother, "what if I had been gone for months, for years, for . . . " (*CSB,* 356). The narrator's reply:

> Tu sais, tu peux te le rappeler, comme je suis malheureux les premiers temps où nous sommes séparés. Puis, tu sais comme ma vie s'organise autrement, et, sans oublier les êtres que j'aime, je n'ai plus besoin d'eux, je me passe très bien d'eux. Je suis fou les huit premiers jours. Après cela je resterai bien seul des mois, des années, toujours. (*CSB,* 356)

> You know, you can recall, how unhappy I am at first when we are separated. Then, you know, I reorganize my life and, without forgetting my loved ones, I don't need them anymore, I can get along quite well without them. I am distraught the first week. After that, I could stay alone for months, years, forever.

Not until the process of mourning is complete can the artist efface himself in deference to his art, can the empty and groundless "je" of the *Recherche* appear—or disappear. In *Santeuil,* writes Serge Gaubert, "he was in the center of the canvas, the person on whom everything reflected; in the *Recherche,* he will be the one who, directing the show, is everywhere present in it without ever being directly represented."[23]

Significantly, both maternal and paternal figures are exorcized simultaneously at the conclusion of the *drame du coucher* narrative that opens *A la recherche du temps perdu,* where the narrator draws a parallel between their death and the mortality of his own *moi.* Recalling the terrifying appearance of his father on the staircase landing where he guiltily awaited his mother, he comments:

> La muraille de l'escalier où je vis monter le reflet de sa bougie n'existe plus depuis longtemps. En moi aussi bien des choses ont été détruites que je croyais devoir durer toujours. . . . Il y a bien longtemps aussi que mon père a cessé de pouvoir dire à maman: "Va avec le petit." La possibilité de telles heures ne renaîtra jamais pour moi. (1: 37/1: 39-40)

> The wall of the staircase up which I had watched the light of his candle gradually climb was long ago demolished. And in myself, too, many things have perished which I imagined would last for ever. . . . It is a long time, too, since my father has been able to say to Mamma: "Go along with the child." Never again will such moments be possible for me.

In the *Recherche,* that inaugural scene represents not the recovery but the renunciation of the past, and all its ontological security. For although the protagonist is excused for his "involuntary ailment"–and, despite having committed "a sin so deadly that I expected to be banished from the household" (1: 37-38/1: 40-41), is paradoxically awarded with total possession of his mother for one night–he neither considers himself disculpated, nor does he accede to the role of the Law, as does the hero of *Jean Santeuil.* Whereas the exonerated Jean triumphantly assumes the status of a "new government," Marcel, chagrined by his mother's acquiescence ("I ought to have been happy; I was not" [1: 38/1: 41]), attains the more modest rank of "a grown-up person" with a painful sense of having indulged in a guilty pleasure. Thus the narrator opens his novel by accepting and reaffirming his guilt vis-à-vis the Father, rather than usurping his role. But as Deleuze has shown, that refusal to interiorize the Law is the inaugural gesture of *humour masochiste,* by means of which the ego expels the Father from the symbolic sphere. It is no accident that the father, who plays a weak role in the bedtime scene of *Jean Santeuil,* and a relatively important one in a number of other passages, is explicitly identified with the patriarch Abraham in the initial scene of the *Recherche,* only to become a relatively insignificant figure in relation to the mother throughout the remainder of the novel. "In the case of masochism, the law is transferred to the mother"; "the mother . . . incarnates the superego, but in a parodic fashion" (*SM,* 79, 107). In that opening passage, Proust announces his refusal to write the *roman familial*–a refusal that is at the same time a rejection of mimetic art. The *drame du coucher* narrative, it will be recalled, is presented as the narrator's sole *voluntary memory* of Combray—that is, exactly the sort of experience that is not the matter of art, and that must be forgotten before writing can begin. The mother is everywhere "present" in the rest of the *Recherche,* but as an emblem of the relinquishment of the Real, the assumption of the Absence that is the condition of art. Thus the narrator of *Le Temps retrouvé,* on the point at last of commencing his work, makes a final allusion to that paradise lost: "And I would finally achieve what I had so ardently desired in my walks on the Guermantes way and thought to be impossible, just as I had thought it impossible, as I came home at the end of those walks, that I should ever get used to going to bed without kissing my mother" (3: 1035/3: 1091).[24]

Indeed the *drame du coucher* is already a parody of the Law, insofar as it illustrates the practice of writing of which the narrator is only beginning to elaborate the theory. Here, as throughout the *Recherche,* the traditional "logical," or "normal" hierarchy of textual functions is inverted. "Metaphor," rather than being subordinated to the narrative, or referential function of the text, as it is in *Santeuil,* takes on a primary role, narrative being reduced to a mere pretext for the elaboration of those Proustian analogies or laws which, by subsuming the individual in the universal, serve to nullify the singularity and unicity of the narrator/protagonist. Hence the practice of the novel is as essential to the conception of subjectivity developed therein as are the theories set forth in support of that conception. The Proustian subject, like the "objective reality" in which he is immersed, is spatially dispersed and temporally discontinuous. Only language can cement together the disparate fragments of experience. This is why the *baiser du soir* episode that initiates the *Recherche* is introduced by an account of the narrator's experience of awakening, as he tries to assemble the scattered fragments of his *moi*—this process will become a model for his activity as a writer. It is memory that comes to the rescue of the awakening narrator, but memory, we know, will later become a mere clue leading to the discovery of the powers of metaphor. The "informed narrator"[25] who is identified in the prefatory pages of *Jean Santeuil* is succeeded in the *Recherche* only by a dispersed "I" in the process of trying to reconstitute an identity. He will begin his search by appealing to memory: the result, of course, is the bedtime scene.

But the scenario has undergone considerable transformations since we last read it in *Jean Santeuil.* The nine-page account has ballooned into thirty-four pages of text. "Ballooned," and not just lengthened, for the twenty-five "extra" pages devoted to the *drame du coucher* in the *Recherche* may entail some variations in the diegesis, but do little to complicate or expand it; they do not represent an attempt to *better describe* the incident by recounting it in greater detail. The new material consists principally of what, by the standards of the classic linear, chronologically ordered narrative, would have to be considered digressions. Thus the account opens on page 9—in the imperfect, or "iterative" mode[26]—with a lengthy evocation of the magic lantern show used to divert Marcel from his anxiety over his impending bedtime. With the phrase "after dinner, alas, I was soon obliged to leave Mamma, who stayed talking with the others" (1: 10/1: 11), the narrative returns to the plight of the unhappy protagonist, only to abandon him forthwith in favor of the grandmother, whose habits and relationships with her family are the subject of the three succeeding pages. With "My only consolation when I went upstairs for the night was that Mamma would come in and kiss me after I was in bed" (1: 13/1: 13) having set the narrative back on course, Marcel's bedtime ritual is accorded nearly a page, but the specification that when there was company—namely, Swann—at dinner, the mother did not come up to kiss him, introduces a nine-page parenthesis devoted to Swann, the family's image of him, and the worldly socialite they scarcely suspect. We rejoin Marcel briefly via "the only one of us in whom the prospect of Swann's arrival gave rise to an unhappy foreboding was myself. . . . because on the evenings when there were visitors, Mamma did not come up to my room" (1: 23/1: 24), but our attention is soon diverted by the appearance of Swann at the garden gate and his subsequent conversations with his hosts—though this does not constitute a digression in the same sense as the previous examples: with Swann's arrival the narrator has shifted to the *passé simple*, so that the scene presented here does not disrupt the chronology of the narrative; Marcel is in fact present, albeit as a supernumerary. He reassumes the leading role with "I never took my eyes off my mother. I knew that . . . I would not be permitted to stay there for the whole of dinner-time" (1: 27/1: 29).

While the narrative proceeds somewhat less circuitously from this point on, it is nonetheless "interrupted" at several points, most notably by an extensive commentary on the mysteriously archaic codes governing Françoise's behavior and on the basis of which she might refuse to deliver Marcel's note to his mother at dinner (1: 28–29/1: 30–31) and further on—the note delivered and Marcel anxiously awaiting a response—an intricate analogy demonstrating the identity of the protagonist's sufferings with those of Swann-in-love, and ultimately with a universal experience of unrequited love. The note having failed to bring his mother to his side, Marcel determines in desperation to await Swann's departure in order to intercept her on the stairs to her room, this despite his fear of his father's wrath. The outcome is of course a

dramatic reversal: the terrible patriarch urges the mother to stay with
the child, a *coup de théâtre* that the narrator does not fail to reflect
upon at length. In *Jean Santeuil,* however, the episode concludes with
the mother leaving the sleeping Jean to rejoin her guests, whereas
Marcel's mother spends the night at his side, reading from *François le
Champi,* one of the books his grandmother has chosen for him as gifts
for his *fête.* This serves as a pretext for both a digression on the grandmother's notions of art (1: 39–41/1: 42–44) and a commentary on the
narrator's own naïve response to his first novel (1: 41–43/1: 44–46) —
thereby introducing the real subject of the *Recherche:* the novel itself.

Thus the *drame du coucher* narrative has been expanded by means of
a process of ramification which, for readers of the *Recherche,* has
become the hallmark of Proustian style, but which occurs rarely in
Jean Santeuil. This process inevitably obeys the principles of Proustian
metaphor, a fact that is in some instances more readily apparent than
in others. The comparison of the narrator preparing his mind for the
fleeting pleasure of his mother's kiss to a painter readying palette and
canvas for a rare and brief sitting (1: 27/1: 29) offers an obvious example
of a Proustian analogy. Similar, if more elaborate, analogies nourish
the narrator's aside on Françoise's idiosyncratic system of etiquette:

> Elle possédait à l'égard des choses qui peuvent ou ne peuvent pas se
> faire un code impérieux, abondant, subtil et intransigeant sur des
> distinctions insaisissables ou oiseuses (ce qui lui donnait l'apparence
> de ces lois antiques qui, à caté de prescriptions féroces comme de
> massacrer les enfants à la mamelle, défendent avec une délicatesse
> exagérée de faire bouillir le chevreau dans le lait de sa mère, ou de
> manger dans un animal le nerf de la cuisse). Ce code, si l'on en
> jugeait par l'entêtement soudain qu'elle mettait à ne pas vouloir faire
> certaines commissions que nous lui donnions, semblait avoir prévu
> des complexités sociales et des raffinements mondains tels que rien
> dans l'entourage de Françoise et dans sa vie de domestique de village
> n'avait pu les lui suggérer; et l'on était obligé de se dire qu'il y avait
> en elle un passé français très ancien, noble et mal compris, comme
> dans ces cités manufacturières où de vieux hôtels témoignent qu'il y
> eut jadis une vie de cour, et où les ouvriers d'une usine de produits
> chimiques travaillent au milieu de délicates sculptures qui représen-
> tent le miracle de saint Théophile ou les quatre fils Aymon. (1: 28–
> 29/1: 30–31)

On the subject of things which might or might not be done she
possessed a code at once imperious, abundant, subtle, and uncom-
promising on points themselves imperceptible or irrelevant, which
gave it a resemblance to those ancient laws which combine such
cruel ordinances as the massacre of infants at the breast with prohi-
bitions of exaggerated refinement against "seething the kid in his

mother's milk," or "eating of the sinew which is upon the hollow of the thigh." This code, judging by the sudden obstinacy which she would put into her refusal to carry out certain of our instructions, seemed to have provided for social complexities and refinements of etiquette which nothing in Françoise's background or in her career as a servant in a village household could have put into her head; and we were obliged to assume that there was latent in her some past existence in the ancient history of France, noble and little understood, as in those manufacturing towns where old mansions still testify to their former courtly days, and chemical workers toil among delicately sculptured scenes from *Le Miracle de Théophile* or *Les quatre fils Aymon.*

It is scarcely necessary to point out the difference between such comparisons and the stereotypical similes that appear in the *Jean Santeuil* version. The "Proustian" metaphor, insofar as it avoids the banal predictability of the commonplace, disconcerts because it defies our habits of perception. Its effect is therefore to draw attention to the narrative instance itself, that is, to the text, as opposed to the diegesis (which is precisely what "realist" discourse seeks to avoid), and consequently to inject an element of *humor* into the Proustian narrative. *A la recherche du temps perdu* is an eminently humorous text not only in the narrow sense, because the unfamiliar or incongruous (when not threatening) is perceived as funny, but also in the larger, theoretical, sense, for the logic of the signifier there tends to prevail over the logic of the signified.[27] The analogies just cited trouble the coherence of the diegesis (thereby undermining the referential function of the text) by introducing thematically heterogeneous elements (antique codes, court life, chemical factories); others disrupt the narrative even more dramatically by importing new diegetic material belonging to another space and a different time—or perhaps to an undefined space and time which we can only presume to have constituted a segment of the narrator's experience.[28] Such is the passage in which Proust relates Marcel's anguish first to Swann's past experience (thus presaging the parallel between Swann's passion for Odette and the narrator's for Albertine), and then to the torments of any jealous lover ("on" or "nous"). Hence an important consequence of the introduction of metaphor into the text of the *Recherche* is that the *coucher* incident has been divested of its status as a personal tragedy, to become an illustration of a universal law of desire.

Even those "digressions" that do not serve primarily to develop an analogy, however, explode the spatial and temporal limits of any given episode, superimposing disparate points in time and space; insofar as they, too, bring together distinct elements in an *apparently necessary* unity, such passages may be designated—if only "metaphorically"—as a form of Proustian "metaphor." The narrator's excursus explaining the grandmother's aesthetic convictions is exemplary. The content of the passage has little "to do" with the account of the narrator's night with his mother; yet from the titles of the books, to the reasons why they were chosen, to the aesthetic hierarchy that determined that choice, the text unfolds in a seductively logical movement which, like the second chauffeur's song, leads us far from our point of departure,[29] and appears digressive only when abruptly interrupted by the resumption of the bedtime narrative: "Mamma sat down by my bed" (1: 41/1: 44). Once again the "digression" is in fact less a departure from than a return to the real "story" recounted in the *Recherche*, the development of an idea, not that of a character. Both the long aside on the grand-mother's notions of art and the subsequent commentary on Marcel's perception of *François le Champi* are episodes in the narrator's appren-ticeship of signs. The protagonist/narrator himself is already scarcely more than a phantom interpreter, rather than an actor in the drama of his life. His activity consists primarily of emitting messages and re-ceiving them.

In using the past—the classic *récit d'enfance*, or childhood narrative[30]—as a pretext for the pleasure of writing, Proust is already demonstrat-ing his independence vis-à-vis the ostensible referent, and by implica-tion, vis-à-vis the mother, or archetypal lost object. Thus of course the narrator's gradual emancipation from his infatuation with the mother and all her avatars (Gilberte, Albertine, the duchess of Guermantes . . .) will parallel his progressive discoveries about the truth of art. Hence the importance of the theme of snobism—i.e., the belief that the more inaccessible the Other, the more inherently desirable he or she is, and the consequential desire for recognition as an equal by that Other—will have in the *Recherche*. Snobism is everywhere evident in *Jean San-teuil*, although it is unnamed as such: the aristocrats are portrayed as possessing all the noble traits ascribed to them by the hero, who rapid-ly proves himself to be a kindred spirit—this despite the fact that Jean (and presumably Proust) is beginning to realize that the charm of the objects of our desire is not essential to them. In *Contre Sainte-Beuve*, however, Proust integrates the phenomenon of snobism into a theory of writing:

> Cette vérité des impressions de l'imagination, si précieuse, l'art qui prétend ressembler à la vie, en la supprimant, supprime la seule chose précieuse. Et en revanche s'il la peint, il donne du prix aux choses les plus vulgaires; il pourrait en donner au snobisme, si au lieu de peindre ce qu'il est dans la société, c'est-à-dire rien, comme l'amour, le voyage, la douleur réalisés, il cherchait à le retrouver dans la

couleur irréelle—seule réelle—que le désir des jeunes snobs met sur la comtesse aux yeux violets, qui part dans sa victoria les dimanches d'été. (*CSB,* 99–100)

In omitting this precious truth that comes from the impressions of the imagination, art that claims to resemble life omits the only precious thing. On the other hand, if art does try to present that truth, it accords a value to the most ordinary things; it might even give snobism a certain value, if, instead of describing what it is in society—that is, nothing, like love, travel, or suffering, once they are realized—it sought to find it in the unreal tinge (in fact the only real one) that the desire of young snobs gives to the blue-eyed countess setting out in her victoria on Sunday mornings in summer.

A la recherche du temps perdu will follow this prescription, using the protagonist's own snobism and his long-sought, hard-won *succès mondain* as one means of simultaneously exposing the nullity of the object and demystifying the referent. Nowhere, perhaps, is the connection between this theme and Proust's practice of writing more apparent than in his treatment of the protagonist's evening at an opera gala—a vastly transformed "version" of the *Frédégonde* episode of *Jean Santeuil.* Whereas Jean was the principal actor in the spectacle, Marcel is demoted to *voyeur.* From his seat in the orchestra, he contemplates from afar the society of aristocrats gathered in their boxes (which in French have the amusing distinction of sharing the signifier *baignoires* with bathtubs), his gaze transforming them into a shimmering assembly of aquatic gods and goddesses, in one of the longest and most elaborate *métaphores filées* of the novel. To quote only a few lines:

Mais, dans les autres baignoires, presque partout, les blanches déités qui habitaient ces sombres séjours s'étaient réfugiées contre les parois obscures et restaient invisibles. Cependent, au fur et à mesure que le spectacle s'avançait, leurs formes vaguement humaines se détachaient mollement l'une après l'autre des profondeurs de la nuit qu'elles tapissaient et, s'élevant vers le jour, laissaient émerger leurs corps demi-nus et venaient s'arrêter à la limite verticale et à la surface clair-obscur où leurs brillants visages apparaissaient derrière le déferlement rieur, écumeux et léger de leurs éventails de plumes, sous leurs chevelures de pourpre emmêlées de perles que semblait avoir courbées l'ondulation du flux. . . . Les radieuses filles de la mer se retournaient à tout moment en souriant vers des tritons barbus pendus aux anfractuosités de l'abîme, ou vers quelque demi-dieu aquatique ayant pour crâne un galet poli sur lequel le flot avait ramené une algue lisse et pour regard un disque en cristal de roche. . . . Comme une grande déesse qui préside de loin aux jeux des divinités inférieures, la princesse était restée volontairement un peu au fond sur le canapé latéral, rouge comme un rocher de corail. . . . Sur la chevelure de la princesse, et s'abaissant jusqu'à ses sourcils, puis reprise plus bas à la hauteur de sa gorge, s'étendait une résille faite de ces coquillages blancs qu'on pêche dans certaines mers australes et qui étaient mêlés à des perles, mosaïque marine à peine sortie des vagues. (2: 40–41/2: 35–37)

But in the other boxes, almost everywhere, the white deities who inhabited those sombre abodes had taken refuge against their shadowy walls and remained invisible. Gradually, however, as the performance went on, their vaguely human forms detached themselves languidly one after the other from the depths of the night which they spangled, and, raising themselves toward the light, allowed their half-naked bodies to emerge into the chiaroscuro of the surface where their gleaming faces appeared behind the playful, frothy undulations of their ostrich-feather fans, beneath their hyacinthine, pearl-studded headdresses which seemed to bend with the motion of the waves. . . . The radiant daughters of the sea were constantly turning round to smile up at the bearded tritons who clung to the anfractuosities of the cliff, or towards some aquatic demi-god whose skull was a polished stone on to which the tide had washed a smooth covering of seaweed, and his gaze a disc of rock crystal. . . . Like a tall goddess presiding from afar over the frolics of the lesser deities, the princess had deliberately remained somewhat in the background on a sofa placed sideways in the box, red as a coral reef. . . . Over her hair, reaching in front to her eyebrows and caught back lower down at the level of her throat, was spread a net composed of those little white shells which are fished up in certain southern seas and which were intermingled with pearls, a marine mosaic barely emerging from the waves.

Proust pursues the analogy throughout his "description" of the denizens of the *baignoires* (2: 40–44/2: 35–40), abandoning it for the duration of a nine-page meditation on the dramatic art of la Berma, and then resuming it briefly (2: 52–54/2: 49–50) to describe the arrival of the duchess of Guermantes in the box of her cousin the princess. The aquatic theme is absent from the subsequent pages, devoted chiefly to Mme de Cambremer, but like a leitmotif ("Siegfried's theme") destined to evoke the Guermantes presence, it recurs at the conclusion of the episode when the duchess looks out upon "the nameless, collective madrepores of the audience in the stalls" (her gaze doubtless communicating to them a limited measure of her aquatic essence) and recognizing "the protozoon devoid of any individual existence which was myself"–the narrator–"showered upon me the sparkling and celestial torrent of her smile" (2: 58/2: 54–55).

In the four pages of the *Frédégonde* narrative, an entire social drama is played out; in twenty-three pages on la Berma's appearance at the *Opéra*, virtually nothing "happens"—if we qualify as "events" only those changes that affect the diegesis. The two passages are products of radically different aesthetic enterprises; if nothing "happens" in the *Recherche* account, it is because Proust is telling us that nothing *does* happen in "reality," or at least that *what* happens is irrelevant for the artist. In this respect, the relative "content" of the two passages is of course not entirely indifferent for our analysis: the one consists solely of the rapid-fire enumeration of actions, while in the other, the vast majority of the text is given over to commentary, to reflection—that is, to "theory."

As a closer study of the language in the *Recherche* version reveals, the entire metaphorical mechanism is set off by the word *baignoire*, which strikes the narrator's fancy as he enters the opera. The term is in fact already associated in the narrator's mind with the hallowed name of the duchess of Guermantes, whose various haunts he has vainly sought to represent to himself: "That villa, that opera-box, into which Mme de Guermantes transfused the current of her life, must, it seemed to me, be places no less magical than her home" (2: 35/2: 30–31).[31] Hence the dramatic effect produced by the words of a personage he presumes to be the prince of Saxony requesting a box which may be the princess of Guermantes' *baignoire*:

> En disant cette phrase au contrôleur, il embranchait sur une vulgaire soirée de ma vie quotidienne un passage eventuel vers un monde nouveau; le couloir qu'on lui désigna après avoir prononcé le mot de baignoire, et dans lequel il s'engagea, était humide et lézardé et semblait conduire à des grottes marines, au royaume mythologique des nymphes des eaux. Je n'avais devant moi qu'un monsieur en habit qui s'éloignait; mais je faisais jouer auprès de lui, comme avec un réflecteur maladroit . . . l'idée qu'il était le prince de Saxe et allait voir la duchesse de Germantes. (2: 38/2: 33)

> In uttering this sentence to the attendant, he grafted on to a commonplace evening in my everyday life a potential entry into a new world; the passage to which he was directed after having spoken the word "box" and along which he now proceeded was moist and mildewed and seemed to lead to subaqueous grottoes, to the mythological kingdom of the water-nymphs. I had before me a gentleman in evening dress who was walking away from me, but I kept playing upon and around him, as with a badly fitting projector . . . the idea that he was the Prince of Saxony and was on his way to join the Duchesse de Guermantes.

In what is essentially a prologue to the *baignoire* scene, therefore, the narrator is announcing what the succeeding pages will illustrate:

that the beings who populate the boxes, like the "gentleman in evening dress" are but insignificant surfaces onto which the narrator projects the images conjured up by his desire. There is never any question of his having perceived or divined some essential quality of the occupants of the *baignoires* that grounds the analogy in a heretofore hidden reality; the entire process is motivated at the level of the signifier. The reader who prizes Proust for his vivid depictions of contemporary society may be certain that if "polished stones" (or some other shiny objects) were not associated with seashores, then there would have been no balding heads in the boxes that evening, and that if the princess of Guermantes chose to adorn herself with shells and pearls rather than with diamonds and emeralds, it was only in deference to the aquatic origins of the former.[32] Might not Barthes, in substituting *pleasure* for *expressivity* as the supreme value of writing, have been referring to Proust? "You don't elaborate in order to be more precise, more true to life; from expression to expression, you elaborate to exhibit metaphors, that is, felicitous expressions, or, again, expressions as felicities."[33]

A single concrete detail from the *Jean Santeuil* scene survives in *Le Côté de Guermantes,* but so transformed as to be emblematic of the disparity between the two versions: in both, the aristocrats eat candy. But whereas in *Santeuil* this is presented as the banal activity that it is, the bedazzled narrator of the *Recherche* can only assume that the princess of Guermantes merely feigns to distribute sweets in conformation with some enigmatic ritual:

> Je la voyais en train d'offrir des bonbons glacés à un gros monsieur en frac. Certes j'étais bien loin d'en conclure qu'elle et ses invités fussent des êtres pareils aux autres. Je comprenais bien que ce qu'ils faisaient là n'était qu'un jeu. (2: 42/2: 38)

> I saw her engaged in offering crystallised fruit to a stout gentleman in tails. Certainly I was very far from concluding that she and her guests were mere human beings like the rest of the audience. I understood that what they were doing there was only a game.

Here the narrator stands in the same relationship to his protagonist as does the author of the *Recherche* to the author of *Jean Santeuil* (or at least, the author implied by that text). Less enlightened than the narrator, Marcel still believes in "the transcendence of the Other."[34] And while the narrator cannot directly denounce Marcel's mystification until *Le Temps retrouvé,* he can demonstrate it: he may show, not tell. For the author of *Jean Santeuil,* the world conceals as many mysteries as do the opera boxes for Marcel, a fact to which his writing bears constant testimony. And as though to commemorate that moment in his own quest in the pages of the novel he is writing, Proust places a nameless "young man with fair hair" [*jeune homme blond*] (2: 53/2: 49) on the first row of the Guermantes' box, where the duchess greets him with a "deep curtsey" before the envious eyes of the world—and of Marcel. Thus it is an Other who, in the *Recherche,* enjoys the maternal presence that Jean himself (whose "small pale face" [*petite figure blonde*] had summoned his mother from the bedroom window in the *coucher* scene [*JS,* 204/27] recovered in the person of the duchess of Réveillon.[35] The young man in the duchess's box is as much a projection of the protagonist's desire as is the aura—"la couleur irréelle"—that surrounds the Guermantes, an objectification of the ego that Marcel is still seeking to establish as a source of his works. Not until the "Goncourt" passage early in *Le Temps retrouvé* does he relate his earlier realization that the capacity to *briller* in society (as Beyle would have said) is no index of artistic talent to the discovery that the artist's choice of model is equally unimportant for the work of art.[36] Little more than a hundred pages later (an instant in Proustian time) will come the final revelation that he must forget the past—and the present, which is only a potential past—before he can write.

A Remembrance of Things Past is precisely what *A la recherche du temps perdu* is not; nor is it the novel the narrator is going to write, once the past is forgotten. It is a novel about forgetting: forgetting other people—*maman,* Gilberte, Albertine—but most of all, about forgetting oneself in order to "open oneself to the violence of signs," as Deleuze would say. The *Recherche* is not an autobiography—as any number of critics have proclaimed by now—but this is not merely because the material is "fictionalized." It is because the notion of "self" it implies is antithetical to any classical concept of autobiography. Nor can it be a novel in the traditional sense, since it rejects the principle of referentiality. For the Proustian subject, divested of "the time of the narrative (of the imagery)," writing is not the child of a nostalgic quest for a lost self, an anxious rehashing of the family romance; for "the Text can recount nothing . . ."—but this is not Marcel Proust, it is Roland Barthes, introducing his "autobiography" *Roland Barthes* (*RB,* 6/3-4). If, in retrospect, those words seem surprisingly relevant to the Proustian text, it is because *A la recherche du temps perdu* (simultaneously autobiography, novel, and literary theory) recounts, in a fictional mode, and *avant la lettre,* the gradual "humorous" relinquishment of the ego that was to constitute the essential feature of the shift from modern to postmodern mentality—and from a theory of the literary *work* to that of the *text.* It is no mere coincidence that in the opening pages of *Roland Barthes,* next to photographs of the author as a young child, there appears the caption: "Contemporaries? I was beginning to walk, Proust was still alive, and was finishing *A la Recherche du Temps Perdu*" (*RB*, 27/23). For Barthes—the iconoclastic advocate of nonreferential literature, conspirator in the death of the author, and hedonistic champion of the pleasure of the text—was certainly Proust's greatest, perhaps his only, disciple.

6 : Barthes
Ecrire le Corps

Lorsque je feins d'écrire sur ce que j'ai autrefois écrit, il se produit
... un mouvement d'abolition, non de vérité. Je ne cherche pas à
mettre mon expression présente au service de ma vérité antérieure
(en régime classique, on aurait sanctifié cet effort sous le nom d'*au-
thenticité*), je renonce à la poursuite épuisante d'un ancien morceau
de moi-même. ... Je ne dis pas: "Je vais me décrire," mais: "J'écris un
texte, et je l'appelle R. B." ... Ne sais-je pas que, *dans le champ du
sujet, il n'y a pas de référent?* Le fait (biographique, textuel) s'abolit
dans le signifiant, parce qu'il *coïncide* immédiatement avec lui: en
m'écrivant, je ne fais que répéter l'opération extrême par laquelle
Balzac, dans *Sarrasine,* a fait "coïncider" la castration et la castrature.
(*RB*, 61–62/56)

When I pretend to write on what I have written in the past, there
occurs ... a movement of abolition, not of truth. I do not strive to
put my present expression in the service of my previous truth (in
the classical system, such an effort would have been sanctified under
the name of *authenticity*), I abandon the exhausting pursuit of an
old piece of myself. ... I do not say: "I am going to describe myself," but: "I am writing a text, and I call it R.B." ... Do I not know
that, *in the field of the subject, there is no referent?* The fact (whether
biographical or textual) is abolished in the signifier, because it immediately *coincides* with it: *writing myself*, I merely repeat the extreme operation by which Balzac, in *Sarrasine,* has made castration
and castrature "coincide."

The fragment entitled "La coïncidence" of Barthes's *Roland Barthes*
defines his autobiographical project in opposition to precisely the type
of document Beyle set out to produce in the *Vie de Henry Brulard:* a
true confession, a totalizing representation of his past self. It is impossible to write a classic autobiography today, because, as Barthes puts it
in another fragment, "we have a different knowledge today than yesterday" (*RB*, 124/120)—a new "knowledge" or what might be more appropriately called a new paradigm, within which the subject is treated, not
as a referent, an extralinguistic entity, but as "an effect of language"
(82/79). In other words, the author of *Roland Barthes* rejects an ironic
approach to autobiography in favor of a humorous one.

Those "other words" are not merely my own, into which I have translated Barthes's language, for, although he does not label his own approach "humor," the conception of subjectivity that he denounces here is the same deluded belief in an autonomous ego that he identified in *S/Z* as the motive of irony. To recall a passage from that essay cited in Chapter Two above, classic irony is for Barthes the stereotypical parodic utterance of "a subject that puts its imaginary elements [*son imaginaire*] at the distance that it pretends to take with regard to the language of others, thereby making itself even more securely a subject of discourse" (*SZ*, 52/45). Or (still in Barthes's terms), irony is a discourse by means of which one subject seeks to establish its superiority over—"avoir barre sur"—others (212/206).

Given the explicit analogy drawn in the "Coïncidences" fragment between *Sarrasine* and *Roland Barthes*, it would be difficult not to perceive the theoretical continuity that links—via *Le Plaisir du texte*—the two works. For *Roland Barthes* is, among other things, an attempt to apply to autobiographical writing the principles of textuality (as well as much of the critical terminology) developed in *S/Z*. And one of Barthes's primary preoccupations during the period which produced *S/Z* (his "post-semiological" phase, *remise-en-cause* of his earlier structuralism) was the problem of how to avoid irony, in at least two related senses: first, the arrogance[1] of a discourse with pretensions to scientificity (e.g., early structuralism) and second, the superciliousness of a discourse which would establish its distance in relation to other discourses by claiming the status of a metalanguage (e.g., a self-satisfied poststructuralism)—yet to avoid these without lapsing into the stoic-heroic irony of silence. Whereas the text of *Brulard* became increasingly reflexive as Beyle encountered the various stumbling blocks of autobiography, *Roland Barthes* is throughout a reflection on autobiographical writing—or the impossibility of it. Both an autobiography and a book about an autobiography to be written, it is closer to Proust's novel about (not) writing a novel than to any classic example of the autobiographical genre.

Thus the fundamental problem and principal theme of *Roland Barthes* will be how to talk about oneself without the arrogance of irony. The central theme/concept of *S/Z*, castration, will also come prominently into play in the development of this problematic in the autobiography. Already, in Barthes's reading of *Sarrasine*, castration was a multivalent term. As the absence of the phallus, psychoanalytic symbol of the ultimate signified, it was emblematic of the illusion of referentiality produced by the text, and the delusion of the reader who would look *behind* the text in search of a final truth. As the parodic, mocking voice of irony, it was the "castrating gesture" (*SZ*, 166/160) by which one code attempts to dominate ("avoir barre sur") all others, in order to "abusively clos[e] off the plurality of codes" (212/206). Finally, it was the condition of the being who is excluded from society (conceived of as a system of intelligible, because stereotypical, signs) because he lacks a phallus, or social identity. In *Roland Barthes*, the term *castration* will function in all these senses as well as in a more positive one, as Barthes both thematizes and seeks to put into practice an autobiographical discourse that is neither banally referential nor smugly parodic, neither comfortably included in nor dramatically excluded from the domain of intelligibility. In other words (Barthes's), he must "exorcize [*déjouer*] the double violence of overwhelming meaning and of heroic non-meaning" (*RB,* 122/118).

Two fragments of Barthes's autobiography thematize his position vis-à-vis other discourses in terms of a favorite analogy:

> Quand je jouais aux barres au Luxembourg, mon plus grand plaisir n'était pas de provoquer l'adversaire et de m'offrir témérairement à son droit de prise; c'était de délivrer les prisonniers—ce qui avait pour effet de remettre toutes les parties en circulation; le jeu repartait à zéro.
>
> Dans le grand jeu des pouvoirs de parole, on joue aussi aux barres; un langage n'a barre sur l'autre que temporairement; il suffit qu'un troisième surgisse du rang, pour que l'assaillant soit contraint à la retraite: dans le conflit des rhétoriques, la victoire n'est jamais qu'*au tiers langage.* Ce langage-là a pour tâche de délivrer les prisonniers, d'éparpiller les signifiés, les catéchismes. . . . Que la différence ne se paye d'aucune sujétion, pas de dernière réplique. (*RB,* 54–55/50)

> When I used to play prisoner's base in the Luxembourg, what I liked best was not provoking the other team and boldly exposing myself to their right to take me prisoner; what I liked best was to free the prisoner—the effect of which was to put both teams back into circulation: the game started over again at zero.
>
> In the great game of the powers of speech, we also play prisoner's base: one language has only temporary rights over another; all it takes is for a third language to appear from the ranks for the assailant to be forced to retreat: in the conflict of rhetorics, the victory never goes to any but the *third language.* The task of this language is to release the prisoners: to scatter the signifieds, the catechisms. . . . Difference should not be paid for by any subjection: no last word.

> Le mouvement de son oeuvre est tactique: il s'agit de se déplacer, de barrer, comme aux barres, mais non de conquérir. . . . Cette oeuvre se définirait donc comme: *une tactique sans stratégie.* (*RB,* 175/172)

> The movement of his work is tactical: a matter of displacing himself, of obstructing, as with bars, but not of conquering. . . . This work would therefore be defined as: *a tactics without strategy.*

To take an oppositional stance without instituting a master-slave dialectic, to be ever an adversary but never a victor: this was precisely the tactic ("oppose without appeal to force") prescribed in *S/Z* (212/ 206) for the critic who would avoid irony. For Barthes, as we shall see, it entails a game of *barres* in another, linguistic sense. His texts are inevitably structured around series of dichotomies represented in the classic manner as two opposing terms separated by a bar. Among the most prominent of these in *Roland Barthes: signified/signifier, self/other, mind/body, work/text, doxa/paradoxa, metaphor/metonymy;* all exemplify the paradigm *irony/humor*. In each case, the second term is endowed with positive connotations, and ostensibly supersedes the first in a Barthesian hierarchy of values; at closer reading, however, it becomes apparent that in Barthes's usage, the second term is never simply the antithesis of the other, but also represents the undoing of the very dichotomy to which it belongs—the dissolution of the *barre* that marks the distinction between terms. Thus, what was apparently a simple dialectical movement becomes "another dialectic . . . the contradiction of the terms yields in his eyes by the discovery of a third term, which is not a synthesis, but a *translation*" (*RB*, 73/69).

If the process sounds familiar, if the nonantithetical interrelationship of Barthesian dichotomies evokes Derridean deconstruction, with its most celebrated dichotomy, *parole/écriture*—in which *écriture* is both the Other of parole, and its condition of possibility (which is to say, the *impossibility* of maintaining the distinction)—it is of course because, as Barthes himself points out (*RB*, 148/145), Derrida is a major contributor to the intertext of Barthes's post-semiological phase. In the Barthesian "version" (a translation, as in *thème et version*) of deconstruction, as with his adoption of the term *écriture*, there is no pretense of "originality," since the opposition self/other is no more stable than any other of Barthes's dichotomies, a principal tenet of his theory of textuality being that at the "center" of the subject is the discourse of the Other (and here the intertext is Lacan; the intertext of "intertext" is Kristeva . . .). The singularity of the Barthesian text resides solely in the manner in which it appropriates the language of the other, according it a notoriously indecisive status.[2] Barthes seems to speak Marxism, linguistics, psychoanalysis, and deconstruction fluently; is it only a semblance? To the reader of Barthes who wonders whether his use of concepts borrowed from other disciplines is to be taken "seriously" or not, the response must be: both. When an actor speaks French in a play, he may only be acting, but he is still speaking French. "Can one pretend to speak a language?" wondered the author of *L'Ecriture et la différence*.[3] The idea of the feint appealed to the author of *Roland Barthes:* "It always comes down to this: what is the project of writing which will present, not the best pretense [*la meilleure feinte*], but simply an *undecidable pretense* [*une feinte indécidable*] (as D. says of Hegel)?" (124/121).

"Phases" is a commentary on the nature of Barthes's textual borrowings: "The intertext is not necessarily a field of influences; rather it is a music of figures, metaphors, thought-words [*pensées-mots*]; it is the signifier as *siren*" (*RB*, 148/145). Language is, above all, an object of desire; therein lies the undoing of innumerable dichotomies, of which two in particular (both counterparts of the archetypal reality/appearance dichotomy) play an essential role in the Barthesian autobiography: signified/signifier and mind/body.

Relatively solid in *Mythologies,* the bar separating signified and signifier was already crumbling in the supposedly scientific *Système de la mode,* in which the object under analysis was not in fact fashion itself, but language about fashion. *S/Z* was the tale of that bar's catastropic dissolution, the "unrestrained metonymy" that leads to the breakdown of all economies: "By abolishing the paradigmatic barriers [*les barres paradigmatiques*], this metonymy abolishes the power of *legal substitution* on which meaning is based: . . . it is then no longer possible to *represent*" (*SZ*, 221–22/216). If it is no longer possible to distinguish words from concepts, copies from originals, paper money from gold, appearance from reality, on what are to be founded science, philosophy, theology? This disastrous hemorrhaging of values was incarnated, for Plato and Aristotle, by the Sophists, for Christian moralists and theologians by ironists and punsters, and for some contemporary critics by Barthes (Derrida, etc.).

His habit of tampering with paradigms is a leitmotif (without tragic undertones) of Barthes's *Barthes:*

> Mon discours contient beaucoup de notions couplées. . . . Ces oppositions sont des artefacts: on emprunte à la science des manières conceptuelles, une énergie de classement: on vole un langage, sans cependant vouloir l'appliquer jusqu'au bout: impossible de dire: ceci est de la dénotation, ceci de la connotation, ou: un tel est écrivain, un tel écrivant, etc.: l'opposition est *frappée* (comme une monnaie) mais on ne cherche pas à *l'honorer.* A quoi sert-elle donc? Tout simplement à *dire quelque chose:* il est nécessaire de poser un paradigme pour produire un sens et pouvoir ensuite le dériver. (*RB,* 95–96/92)

> My discourse contains many coupled notions. . . . Such oppositions are artifacts: one borrows from science certain conceptual procedures, an energy of classification: one steals a language, though without wishing to apply it to the end: impossible to say: this is denotation, this connotation, or: this passage is readable, this writable, etc.: the opposition is *struck* (like a coinage), but one does not

seek to *honor* it. Then what good is it? Quite simply, it serves *to say something:* it is necessary to posit a paradigm in order to produce a meaning and then to be able to divert, to alter it.

Barthesian categories are "forgeries" (title of the previous fragment) because they are not backed by "gold," that is, a stable meaning; rather their value (a term of Saussurean coinage) varies at the whim of the speaker: they function within a given context, but cannot be exchanged for referents, like poker chips that cannot be cashed in when the game is over.

Seduced by signifiers, Barthes "pays his visits, i.e., his respects, to vocabularies. . . . but the intertext thereby created is literally *superficial*" (*RB,* 78/74); philosophy, linguistics are merely a "reservoir of images" (103, 127/99, 124) for the Barthesian text. At first glance, then, Barthes's self-proclaimed "superficiality" appears to be just that: a reversal of the traditional hierarchy that subordinates signifier to signified, a defiant *parti pris* for words *instead of* ideas, for pure "formalism," "art for art's sake," etc. But of course it is not so simple. Initially, Barthes does accord priority to the signifier, inasmuch as the word is never treated as a mere label for a concept. As Deleuze might put it, Barthes's mind works *dans le mauvais sens*—in the wrong direction: "He rarely starts from the idea in order to invent an image for it subsequently; he starts from a sensuous object, and then hopes to meet in his work with the possibility of finding an *abstraction* for it" (103/99). In fact Barthes is only capitalizing on what, in *Critique et vérité,* he called the "symbolic" function of language (much like Jakobson's poetic function)—that is, the inevitable implication of the physical properties of words in the thought process. Barthesian *écriture,* as analyzed by Barthes *lui-même,* is a practice of deliberate, elaborate Cratylism:

> Le "raisonnement" est fait en somme d'un enchaînement de métaphores: il prend un phénomène (la connotation, la lettre Z), et il lui fait subir une avalanche de points de vue; ce qui tient lieu d'argumentation, c'est le dépliement d'une image: Michelet "mange" l'Histoire; donc il la "broute"; donc il "marche" en elle, etc.: tout ce qui arrive à un animal paissant sera ainsi *appliqué* à Michelet: l'application métaphorique tiendra le rôle d'une explication.
>
> On peut appeler "poétique" (sans jugement de valeur) tout discours dans lequel le mot conduit l'idée: si vous aimez les mots au point d'y succomber, vous vous retirez de la loi du signifié, de l'écrivance. (155/152)

The "reasoning" consists, in short, of a series of metaphors: he takes a phenomenon (connotation, the letter Z) and he submits it to an avalanche of points of view; what replaces argumentation is the unfolding of an image: Michelet "eats" History; hence he "grazes" on it;

hence he "walks" in it, etc.: everything that happens to an animal put out to pasture will thus be *applied* to Michelet: the metaphoric application will play the part of an explanation.

One might call "poetic" (without value judgment) any discourse in which the word leads the idea: if you like words to point of succumbing to them, you exclude yourself from the law of the signified, from *écrivance*.

As a result, the Barthesian "unit of thought" is not the concept in the classic sense, but something Barthes has dubbed the "objet intellectuel" or "pensée-mot," in which signifier is indistinguishable from signified, and the question of the priority of conceptualization or language, a chicken-or-the-egg problem. In his theory as well as in his practice, Barthes progressively abandons a "metaphorical" or "vertical" notion of language (in which word represents idea) for a "metonymical" or "horizontal" one, in which signifier and signified are continuous, occupying the same plane: a signified is always also the signifier of another signified, which is always also a signifier, etc. A popular model for this phenomenon is the dictionary, in which the search for the meaning of a word sets off a potentially endless process of referral—and thus deferral of meaning—words being defined by other words, which are in turn defined by, etc. A more contemporary and perhaps more intriguing model is provided by the Möbius strip, in which "this" side is continuous with the "other" side.

As signifier is continuous with signified, language is continuous with concrete reality. "My body itself (and not only my ideas) can *make up* to words [*se faire aux mots*], can be in some sense created by them," so that, if R.B. (as the narrator often refers to himself) one day discovers, with a thrill of horror, an *excoriation* on his tongue, it is doubtless for the pleasure of using "that rare, savory word" (*RB,* 155/152); if he has migraines instead of headaches, it is partly because "the word is so lovely," and partly because migraines are the "mythological attribute of the bourgeois woman and of the man of letters" (128/124). In a similar vein, he wonders, of two Bonapartist soldiers who committed suicide for love, "From what language . . . did they draw their passion (scarcely in accord with the image of their class and profession)? What books had they read—or what stories been told?" Here, Barthes explicitly raises the chicken/egg dilemma: "Entanglement of language and the body: which begins?" (95/91). At stake in the dissolution of the language/body dichotomy is the perennial mind/body opposition, for if the body is coextensive with language, it must also be coextensive with thought. This breakdown of the distinction between the abstract and the concrete (the essential and the accidental) is morally disruptive in Platonic-Christian tradition, since it upsets the "natural" order of things: the mind *ought to* "avoir barre sur" the body. Whence the perplexity, even dismay, of Barthes's readership when confronted with his claim that "writing proceeds through the body" [*l'écriture passe par le corps*]: "Public opinion has a reduced conception of the body: it is always, apparently, what is opposed to the soul: any somewhat metonymic extension of the body is taboo" (83/80).

Indeed, *le corps* is, in *Roland Barthes,* the principal figure for the "unbridled metonymy" that characterizes the logic of the text. By its very mutability, it is a fitting emblem of Barthes's critical tactics:

> Dans le lexique d'un auteur, ne faut-il pas qu'il y ait toujours un mot-mana, un mot dont la signification ardente, multiforme, insaisissable et comme sacrée, donne l'illusion que par ce mot on peut répondre à tout? Ce mot n'est ni excentrique ni central; il est . . . à la fois reste et supplément, signifiant occupant la place de tout signifié. Ce mot est apparu dans son oeuvre peu à peu; . . . maintenant, il s'épanouit; ce mot-mana, c'est le mot "corps." (*RB,* 133/129–30)

> In an author's lexicon, will there not always be a word-as-mana, a word whose ardent, complex, ineffable, and somehow sacred signification gives the illusion that by this word one might answer for everything? Such a word is neither eccentric nor central; it is . . . at once remainder and supplement, a signifier taking up the place of every signified. This word has gradually appeared in his work; . . . now it blossoms, it flourishes; this word-as-mana is the word "body."

Now the notion of a "mot-mana" is not to be confused with that of a "mot-clef," or "key word." The latter is a "full" term, with a stable meaning, the index of an ultimate signified—an idea, concept, person, or thing around which a work is organized or which serves as a principle of its explanation ("rosebud" comes to mind). The mot-mana "corps" is a Barthesian version of Lévi-Strauss's empty, floating signifier, index of an unknown or missing signified, a value "in itself devoid of meaning and thus capable of receiving any meaning," which Deleuze identifies with the "paradoxical element" essential to the functioning of any structure and which determines the production of meaning, the element whose fundamental property is to "'be missing from its own place,' never resembling itself, always in disequilibrium. . . . It is at once word and object: esoteric word, exoteric object" (*LS,* 64–66).

While it would no doubt be useless to try to take the allusion to Lévi-Strauss too "seriously," it is clear that the "objet intellectuel," "pensée-mot" *corps* is a kind of floating signifier in *Roland Barthes,* symbol of the undefinable, the paradoxical instance, the "third term" that undermines all the dichotomies upon which traditional logic is founded; emblem, above all, of the unsignifiable contemporary subject, never in its place, never identical to itself, both absolutely singular and fundamentally plural—that is, penetrated with otherness. The body is both the source and the sign of the slight, almost indiscernible *difference* introduced into the discourse of the Other by the writing subject Barthes:

> Il essaye de tenir un discours qui ne s'énonce pas au nom de la Loi et/ou de la Violence: dont l'instance ne soit ni politique, ni religieuse, ni scientifique; qui soit en quelque sorte le reste et le supplément de tous ces énoncés. Comment appellerons-nous ce discours? *érotique,* sans doute, car il a à faire avec la jouissance; ou peut-être encore: *esthétique,* si l'on prévoit de faire subir peu à peu à cette vieille catégorie une légère torsion qui l'éloignera de son fond régressif, idéaliste, et l'approchera du corps, de la dérive. (*RB,* 87/84)

> He attempts to compose a discourse which is not uttered in the name of the Law and/or of Violence: whose instance might be neither political nor religious nor scientific; which might be in a sense the remainder and the supplement of all such utterances. What shall we call such discourse? *erotic,* no doubt, for it has to do with pleasure; or even perhaps: *aesthetic,* if we foresee subjecting this old category to a gradual torsion which will alienate it from its regressive, idealist background and bring it closer to the body, to the *drift.*

Why *le corps?* Initially, because the body is traditionally opposed to the mind—to reason, rationalism, logic, and consistency. Its status as the tangible, temporal component of our being is exemplified in the ancient doctrine of the bodily humors, thought to determine character and temperament, and generally associated with capricious or irrational behavior, even after medical science had ceased to take them seriously. Thus classical French moralists warned against the insidious influence of the *humeurs:* La Rochefoucauld maintained that "the bodily humors . . . exercise . . . a secret control over us, so that they play a considerable role in all our actions, without our being aware of them."[4] His contemporary La Bruyère, using the term only somewhat more metaphorically, admonished that "those who write according to their humor, are subject to revising their work; since it [their humor] is not always steady and varies in them according to the occasion, they soon tire of the expressions and the terms of which they have been fondest."[5] He, at least, might not have objected to Barthes's claim that "l'écriture passe par le corps," though he doubtless would have frowned upon his hedonistic colleague's enthusiastic approbation of that phenomenon.

It should not be surprising that *humour* is a doublet of *humeur*, the former being simply the English version of the latter, borrowed back by the eighteenth-century French to designate a form of capricious wit which seems to bear the mark of its fluid corporeal origins. The *Robert* defines it as a "type of wit that consists of presenting reality, or of deforming it, in such a manner as to bring out its droll or bizarre aspects," appending the intriguing observation that "modern definitions of humor make of it a notion quite close to the 'absolute comic' of which Baudelaire speaks"—about which, I refer the reader back to Chapter Two above. The *Robert* further remarks that usage has long opposed humor's gratuitousness to irony's tendentiousness: "Humor [is] gratuitous gaiety, engaging nothing . . . irony entails a judgment and always has a victim." All the above seems to provide a rather Barthesian etymological justification for adopting the term *humor* to designate Barthes's policy of critical nonviolence, particularly since his own terminology is but one etymological remove from mine:

> Je puis me révolter de deux manières: en revendiquant, tel un légiste, contre un droit élaboré sans moi et contre moi . . . ou en dévastant la Loi majoritaire par une action transgressive d'avant-garde. Mais lui, il semble rester bizarrement au carrefour de ces deux refus: il a des complicités de transgression et des humeurs individualistes. . . . Tel un *out-sider* intermittant, je puis entrer-dans, ou sortir-de la socialité lourde, selon mon humeur. (*RB*, 134–35/131)

> I can rebel in two ways: by arguing, like a jurist, against a law elaborated without me and against me . . . or by wrecking the majority's Law by a transgressive avant-garde action. But he seems to remain strangely at the intersection of these two rejections: he has complicities of transgression and individualist moods. . . . I can enter into or emerge from the burdensome sociality, depending on my mood.

In Barthes's earliest book, *Le Degré zéro de l'écriture* (1953), *le corps* is very nearly the biological, humoral body of philosophical tradition albeit with a slightly mystical aura. There, it is identified with the author's inner depths, or *profondeur*, ground of his originality because it is the source of his personal style. The body precedes language, that which is given by culture, and makes itself heard through the idiosyncracies of style:

> La langue est donc en deça de la Littérature. Le style est presque au-delà: des images, un débit, un lexique naissent du corps et du passé de l'écrivain et deviennent peu à peu les automatismes de son art. Ainsi sous le nom de style, se forme un langage autarcique qui ne plonge que dans la mythologie personnelle et secrète de l'auteur. . . .

Ses références sont au niveau d'une biologie ou d'un passé, non d'une Histoire: il est la "chose" de l'écrivain, sa splendeur et sa prison, il est sa solitude. . . . Il est la voix décorative d'une chair inconnue et secrète. . . . Le style est proprement un phénomène d'ordre germinatif, il est la transmutation d'une Humeur.[6]

A language is therefore on the hither side of Literature. Style is almost beyond it: imagery, delivery, vocabulary spring from the body and the past of the writer and gradually become the very reflexes of his art. Thus under the name of style a self-sufficient language is evolved which has its roots only in the depths of the author's personal and secret mythology. . . . Its frame of reference is biological or biographical, not historical: it is the writer's "thing," his glory and his prison, it is his solitude. . . . It is the decorative voice of hidden, secret flesh. . . . Style is properly speaking a germinative phenomenon, the transmutation of a Humour.

Not a purely physical entity, the body of *Le Degré zéro* nonetheless remains distinct from language, associated with it primarily through *influence* (from the Latin *influere*, to flow in). Throughout the semiological writings (*Eléments de sémiologie, Système de la mode*), it remains something to be signified through language, but as the "science" of semiology becomes weighted down with "tout un imaginaire" ("a whole repertoire of images") and Barthes shifts his attention from work to text, the *barre* separating body from sign loses its solidity: "One . . . must introduce into this rational image-repertoire [*imaginaire*] the texture of desire, the claims of the body: this, then, is the Text, the theory of the Text" (*RB*, 75/71). The resulting "textuality" phase (see "Phases," *RB*, 148/145), which produced *S/Z* and *Sade, Fourier, Loyola* and *L'Empire des signes*, might well be characterized by the "fusion . . . of discourse and the body" that Barthes admired in Sade's writing.[7] This evolution of the body corresponds, of course, to an evolution in the prevailing conception of subjectivity: language, once exterior to the subject, has become an essential constituent of it, exploding the walls of the subjective "prison" of which Barthes spoke in *Le Degré zéro*. The private person expressed through style is superseded by an individual conceived of as a nodal point, a confluence of discourses in a vast text. This is the subject of *écriture* (a term that supplants the notion of *style*), and as Barthes's writing becomes increasingly "subjective" (or "égoïste," as Todorov has put it),[8] in *Le Plaisir du texte* and then in *Roland Barthes*, the subject under examination will be this plural, "superficial" combination of variables, rather than a singular, intimate self. "Whenever I attempt to 'analyze' a text which has given me pleasure," reads a passage of *Le Plaisir*, "it is not my 'subjectivity' I encounter, but my 'individuality,' the given which makes my body separate from other bodies and appropriates its suffering or its pleasure: it is my body of bliss [*jouissance*] I encounter. And this body of bliss is also *my historical subject*" (*PT,* 98–99/62). Thus, by the time Barthes classifies *Le Plaisir* and the subsequent autobiography together under the genre "morality," cautioning that "*morality* should be understood as the precise opposite of ethics [*la morale*] (it is the thinking of the body in a state of language)" (*RB,* 148/145), the humoral body of the early works has metamorphosed into a "humorous" body, both word and flesh, mind and matter. That is, the humorous body is no longer *simply* the opposite of the spirit (although it is still that, too); in a typically Barthesian fashion, it represents a refusal to honor that opposition.

This is the body that is both the "subject" of *Roland Barthes* (in the sense that one says, "the subject of my book is . . .") and the symbol of Barthes's attempt to produce an autobiographical text, the most fitting epigraph for which would be the author's own aphoristic "Ecrire le corps": "To write the body" (*RB,* 182/180). As I pointed out in my opening remarks, Barthes does define his autobiographical project in opposition to the classical, totalizing "regard en arrière," or retrospective glance, transcribed in the traditional autobiographical work. "Mon présent a-t-il barre sur mon passé?" ("What right does my present have to speak of my past?") he wonders rhetorically in "Lucidité" (124/121). And insofar as the ultimate subject of such a work is the spiritual, not the physical being, the "infinite eternal self" (as Kierkegaard would say) rather than the mutable, phenomenal individual, the *corps* of Barthes's *écrire le corps* does stand for the rejection of an idealist notion of the self and the reaffirmation of a certain materialism. But to read it as the simple reversal of the idealism/materialism dichotomy, or the metaphorical substitution of a concrete intelligible for an abstract one, is simply to miss the point. Stephen Ungar's evaluation of *Roland Barthes* constitutes an exemplary misconstruction of this sort: "As he has attempted to disenfranchise himself from a scientific approach to criticism, Barthes's attentions have moved increasingly toward self-scrutiny and introspection in the guise of anatomical discourse. But . . . Barthes still remains somewhat of a Structuralist . . . who seeks self-knowledge by trying to make himself into a kind of text: a body to be observed, analysed and ultimately understood."[9] This is in fact precisely what Barthes is trying not to do, and while one might wish to argue that that attempt is not entirely successful, any argument to that effect should recognize at the outset that the *corps* of *Roland Barthes* is anything but the observable, analyzable organic unity suggested by Ungar's comment. The ever-present, almost irresistible temptation is, of course, to make it into one, and if there is one dominant theme of Barthes's autobiography, it is the difficulty, perhaps even futility, of that effort to avoid hypostatizing the subject by falling prey to the lure of *l'imaginaire*.[10]

L'imaginaire is another slippery Barthesian term, of Lacanian inspiration, Sartrian overtones, and multidisciplinary connotations: it comprises the subject's identification with an illusory self-image, and its concomitant blindness to the images imposed on it by the other, as well as any naïve delusion of "self-possession" in the form of self-knowledge and/or freedom from the "look" of the Other. From there *l'imaginaire* extends to any delusion of mastery, or conviction that one has found the center or the outside, any reification of concepts, categories, or systems, or belief in absolutes: science and religion are virtually synonymous with *l'imaginaire* in Barthes. It could be said that living in *l'imaginaire* is taking oneself too seriously; Barthes himself observes that it is sometimes equivalent to classic "amour-propre," or self-esteem (*RB*, 78/74). Thus, in his comment that the ironist is he who "puts its *imaginaire* at the distance that it pretends to take with regard to the language of others" (*SZ*, 52/45), the imaginary is both the subject's illusion of possessing an autonomous ego and its pride at having stepped outside (of language, hence of itself, of intersubjectivity, and of intertextuality)—in effect having mastered the discourse of the Other.

Ungar's reduction of R.B.'s body to an object of observation is a fine example of the imaginary at work, as is no doubt my own essay on the subject, scholarly writing being bound as it is to act like a metalanguage: to feign, at least, to take itself seriously. The traditional autobiographical project constitutes an attempt to apply an equally reductive operation to the self: "*myself by myself*? But that is the very program of the image-system [*imaginaire*]!" (*RB*, 156/153). Beyle was voicing the same objection in more classical terms with his "What eye can see itself?" The time-honored canon of "sincerity" in autobiographical writing is but a sanction for self-delusion, since the subject is never fully aware of its own motives (*humeurs*, perhaps, in the parlance of another era?): "The more 'sincere' I am, the more interpretable I am, under the eye of other examples [*instances*] than those of the old authors, who believed they were required to submit themselves to but one law: *authenticity*. Such examples are History, Ideology, the Unconscious" (124/120). History, ideology, the unconscious—names for the other that inhabits the center of the subject, speaking for us, so that the "instinctive" utterance is also the least original, the most banal. Ideology is "ce qui se répète et *consiste*" ("what is repeated and *consistent*" [108/104]), via the spontaneous parroting of commonplaces: what "they say," what "everyone knows"—that universal common sense designated by the Barthesian coinage, *doxa:*

La Doxa, c'est l'opinion courante, le sens répété, *comme si de rien n'était.* C'est Méduse: elle pétrifie ceux qui la regardent. Cela veut dire qu'elle est *évidente.* Est-elle vue? Même pas, c'est une masse gélatineuse qui colle au fond de la rétine. (126/122)

The *Doxa* is current opinion, meaning repeated *as if nothing had happened.* It is Medusa: who petrifies those who look at her. Which means that it is *evident.* Is it seen? Not even that: a gelatinous mass which sticks onto the retina.

The *doxa* is what comes "naturally," the body of conventions that we take to be eternal laws, of relatives we mistake for absolutes. Because the recourse to *doxa* precludes reflection (the eye cannot see that which is in itself) it stupefies; hence another of its synonyms: *la bêtise.* The ideologue is *bête* because he is *"consistant,"* mechanically repeating stereotypes, or fixed, set phrases (*"stereos* means *solid"* [63/58]), all the while believing he speaks for himself. Ideology and the *imago* are two variations of the stereotype: "L'idéologique, c'est quoi? c'est ce qui fait consister l'idée. Et l'Imaginaire? Ce qui fait consister l'image" ("What is the ideological? It is what makes ideas consistent. And the imaginary? What makes images consistent").[11]

Irony, it will be recalled, is the form of *bêtise* that consists of flaunting one's intelligence, i.e., difference, by declaring everyone else *bête*— that is, of demonstrating one's own lucidity by pointing out the blindness of others. But insofar as that very difference constitutes a self-image, it is as stereotypical as the stereotypes it is denouncing, and is perpetually in danger of being labeled by the other as such. The blind spot at the source of every subject's vision—its own *doxa,* or the presuppositions that filter its perception—constitutes its *imaginaire,* always visible to the Other: "The image-system, one's imaginary life [*l'imaginaire*], is the very thing over which others have an advantage [*ont barre*]" (*RB,* 85/82). There is a Sartrian preoccupation with the Other in *Roland Barthes,* a recurrent allusion to the intersubjective struggle between myself and the other who relentlessly threatens to reduce me to a thing *en soi.* R.B. admits to his own fascination with the *miroir aux alouettes* that is the look of the other (representative of the Supreme Other, the paternal instance, or Law) and intermittently reflects on the means of escaping its allure. In "Eloge du contrat," he proposes an alternative reminiscent of the "masochistic" tactics of Deleuze's humorist, who invests authority in the maternal instance via the *pact,* thereby displacing the absolute with the conventional.[12] The contract of prostitution is for Barthes the model of the "good contract," "since the body intervenes directly here"; it liberates interpersonal relationships from the tyranny of the *imaginaire,* in the form of the inevitable and insatiable need to know *"what I am for him"* (63–64/59).

To submit to the authority of the Other as sole arbiter of the self is to sentence oneself to self-reflection *in perpetuum,* like the dandy frozen before his mirror, or Estelle and Garcin of *Huis clos,* desperately seeking their images in the eyes of those around them. It is, like Kierkegaard's aesthete or de Man's ironist, to be caught in the spiral of a "self-escalating act of consciousness," first observing the self to evaluate and criticize the image it is projecting, then splitting again to observe the observing self, denouncing any self-delusions it might harbor, then redoubling oneself, and so on, *ad infinitum.* The autobiographer, it seems, is condemned to this fate—if, that is, he would have *"the last word"* (*RB,* 124/120). Thus R.B. mimes the spiraling of irony, following a "lucid" third-person analysis of his motives with a second-person rebuke for his continued self-mystification: "So you make a declaration of humility; you still don't escape the image-system [*l'imaginaire*]"—countering with a first-person "But, in saying as much, I escape . . . ," finally abandoning the game with a resigned "etc. (*the ladder continues*)" (106/102). "The book . . . proceeds by impulses of the image-system [*imaginaire*] pure and simple and by critical approaches [*accès critiques*]," he comments in another fragment, "but these very approaches are never anything but effects of resonance: nothing is more a matter of . . . the imaginary than (self-) criticism" (123–24/120).

Always deluded in some respect, always blind to itself in its most lucid moments, the Barthesian subject knows only one thing about itself with certitude: that it cannot escape from the imaginary, and that every stroke of the autobiographical pen produces more images:

> Comment écrire, à travers tous les pièges que me tend l'image collective de l'oeuvre? — Eh bien, *aveuglément.* A chaque instant du travail, perdu, affolé et poussé, je ne puis que me dire le mot qui termine le *Huis-clos* de Sartre: *continuons.* (*RB,* 140/136)

> How to write, given all the snares set by the collective image of the work? —Why, *blindly.* At every moment of the effort, lost, bewildered, and driven, I can only repeat to myself the words which end Sartre's *No Exit:* Let's go on.

But when Garcin pronounces the *"continuons"* that interrupts, rather than ends, an endless intersubjective play, it is with a kind of despairing hope that "one day" he will capture the image that eludes him. R.B., in resigning himself to writing *blindly,* is relinquishing possession of his ego, turning his back to the mirror—and to the Other. *Roland Barthes* will be a collection of images exposed to the public view—"the vital effort of this book is to stage an image-system [*imaginaire*]"

(109/105)—but the author can never see these images as the reader does, never classify or demythify them:

> Ce livre est fait de ce que je ne connais pas: l'inconscient et l'idéo-logie, choses qui ne se parlent que par la voix des autres. Je ne puis mettre en scène (en texte), *comme tels,* le symbolique et l'idéologique qui me traversent, puisque j'en suis la tache aveugle (ce qui m'appar-tient en propre, c'est *mon* imaginaire, c'est *ma* fantasmatique: d'où ce livre). De la psychanalyse et de la critique politique, je ne puis donc disposer qu'à la manière d'Orphée: sans jamais me retourner, sans jamais les regarder, les déclarer (ou si peu: de quoi remettre encore mon interprétation dans la course de l'imaginaire). (155-56/152-53)

> This book is made of what I do not know: the unconscious and ide-ology, things which utter themselves only by the voices of others. I cannot put on stage (in the text), *as such,* the symbolic and the ideo-logical which pass through me, since I am their blind spot (what actually belongs to me is *my* image-repertoire, *my* phantasmatics: whence this book). I can make use of psychoanalysis and of political criticism, then, only in the fashion of Orpheus: without ever turn-ing around, without ever looking at them, declaring them (or so lit-tle: just enough to restore my interpretation to the course of the image-system).

To write "lucidly"—and such is the goal of the traditional autobiog-rapher—would be to identify and label the various manifestations and degrees of one's *imaginaire* (something like measuring the level of one's bad faith), distancing oneself from them by means of a "metalinguistic operator": quotation marks, which serve to attribute utterances to an*other,* or parentheses in which to formulate reservations, isolating one's commentary from the discourse-object. The *imaginaire* is essen-tially what it embarrasses one to write about oneself (e.g., an admis-sion or manifestation of error, stupidity, naïveté, etc.); the use of quotation marks, i.e., irony, distances the now-enlightened writing subject from its formerly (or even presently) mystified self. But be-cause "lucidity" is also an *imaginaire,* the only means of interrupting the endless spiraling or layering process is to subvert it by abolishing or at least obscuring the distinctions among levels (just as removing the paradigmatic *barre* undermines classic dichotomies): "Hence the ideal would be: neither a text of vanity, nor a text of lucidity, but a text with uncertain quotation marks, with floating parentheses (never to close the parenthesis is very specifically: to drift)" (*RB,* 109–110/106). The text Barthes is describing here is quite simply a *Texte* (as opposed to an *oeuvre*), that multivalent network of discourses of which it is im-possible to say *who is speaking.* One never knows whether or not to take the author of the text "seriously," for *"one never knows if he is*

responsible for what he writes (if there is a subject behind his language)"
(*SZ*, 146/140). To write blindly is to practice *écriture*, the production of
texte.

The "sincere," "authentic" autobiography is, by definition, an *oeuvre:*
a referential, coherent, unified narrative, spoken by a single voice. The
autobiographical work is the totalizing retrospective and introspective
(i.e., self-reflective) account of a *consistent* subject, an intellectual striptease in which the man-behind-the-work bares his soul (his "true,"
incorporeal being). Conceived of as a *representation,* the work presupposes a vertical, metaphorical model of language: signifiers represent
signifieds, words express ideas. The work, then, is founded on what
Barthes, in *Le Plaisir du texte,* defined as "language's image reservoirs
[*imaginaires*]": "the word as a singular unit . . . ; speech as instrument
or expression of thought; writing as transliteration of speech," whereas
the text, radically metonymical, or *symbolique,* "is language without its
image-reservoir [*imaginaire*]" (*PT,* 54–55/33)—that is, the work without
its "message," its "profundity," or its illusion of referentiality, all those
"elsewheres" or "alibis" that back up the word. Superficial, the text has
no alibi—no excuse for its existence. Like the contract of prostitution,
which established a purely superficial (physical, therefore soulless or
"meaningless") relationship, the text frees the subject from the imaginary because it destroys the illusion of a stable ego from which it
emanates:

> L'écriture me soumet à une exclusion sévère, non seulement parce
> qu'elle me sépare du langage courant ("populaire"), mais plus essen-
> tiellement parce qu'elle m'interdit de "m'exprimer": *qui* pourrait-elle
> exprimer? Mettant à vif l'inconsistance du sujet, son atopie, disper-
> sant les leurres de l'imaginaire, elle rend intenable tout lyrisme
> (comme diction d'un "émoi" central). (*RB,* 89/86)

> Writing subjects me to a severe exclusion, not only because it separ-
> ates me from current ("popular") language, but more essentially
> because it forbids me to "express myself": *whom* could it express?
> Exposing the inconsistency of the subject, his atopia, dispersing the
> enticements of the imaginary, it makes all lyricism untenable (as the
> utterance of a central "emotion").

Ecriture is the self-manifestation of the inconsistent subject—not,
warns Barthes, the divided, contradictory person, whose antithetical
tendencies can easily be synthesized into a stereotype of human nature[13] (as Baudelaire criticism has amply proven)—but the dispersed,
diffracted contemporary subject who is, precisely, a *je de l'énonciation.*
The subject of *écriture* is not *represented* in the text, but *figured:* "Figuration is the way in which the erotic body appears . . . in the profile of

the text. For example: the author may appear in his text (Genet, Proust), but not in the guise of direct biography (which would exceed the body, give a meaning to life, forge a destiny)" (*PT,* 88–89/55–56). Once again, the *body* is associated with the text, as that which liberates from *consistency,* escaping the imposition of a final meaning or a fixed destiny (which always have to do with the soul or spirit). Just as the eternal soul constitutes an alibi for the temporal body, justifying its existence, so the message redeems literary language (which is why Barthes defines representation as *"embarrassed figuration"*—one that must excuse itself, with morals, truths, etc. [89/56]).

What is eternal and immutable is, simply . . . dead, disembodied: "*Doxa* . . . is a dead repetition, because it comes from no one's body—except perhaps, indeed, from the body of the Dead" (*RB,* 75/71). To de-banalize the stereotype ("banality is discourse without body" [141/137])[14] and revive language, it suffices to speak it with the body: "If I managed to talk politics *with my own body* . . . with repetition, I would produce Text" (178/175). The subject of classic autobiography is dead, too: *médusé* by the Other, immortalized by the Work.[15] Dissected, classified, labeled, and shelved. R. I. P. That autobiographical writing could be suicidal, Barthes was intensely aware; "écrire le corps" epitomizes his program to revitalize the genre by producing an autobiography that was not also an obituary.

Yet *écriture* is itself a kind of suicide,[16] since it affirms the death of the ego and the relinquishment of authority over one's discourse, and over the reader. It is a social suicide because the writer, by refusing to use language as it *ought to* be used—that is, as everyone else uses it (Law = *Doxa*)—is "barré," "exclu," "coupé" from the linguistic community (*RB,* 89, 126–27/86, 123). Indeed, the writer is "cut off" by the Doxa-Méduse in the most literal sense: "Medusa, or the Spider: castration. She stuns me [*me sidère*] . . . an effect produced by a scene I hear but do not see . . . I remain *behind the door*" (126/123).[17] He who practices *écriture* is castrated for usurping the role of the Father, taking the law into his own hands—and again the most literal connotations apply: writing is a form of onanism, of unproductive eroticism, "perverse expenditure ('for nothing')" (66/62). Playing with language has long been considered as perverse as playing with oneself, and Barthes capitalizes on that moral tradition by playing on the equivalence between the erotic, sterile body and the erotic, sterile text of *Roland Barthes.* Thus "for nothing" ("pour rien") first appears early on, in reference to the author's body, in the caption of a family photograph: "Final stasis of this lineage: my body. The line ends in a being *pour rien*" (23/19), and is echoed in the final pages as a commentary on an authorial doodle: "Doodling [*la graphie pour rien*] . . . or the signifier without the signified" (187–89/187). Castration and sterility, as attributes of the textual body, clearly have positive connotations; like so many of Barthes's notions, castration is an ambivalent term.

For R.B., like the masochist-humorist of Deleuze's *Présentation de Sacher-Masoch*, "good" castration is not exactly a punishment for illicit textuality (the perversion that consists of entertaining an erotic relationship wtih the mother tongue);[18] it is a prerequisite, a *prerequisite punishment*. Masochistic humor is a parodic reversal of the law: "The same law that forbids me to fulfill a desire on pain of a resultant punishment is now a law that puts punishment first, and orders me as a result to satisfy my desire" (*SM*, 78). The *jouissance du texte* presupposes the rejection of the father-phallus-signifier-superego. Indeed, Barthes's renunciation of any pretense of reproducing a self-image in his autobiography—"I abandon the exhausting pursuit of an old piece of myself" (*RB*, 60/56)—is echoed in the most explicit corporeal terms in "La côtelette" ("the rib chop"), an account of his decision, one day, to throw away (out the window, into the public domain) a fragment of rib, "a kind of bony penis," returned to him after surgery (65–66/61).

The self-castration of the humorist is a parodic subversion of castration, because it does not result in the assumption of the role of the father. In the classic Oedipal scenario, the father's intervention to separate the child from the mother constitutes a symbolic castration, following which the child identifies with the symbolic father, internalizing the law. In the masochist version, the father is "expelled from the symbolic order," and the mother is "identified with the law" (*SM*, 61) by means of a humorous pact.[19] "Humorous" castration is a pluralization, rather than a reduction; whereas the "castrating gesture" of *S/Z* (166/160) or the "castrating laughter" of *Le Plaisir du texte* (19/9) referred to the ironist's triumphant imposition of an image, the self-imposed impotence of the writer thematized in *Roland Barthes* is a playful iconoclasm, a shattering of the One into the Many.[20] The notions of sexual and textual plurality are indissociable, Barthes remarks, since both entail the dissolution of stereotypes: "The confrontations and paradigms must be dissolved, both the meanings and the sexes be pluralized" (*RB*, 73/69). Pluralization—textuality—precludes dichotomies, paradigms, and confrontations, and the resulting confusion is, simply, comical; it provokes a different, nontriumphant laughter:

C'est un véritable trésor textuel que *Une nuit à l'Opéra*. Si j'ai besoin, pour quelque démonstration critique, d'une allégorie où éclatera la mécanique folle du texte carnavalesque, le film me la fournira: la cabine du paquebot, le contrat déchiré, le charivari final des décors, chacun de ces épisodes (entre autres) est l'emblème des subversions logiques opérées par le Texte: et si ces emblèmes sont parfaits, c'est finalement parce qu'ils sont comiques, le rire étant ce qui, par un dernier tour, délivre la démonstration de son attribut démonstratif. Ce qui libère la métaphore, le symbole, l'emblème, de la manie poétique, ce qui en manifeste la puissance de subversion, c'est le *saugrenu.* . . . L'avenir logique de la métaphore serait donc le gag. (83–84/80–81)

What a textual treasury, *A Night at the Opera!* If some critical demonstration requires an allegory in which the wild mechanics of the text-on-a-spree explodes, the film will provide it for me: the steamer cabin, the torn contract, the final chaos of opera decors—each of these episodes (among others) is the emblem of the logical subversions performed by the Text; and if these emblems are perfect, it is ultimately because they are comic, laughter being what, by a last reversal, releases demonstration from its demonstrative attribute. What liberates metaphor, symbol, emblem from poetic *mania,* what manifests its power of subversion, is the *preposterous.* . . . The logical future of metaphor would therefore be the gag.

The "gag," like the impotent body, functions as a third term adrift [*en dérive*], the decomposition or derision, of dialectic.[21] To coin an appropriately Barthesian term (perhaps R.B. already has): to the *rire* of irony corresponds the *dérire* of humor.

Barthes's notion of "le carnavalesque," a recurrent one in the autobiography (as above: "texte carnavalesque"), perhaps best corresponds to the humorous, as I have defined it. The carnival is the domain of the *saugrenu* ("the preposterous"), the moment in which the law is derided, but not overturned—except that there lingers a salubrious sense of its absurd arbitrariness, when Carnival is over. Hence the bizarre (and comical) figure—entitled "Ecrire le corps"—of the textual body that follows the final fragments of *Roland Barthes:* an anatomical plate, not of the skeleton (an eminently logical structuralist closure), but of the veins (also a logical emblem of the humorous body). If R.B.'s body is a "metaphor" for the idea, it is akin to the farce, "a metaphor which . . . slackens" [*débande:* literally, "looses its erection"] (*RB,* 92/ 89). Inevitably, one is compelled to read the fragment on the facing page, entitled "The monster of totality," as a commentary on the image (or the image as an illustration of the text): "Totality at one and the same time inspires laughter and fear: like violence, is it not always *grotesque* (and then recuperable only in an aesthetics of Carnival)?" (182/180). There are echoes of Carnival in the caption to the image, which likens it to "a clown's coat" (182/180).

The textual body is thus metaphorically transmogrified into a form of grotesque costume, so that interior becomes exterior, *dessous, dessus,* and flesh, word—or text. Evoking the by now commonplace conception of the text as *tissu*, or woven cloth, the harlequin image also recalls another fragment of *Roland Barthes*, which defines autobiography as a *rewriting* of the self: "Whereby I cast over the written work, over the past body and the past corpus, . . . a kind of patchwork, a rhapsodic quilt consisting of stitched squares. Far from reaching the core of the matter, I remain on the surface" (*RB*, 145/142). The adjective *rapsodique* is eminently appropriate, for its etymological reverberations: "rhapsody" is derived from the Greek *rhaptein*, to sew, stitch together, and *ōidē*, ode, song; whence its archaic meaning, "a literary work consisting of disconnected pieces, medley, jumble"—which is precisely a description of *Roland Barthes*.

But the garment metaphor also evokes another element of the Barthesian intertext, Proust's modest comparison of his work to that of Françoise: "I should work beside her and in a way almost as she worked herself . . . and, pinning here and there an extra page, I should construct my book, I dare not say ambitiously like a cathedral, but quite simply like a dress" (3: 1033/3: 1090).[22] Thus shifting from the sublime to the humorous, he characterizes the writing process as a kind of *bricolage*, with Françoise helping him glue together his torn "paperies" (3: 1034/3: 1090). Indeed Proust goes so far as to compare his work to a dish of *boeuf mode*, completing his deflation of the romantic image of the writer as demiurgic creator.

For his taste for the bizarre and even the preposterous in metaphorical language, Barthes is probably more indebted to Proust than critics have generally recognized,[23] perhaps out of a misguided reverence for the latter, or a conviction that the Proustian analogy expresses some mystical universal "correspondence." But Barthesian and Proustian metaphors are fundamentally alike in that they establish a purely linguistic, superficial (formerly, one might have said "subjective") relationship between the most disparate objects or phenomena. The Barthesian text, however, flaunts its arbitrariness far more than does the Proustian, to avoid creating the illusion that it represents any extra-linguistic totality. Similarly, and for the same reasons, Barthes's fragmented, "patch-work" autobiography stands in sharp contrast to the apparently seamless text of the *Recherche*. Proust pieced together the fragments of his past experience and past writings into the imaginary unity of a *roman*. Yet if Proust is only "figured" in his text, as Barthes said, many have supposed him to be represented there. Barthes has sought in *Roland Barthes* to avoid that fate by resorting to what he terms the *romanesque*, a fracturing of the *roman*.

A la recherche du temps perdu is a narrative about giving up the imaginary and becoming a writer: the narrator is about to begin writing when the novel ends. The opening pages of *Roland Barthes* summarize, in a sense, the "lesson" of the *Recherche,* announcing that the writing will begin when the novel is over:

> On ne trouvera donc ici, mêlées au roman familial, que les figura- tions d'une préhistoire du corps—de ce corps qui s'achemine vers le travail, la jouissance d'écriture. Car tel est le sens théorique de cette limitation: manifester que le temps du récit (de l'imagerie) finit avec la jeunesse du sujet: il n'y a de biographie que de la vie improductive. Dès que je produis, dès que j'écris, c'est le Texte lui-même qui me dépossède (heureusement) de ma durée narrative. Le texte ne peut rien raconter; il emporte mon corps ailleurs, loin de ma personne imaginaire. . . .
> L'imaginaire d'images sera donc arrêté à l'entrée dans la vie produc- tive. . . . Un autre imaginaire s'avancera alors: celui de l'écriture. (*RB,* 5-6/3-4)

So you will find here, mingled with the "family romance," only the figurations of the body's prehistory—of that body making its way toward the labor and the pleasure of writing. For such is the theoret- ical meaning of this limitation: to show that the time of the narrative (of the imagery) ends with the subject's youth: the only biography is of an unproductive life. Once I produce, once I write, it is the Text itself which (fortunately) dispossesses me of my narrative continu- ity. The Text can recount nothing; it takes my body elsewhere, far from my imaginary person. . . . The image-repertoire will therefore be closed at the onset of productive life. . . . Another repertoire will then be constituted: that of writing.

The collection of photographs that makes up the first quarter of the autobiography is virtually a parody of the work-as-representation, and the autobiography as unveiling of the self. It contains all the elements of the classic family romance: mother, family, friends, the sunny land- scapes of childhood. There is something indiscreet about these images, Barthes remarks, because the narrator's body is exposed ("it is my body from underneath which is presented" [*RB,* 6/3] to the mortifying look of the Other, most literally represented by a photograph of mother and child, apparently reflected in a mirror, captioned: "The mirror stage: 'that's you'" (25/21). This indiscretion is precisely what consti- tutes the attraction of narrative as gradual revelation of a truth (or autobiography as baring of one's soul): as Barthes wrote in *Le Plaisir du texte,* narrative suspense *excites* in the same manner as a striptease, arous- ing the desire to see the sexual organ or to know the end of the story. That longing to know the truth (to possess the phallus) is one with the desire to see the Father;[24] thus all narrative is a form of myth insofar as it is an attempt to establish one's origins through representation (i.e., a compensatory substitute for the absence of origin). Barthes draws together the linguistic, economic, social, and sexual implications of the traditional function of writing as a compensatory representation by including among his photographs a reproduction of an I.O.U., in reference to which he reflects:

> L'écriture n'a-t-elle pas été pendant des siècles la reconnaissance d'une dette, la garantie d'un échange, seing d'une représentation? Mais aujourd'hui, l'écriture s'en va doucement vers l'abandon des dettes bourgeoises, vers la perversion, l'extrémité du sens, le texte. (22/18)

> Has not writing been for centuries the acknowledgment of a debt, the guarantee of an exchange, the sign [legal signature] of a representation? But today writing gradually drifts toward the cession of bourgeois debts, toward perversion, the extremity of meaning, the text.

To abandon the Oedipal complex is to turn one's back on the Father, rejecting traditional religious and economic values, and refusing to vouch for the authenticity of one's own word. In the contradiction between the alleged sterility of the text and the claim that writing inaugurates the productive life, we reencounter the ambivalence that characterized Barthes's use of the term *castration:* there is a "good" and a "bad" sterility, the former being a consequence of the writer's self-imposed impotence to produce narrative, or stories about the Origin. The allusion to Proust ("Contemporaries? I was beginning to walk, Proust was still alive, and was finishing *A la Recherche du Temps Perdu*") on page 27/23 of the "novel" (i.e., biographical) portion of *Roland Barthes* situates Barthes's own *corpus* historically in relation to Proust's, suggesting that what follows is both a homage to the *Recherche* and an attempt, however modest, to transcend it. One might read a later fragment as another formulation of that project: "He would have wanted to produce, not a comedy of the intellect, but its *romanesque*" (*RB*, 94/90).

The remaining pages of *Roland Barthes* represent an effort to "thwart Origin" ("déjouer l'Origine") (*RB*, 142/139) by producing an autobiographical text without any vestige of "organic unity." The techniques Barthes devised have been cataloged often enough by critics; foremost among them is the adoption of fragmentary writing (practiced in several earlier works). The use of fragments has the obvious advantage of precluding narrative continuity, particularly given the paratactic structure of the sentences within each fragment, as well as the fact that Barthes resorts to the alphabet to order them in a manner which is "unmotivated" without being "arbitrary" (150/147). He further seeks to avoid consistency—"to keep a meaning from 'taking'"—by rearranging the alphabetical order when undesirable "effects of meaning" (151/148) occur (the fragment entitled "L'alphabet," for example, appears near the end of the text).[25] The technique is certainly effective at some level; it can be quite difficult to locate a passage by any "logical" process, all the more so since the index "is itself a text" (97/93)—a list of terms in impeccable alphabetical order, but which neither covers all the major topics of the text, nor exhausts the occurrences of those terms that are included, nor even refers to the most important of those occurrences. Yet at the same time, the fragments may be said to serve a mimetic function, as a representation of the dispersed subject, so that *Roland Barthes* assumes a degree of referentiality despite itself (see Ungar's comment, quoted earlier); furthermore, as R.B. points out, the fragment itself is ultimately an aphoristic pronouncement, an interpretable rhetorical genre: "By supposing I disperse myself I merely return, quite docilely, to the bed of the imaginary" (99/95). Even the fleeting, monotone vignettes of remembrances past, which he labels "anamnèses," constitute a form of (meaningful) haïku, although he also comments approvingly that they are nearly *matte*: "The more one succeeds in making them *matte*, the better they escape the image-system [*imaginaire*]" (99, 111–14/95, 107–10).

The fact is that the various fragments of *Roland Barthes* do constitute different levels of the imaginary, different degrees of certitude, naïveté, skepticism, or paranoia, without, however, constituting a definitive hierarchy. As in the eternal *jeu de la main chaude* (game of hand-over-hand)—a favorite Barthesian image for the interplay of discourses[26]—no one pronouncement finally comes out "on top." This is also due in part to Barthes's use of pronouns, for he shifts erratically from "I" to "you" to "he," themselves "shifters," multiplying voices to assure that none has the last word. Not a true confession, the autobiography is not precisely a fiction, either; it is "*presque* un roman: un roman sans noms propres":

> Tout ceci doit être considéré comme dit par un personnage de roman—ou plutôt par plusieurs. Car l'imaginaire, matière fatale du roman et labyrinthe des redans dans lequels se fourvoie celui qui parle de lui-même, l'imaginaire est pris en charge par plusieurs masques (*personae*), échelonnés selon la profondeur de la scène (et cependant *personne* derrière). Le livre ne choisit pas, il fonctionne par alternance, il marche par bouffées d'imaginaire simple et d'accès critiques, mais ces accès eux-mêmes ne sont jamais que des effets de retentissement: pas de plus pur imaginaire que la critique (de soi). La substance de ce livre, finalement, est donc totalement romanesque. (*RB*, 123–24/119–20)

All this must be considered as if spoken by a character in a novel—
or rather by several characters. For the image-repertoire, fatal substance of the novel, and the labyrinth of levels in which anyone who
speaks about himself gets lost—the image-repertoire is taken over by
several masks (*personae*), distributed according to the depth of the
stage (and yet *no one—personne,* as we say in French—is behind
them). The book does not choose, it functions by alternation, it
proceeds by impulses of the image-system pure and simple and by
critical approaches, but these very approaches are never anything
but effects of resonance: nothing is more a matter of the image-
system, of the imaginary, than (self-)criticism. The substance of this
book, ultimately, is therefore totally fictive.

The *romanesque,* then, is a novel that constantly destroys the illusion
of referentiality it is continually producing; it is hardly necessary to
point out the affinity between the labyrinthine *nouveau roman* and
Barthes's "*nouvelle autobiographie.*" While *Roland Barthes* displays a
striking superficial coherence, a reassuring recurrence of themes, terms,
and *pensées-mots,* it is as difficult to totalize as it is to make a Robbe-
Grillet novel "come out even." Like a jigsaw puzzle whose pieces
interlock in a variety of fashions, but never all at once, Barthes's autobiography is eminently, but infinitely, analyzable, so that any reading
of it that does not simply "cut the braid" (*SZ,* 166/160) of the text is
ultimately condemned to rambling in endless circles. The only other
possible conclusion, it seems, is: *etc.*

It is the endless interplay among the fragments of the autobiography
that makes it a Text, and I have attempted here, in following some of
the threads of that text, to suggest something of the complexity of
their interrelationship, and to show that the humoral, humorous *corps*
of *Roland Barthes* both thematizes and puts into practice the kind of
nonironic critical discourse Barthes envisioned in *Critique et vérité,*
S/Z, and *Le Plaisir du texte.* Thus it is, in some sense, the culmination
of a certain "evolution" in Barthes's work. But it is the antithesis of a
culmination in the sense of a comprehensive overview that "puts
everything in perspective." What Barthes seeks to accomplish in *Roland Barthes* is—like R.B. playing at *barres* in the Luxembourg garden—
to put everything back into circulation. Any reader in search of "the
last word" on Barthes had best apply elsewhere.

Roland Barthes is perhaps more of an introduction than a conclusion to Barthes, a Barthes "sampler" that gives the reader a taste of, or
for, the Barthesian text. And in this sense there is what one could call
a *figuration* of the "erotic body" of Barthes in his autobiography—or
what he had called, in the preface to *Sade, Fourier, Loyola,* an "amicable
return of the author" in his text (13/8). Indeed, in retrospect, it may be

that preface that formulated most prophetically (and most poignantly) the Barthesian autobiographical project:

> Si j'étais écrivain, et mort, comme j'aimerais que ma vie se réduisît, par les soins d'un biographe amical et désinvolte, à quelques détails, à quelques goûts, à quelques inflexions, disons: des "biographèmes," dont la distinction et la mobilité pourraient voyager hors de tout destin et venir toucher à la façon des atomes épicuriens, quelque corps futur, promis à la même dispersion; une vie trouée, en somme, comme Proust a su écrire la sienne dans son oeuvre. (14/9)

> Were I a writer, and dead, how I would love it if my life, through the pains of some friendly and detached biographer, were to reduce itself to a few details, a few preferences, a few inflections, let us say: to "biographemes" whose distinction and mobility might go beyond any fate and come to touch, like Epicurean atoms, some future body, destined to the same dispersion; a marked life, in sum, as Proust succeeded in writing his in his work.

Postscript

There is no conclusion to be drawn from the foregoing, at least not in the sense of a totalizing statement which follows ineluctably from the preceding arguments, bringing the book to a close with a resounding, and reassuring, Q.E.D. I have not sought to prove anything so much as to understand the popularity and importance of a term which has become ubiquitous in critical literature of the past two decades, and to evaluate what is at stake, ideologically, in the various critical positions taken on the subject of irony. In my readings of Stendhal, Baudelaire, Proust, and Barthes, I have used the opposition irony/humor primarily as a heuristic device by considering which of those paradigms (and the critical categories they imply) better "fits" their works, that is, better describes the mechanisms that apparently determine the production of the text. This can sometimes produce more questions than answers, as is certainly the case with Baudelaire, but I have nevertheless arrived at some conclusions regarding the prevalence of irony or humor in each author.

It should be quite evident by now that irony and humor are not the clearly defined, positively identifiable phenomena one might wish them to be, and that whether a text is perceived as ironic or humorous has much to do with the perspective of the perceiver (once again, this is most evident in my reading of Baudelaire). Hence I have spoken not only of ironic and humorous texts, but also of ironic and humorous critics, according to the assumptions or beliefs about language that inform their readings. Nonetheless, I do think that some readings are more successful than others, if we gauge the success of a reading by its yield of information or relevant commentary about the object text, a yield which is itself in direct correlation to the amount of textual material accounted for. This is why I consider it futile to approach postmodern literature as a form of irony (defined as a disparity between word and meaning), thereby limiting one's reading to the extraction of a coherent message (and if I hope to have "proved," that is, convinced the reader of, anything in these pages, it is this). While it is doubtless possible to unearth a message in any work, for many recent (and some centuries-old) texts this is about as fruitful a critical exercise as, *mutatis mutandis*, seeking to discern figures in abstract painting—except insofar as it teaches us about our perceptive activity. Indeed, our attempts to decipher any work of art may ultimately tell us more about ourselves (as products of our cultures) than about the work in question.

This, of course, is precisely why so much contemporary criticism has, in the wake of phenomenology, tended to emphasize the reader's role in interpretation, and to speak of meaning as a process rather than as a stable given. The same preoccupation with the subject's activity as a meaning-giver manifests itself in recent ("postmodern") literature both thematically and through formal tactics intended to disconcert the reader, such as the exploitation of linguistic polyvalence, the introduction of contradiction, or the violation of textual levels (i.e., the confusion of the "real" and "fictional" worlds)—tactics that force readers into a constant awareness of the expectations and prejudices they bring to a text, and therefore to a consciousness of their own interpretive activity. In a broad sense, then, humor is this postmodern tactic of disconcertion—which is not a mystification (as many would have it), but rather a demystification of the traditional concept of meaning as a transcendental signified. As such, and depending on the specific preoccupation of its various exponents, humor has appeared under a variety of labels—textuality, deconstruction, agonistics, *écriture féminine*, or simply *écriture*—but in all its manifestations, it rejects the postulates underlying the classic concept of irony (primarily, the primacy of signified over signifier and the ipseity and autonomy of the subject) and serves to reassert the power of language in the constitution of "reality" and of the *cogito*.

Thus structuralist-poststructuralist criticism and postmodern literature have collaborated in that redefinition of subjectivity which is one of the most salient features of contemporary thought. And as theory has increasingly become a practice of writing, while literature has grown increasingly self-reflexive, the boundary between literature and criticism, between "fiction" and "expository writing" has blurred. If the New Novel and the New New Novel (etc.) are also, even foremost, critiques of the novel, much contemporary criticism is presented as a form of theoretical fiction. Given this merging of genres, as well as the primary importance accorded to the question of the subject, a book like Roland Barthes's *Roland Barthes*, a theoretical-fictional autobiography, seems an exemplary product of major recent critical trends, and in some ways a culmination of them (provided that "culmination" be taken here in the sense of a momentary peak). This is why it seems as appropriate a choice as any to close, if not conclude, a work that appears in retrospect to have been both a book about literature (a series of readings of literary texts) and a book about literary theory, as well as, to some extent, a book about autobiography. Barthes's *Barthes* somehow ratifies that mélange, and even lends it an air of necessity.

Yet that necessity is more than apparent, I think; it is certainly born of the topic under discussion, which has from its classical beginnings been considered a form of discourse, a mode of being (a manner in which a subject relates to others and to itself), and a critical stance — three aspects of irony whose interrelationship I have attempted to understand and elucidate in these pages. Moreover, it is quite probably because the concept of irony articulates the problems of self-knowledge and self-expression with a theory or theories of language that the term has become so prominent in the discourse of critical theory today. A regrettable consequence of this is, as I have said, the frequent conflation of antithetical notions of and expressions of "subjectivity" under the rubric "irony."

Thus I return to my original thesis, that postmodern literature's and poststructuralist theory's preoccupation with language and subjectivity has nothing in common with the narcissistic, onanistic, and potentially solipsistic discourse commonly termed romantic irony. Yet it could be argued that the wholesale adoption of relativity and superficiality ("it's all language") that has resulted from the popularization of recent Continental theories has given rise to a critical discourse so self-conscious, polyvalent, and recondite that it has been reduced to a futile, circular chatter about language. This, and not cries of blasphemy or perversity, constitutes the most damning charge that might be leveled at "humorous" criticism. Directed at the originators of structuralist and poststructuralist theory, it is largely unjustified; however, many would-be disciples of Derrida or Barthes probably deserve censure, for pun-laden pages that deconstruct nothing.

This is partly because imitators rarely achieve more than a superficial resemblance with their model. More important, though, with the importation of Continental critical concepts, something has been lost in the translation. Doubtless what has fallen by the wayside is the intellectual and political context within which structuralism and its ulterior developments emerged. A fundamental premise of Continental theory that has been lost, ignored, or misunderstood by those who accuse it of aesthetic solipsism is that any critique of discourse is also necessarily a critique of the power structures that support and are supported by the discourse in question. The equation — now a commonplace of Continental theory — of Father, Law, and transcendent signified, is not "merely" metaphorical. The maintenance of the political status quo depends upon the political subjects' continued belief in the referentiality (i.e., the necessity) of the discourse of the Law/Father, just as the power of a religious doctrine is founded on the believers' continued confidence in the referentiality of Scripture. To shake that confidence is to undermine the political edifice it upholds. Thus the emphasis on the illusoriness of the referent that plays an essential role in poststructuralism is in fact part of a political strategy, and not, as some have apparently thought, a pretext for retreating from the world into a form of idealism. Naturally, this is a somewhat simplistic formulation, which moreover fails to take into account the complexities of the interrelationships linking the political power structure, the critical faculties, and the "subjects," not to mention the organization and regulation of the means of communication among them. That is the subject of another book. Suffice it to point out here that in France the "critical faculties"—in the form of academic institutions—have a much more direct and more clearly defined (therefore more obvious) relationship with the government. Whence at least one major reason why the political implications of critical theory are far more evident in that context than in the United States. Add to that the greater interpenetration of disciplines (at least in the theoretical discourses elaborated around them) and the somewhat less pronounced division between the academic and social spheres in France than in this country, and critical theory appears to occupy a radically different political position on the two sides of the Atlantic.

It would be an error to assume that critical theory—in the form of a critique of discourse—is without political implications in the United States. Nevertheless, while it is easy to assert that it has implications, one may still wonder if it does, or can, have consequences, and what those consequences might be. It certainly will not have any if it stagnates into an endless series of deconstructions of literary texts and de-deconstructions of those deconstructions—in short, a self-escalating spiral of irony (and this is just as true on the Continent as in America).

"The text risks paralysis; it repeats itself, counterfeits itself in luster-less texts, testimonies to a demand for readers, not for a desire to please: the Text tends to degenerate into prattle (*Babil*). Where to go next?" (*RB*, 75/71). Barthes's warning against theoretical stagnation, though directed at himself, in *Roland Barthes*, in 1974, might certainly be generalized to include a great many proponents of textuality today. The answer to the question "où aller?" seems to me to be that we should explore the political consequences of critical theory—consequences that French "humorists" such as Lyotard, Deleuze, Derrida, and even Barthes (his avowed "desire to please" notwithstanding) have long assumed. To use Sartrian–de Manian terms again, perhaps what most sharply distinguishes humor from irony is that the former operates *in the world*. Hence its affirmation of ongoing process, of incompleteness (there can be "no last word," as Barthes put it [*RB*, 55/50]). It is this characteristic of critical humor that its detractors have missed, I think—but that is perhaps because we have not known how to adapt it to *our* political reality. However, a number of critics *have* begun to address the question of the relationship between critical theory and politics in this country, and a perusal of recent publications in the field indicates that more and more are doing so. It seems reasonable to expect that this trend may lead to some of the most interesting developments in critical theory in the years to come.

Notes

Introduction

1. See Derrida's chapter entitled "Ce dangereux supplément," in his *De la grammatologie* (Paris: Minuit, 1967), 203–34.

2. As I point out in Chapter Two, the use of indecipherable or prolonged irony has long been condemned by moralists on much the same grounds as falsehood—another form of misrepresentation, or misuse of language, whose theologically proper function is to purvey truth. Likewise, verbal humor, particularly punning, or the gratuitous use of words for pleasure, has traditionally been condemned as a perversion of language. (Thus the term *humor,* used to designate the prioritizing of the signifier, is actually not far removed from its common usage.) Indeed, all forms of discourse in which the letter does not correspond to the spirit, or worse, perhaps, in which the word, liberated from its ancillary function as servant of thought, becomes an object in itself, a source of enjoyment, have traditionally been judged morally reprehensible.

3. "If it were simply a matter of expressing [*exprimer,* i.e., express or squeeze out] (like a lemon) equally 'full' subjects and objects, through 'images,' what good would literature be?" Roland Barthes, *Critique et vérité* (Paris: Seuil, 1966), 70–71.

4. Roland Barthes, *Roland Barthes* (Paris: Seuil, 1975), 148/145. Hereafter cited in the text as *RB.* All English translations are quoted, with rare modifications, from *Roland Barthes by Roland Barthes,* trans. Richard Howard (New York: Hill and Wang, 1977).

Chapter One   Kierkegaard: The Concept of Irony

1. Søren Kierkegaard, *The Concept of Irony, with Constant Reference to Socrates,* trans. Lee M. Capel (Bloomington: Indiana University Press, 1968), 47. Hereafter cited in the text as *CI.*

2. To the two dialectics correspond two theologies: "The dialogue . . . is symbolic of the Hellenic conception of the relation between man and the deity. Although this relationship has reciprocity, it contains no moment of unity (neither the immediate nor the higher)" (*CI,* 73). The "higher unity" will be realized in the person of Christ, the God-Man (or the Idea born into the phenomenon); the Hegelian dialectic is thus the philosophical manifestation of the kind of onto-theological thought that is Christianity's condition of possibility.

3. The biblical allusion is eminently appropriate, for the Sophists represent the folly of self-dispersion in the multiplicity of the empirical, to be voided by the "higher madness" of irony (*CI*, 274). In one respect Sophistry constituted the awakening of reflection from the sleep of Hellenic immediacy, but it never attained that self-conscious moment at which actuality loses validity: "That life is full of contradictions seems to escape the notice of immediate consciousness, and it confidently and trustingly clings to its inheritance from the past like a sacred relic; reflection, by contrast, discovers this fact at once. It discovers that what should be absolutely certain, the determining principle for men (laws, statutes, etc.), brings the individual into contradiction with himself. It also discovers that all this is external to man and as such cannot be accepted. But if it exposes the fault, it also has a remedy near at hand: it teaches how to give reasons for everything" (227).

4. "He deceived the youth and awakened longings which he never satisfied, allowed them to become inflamed by the subtle pleasures of anticipation yet never gave them solid and nourishing food. He deceived them . . . as he deceived Alcibiades, who . . . observes that instead of the lover, Socrates became the beloved" (*CI*, 213). Socrates' "intellectual pederasty" (216) in his relationship with his pupils is emblematic of the Greek deity's relation to man, in which there is "no moment of unity" (73)—whereas the true bearer of wisdom, Christ, incarnates the Christian God, who inseminated the Verb in the world.

5. "The individual must no longer act out of respect for the law, but must consciously know why he acts" (*CI*, 249).

6. Death itself is without seriousness for Socrates. Ignorant of what it may bring, he can neither fear it nor look forward to it (as opposed to the Christian): "What characterizes the irony [in the *Phaedo*] most perfectly is the abstract criterion whereby it levels everything, whereby it masters every excessive emotion, and hence does not set the pathos of enthusiasm against the fear of death, but finds it a most curious experiment to become nothing at all" (*CI*, 115).

7. "But as the concept of irony has so often acquired a different meaning, it is essential that one does not come to use it . . . in a wholly arbitrary fashion. To the extent that one subscribes to the ordinary use of language, therefore, it is essential to see that the various meanings it has acquired in the course of time can all be accommodated here" (*CI*, 262).

8. Kierkegaard points out that a similar disparity between truth and appearance characterizes a number of other phenomena frequently identified with irony, such as dissemblance, Jesuitism, hypocrisy, persiflage, etc., but insists that irony is distinct from these in that it has no purpose external to itself, no end other than a metaphysical freedom. Whereas the hypocrite, for instance, seeks to convince others that he is good while remaining evil, the ironist wishes only to appear "other" than he is (see *CI*, 272–75).

9. For a development of the concept of despair, see *The Sickness unto Death*.

10. See also *CI*, 301: "[The ironist] lives completely hypothetically and subjunctively."

11. See, however, *The Sickness unto Death*, where despair is qualified as "the sin of poetizing instead of being" (trans. Walter Lowrie [Princeton: Princeton University Press, 1968], 208).

12. Both Kierkegaard's romantic ironist and Sartre's man in bad faith are of course descendants of Hegel's "beautiful soul," "self-consciousness withdrawn into the inmost retreats of its own being," for which the world is but the dying echo of its own voice returning to it: "This return does not therefore mean that the self is there in its true reality (*an und für sich*): for the real is, for it, not an inherent being, is no *per se*, but its very self. . . . It lacks force to externalize itself, the power to make itself a thing, and endure existence. It lives in dread of staining the radiance of its inner being by action and existence. And to preserve the purity of the heart, it flees from contact with actuality, and steadfastly perseveres in a state of self-willed impotence." G. W. F. Hegel, *The Phenomenology of Mind*, trans. J. B. Baillie (New York: Harper, 1967), 666.

In the section of *L'Etre et le néant* (Paris: Gallimard, 1970) devoted to *mauvaise foi*, Sartre remarks that irony, like bad faith, is an "attitude of negation toward oneself" (p. 83), but he does not elaborate.

13. Schlegel's *Lucinde*, for instance, is judged "a very obscene book" (*CI*, 103), because it portrays—and exalts—the romantic-poetic life in all its "aesthetic stupor" (*CI*, 311). The character of Lisette, in particular, incarnates the ironist: she refers to herself in the third person, leads the vegetative existence of a hot-house plant in a sensuous, mirror-studded Oriental decor, and finally takes her own life (with a cry of "Lisette must die, must die now! An inexorable fate requires it!") in a poetically correct manner (*CI*, 302-16).

14. The final chapter of *The Concept of Irony* is entitled "Irony As a Mastered Moment: The Truth of Irony" (*CI*, 336–42).

15. However, irony and doubt are not to be confounded: "With doubt the subject constantly seeks to penetrate the object. . . . With irony, on the other hand, the subject is always seeking to get outside the object. . . . With doubt the subject is witness to a war of conquest in which every phenomenon is destroyed, because the essence always resides behind the phenomenon. But with irony the subject constantly retires from the field and proceeds to talk every phenomenon out of its reality in order to . . . preserve himself in his negative independence of everything" (*CI*, 274).

16. The translator's notes direct us to Kierkegaard's early journals for numerous reflections on the relation between irony and "humour." In addition, Capel demonstrates that the final paragraph of *The Concept*, which concludes upon a reference to Hans Lasson Martensen (a former tutor and later intellectual rival of Kierkegaard's, hence a constant target of his satirical barbs), contains a series of complexly ironic allusions to Martensen's own conception of "humour" (*CI*, 426-29, n. 15).

17. The biblical reference reads: "Jesus saith unto him, I am the way, the truth, and the life; no man cometh unto the Father, but by me" (John 14:6). Thus the allusion to John the Baptist is roundabout, but clear, since he has already been identified as he who negated Judaic positivity in preparation for Christ.

This of course implies a most feasible analogy between grace and "humour," and thus another between the Law and irony. In fact, Kierkegaard refers explicitly to the similarity between the Law and irony: "As irony resembles the Law, so the Sophists resemble the Pharisees" (*CI*, 236). However, it is clear from this passage that the similarity lies in the fact that the Law bore irony within it as the agent of its own destruction (the irony was that it could not be fulfilled— see *CI*, 280)—just as the Sophists' own argumentation was the instrument by which Socrates would destroy them. A further analogy could be logically inferred from all the above, that obtaining between Plato and Christ. This, too, is obviously valid in a certain sense, yet, of course, ultimately invalid; Plato did not bring the Idea into the world in the same sense that Christ did. My point is to warn against reading the various "levels" of Kierkegaard's text as a layering of contents which are strictly equivalent but in different domains. The numerous homologous relationships set up in *The Concept* are just that—relationships—so that the only accurate means of drawing comparisons among them consists in establishing, not a one-to-one correspondence among the *terms* of the various groups, but rather the equivalence of the *relationships* uniting those terms.

18. Sophist discourse is "eloquence that longs for . . . abstract beauty, *versus inopes rerum nugaeque canorae* (verses void of thought, and sonorous trifles)" (*CI*, 70; see also 373, n. 23).

19. Cf. *Republic* I, 337a; *Symposium*, 216e–218d; *Gorgias*, 489e; *Apology*, 38a, for allusions to Socrates' irony. In the *Euthydemus*, 302b, Dionysodorus is accused of behaving ironically, as is Cratylus, in the *Cratylus* 384a.

20. The English translations of Plato cited here are from *The Collected Dialogues of Plato, Including the Letters*, eds. Edith Hamilton and Huntingdon Cairns (New York: Pantheon, 1961).

21. Hegel condemned the romantics for corrupting truth into mere appearance, a charge from which he exonerated Socrates; hence his refusal to identify the latter's standpoint as irony (see *CI*, 285).

22. See Kierkegaard's discussion of Alcibiades' relationship to Socrates, *CI*, 84–89.

23. Hence the tragic mentality of metaphysical man, the moroseness of conceptual thought which Nietzsche rejected in favor of Hellenic "superficiality": "Oh, those Greeks! They knew how *to live*: for that purpose it is necessary to keep bravely to the surface, the fold and the skin; to worship appearance, to believe in forms, tones, and words, in the whole Olympus of appearance! Those Greeks were superficial—*from profundity!*" *The Joyful Wisdom*, vol. 10 of *The Complete Works of Friedrich Nietzsche*, ed. Oscar Levy (London: George Allen and Unwin, 1910), 10.

24. Less adept perhaps than Kierkegaard, Solger foundered in the quicksand of negativity. See thesis 14: "Solger adopted acosmism not out of piety, but seduced by envy because he could not think the negative nor subdue it by thought" (*CI*, 349).

25. On Plato's recuperation of negativity and Socratic irony—in the guise of "writing" and "play"—through dialectic, see Jacques Derrida's essay "La Pharmacie de Platon," in *La Dissémination* (Paris: Seuil, 1972); quoted here in English from "Plato's Pharmacy," in *Dissemination*, trans. Barbara Johnson (Chicago: University of Chicago Press, 1981). Derrida traces the shift in Plato's text from writing conceived as a "bad" *pharmakon* (a corruption of the truth

by signs fatally distant from the vital logos, hence a sterile game of expenditure without return) to the rehabilitation of a certain writing as "good" *pharmakon* (the revelation, or rendering *present* of an already constituted truth, thus a productive form of play):

> This authority of truth, of dialectic, of seriousness, of presence, will not be gainsaid at the close of this admirable movement, when Plato, after having in a sense reappropriated writing, pushes his irony—and his seriousness—to the point of rehabilitating a certain form of play [*jeu*]. Compared with other pastimes, playful hypomnesic writing, second-rate writing, is preferable, should "go ahead." Ahead of the other brothers, for there are even worse seeds in the family. Hence the dialectician will sometimes write, amass monuments, collect *hupomnemata,* just for fun. But he will do so while still putting his products at the service of dialectics and in order to leave a trace (*ikhnos*) for whoever might want to follow in his footsteps on the pathway to truth. The dividing line now runs less between presence and the trace than between the dialectical trace and the non-dialectical trace, between play in the "good" sense and play in the "bad" sense of the word. (178–79/154–55)

Similarly, contemporary critical theoreticians such as Booth distinguish between a "good" irony and a "bad" irony—the former fulfilling the same productive function as doubt in philosophical speculation, leading to positive knowledge, and the latter serving only as a perpetual *remise-en-question* of all assumptions—an irony for which "all is true" (as Kierkegaard said of the Sophists [*CI,* 228]), because nothing is absolutely true or false.

26. The interested reader should consult the extensive informative notes accompanying Lee M. Capel's English translation.

27. "Irony, like prayer, belongs to non-thetic discourse," writes Sylviane Agacinski in *Aparté: Conceptions et morts de Søren Kierkegaard* (Paris: Flammarion, 1977), 51. The "irony" in question here corresponds to what I have called "humor." I recommend Agacinski's interesting chapter on *The Concept of Irony,* which emphasizes Kierkegaard's vacillation between a recuperable and an irreducible, or undialecticizable, irony ("non dialectiquement 'relevable,'" [43]); I disagree, however, with her assertion that the line of demarcation falls between philosophy and religion. Both metaphysics and religion aim at the recuperation of a lost unity (paradise) and the suppression of difference, negativity (death). The discourse of prayer, like the truth of metaphysics, is thetic: positing transcendent truth in the person of the interlocutor, God, prayer represents the accomplishment of the subject's desire for totality.

Chapter Two   Irony/Humor

1. Pierre Fontanier's definition of irony is typical of the classical dictionary of rhetorical terms: "Irony . . . consists in saying, with playful or serious mockery, the opposite of what one thinks, or of what one wishes the hearer to think." *Les Figures du discours* (Paris: Flammarion, 1968), 145–46. In *The Compass of Irony* (London: Methuen, 1969), D. C. Muecke follows a similar

definition of irony (see page 9). I should note, however, that in his later *Irony and the Ironic* (London: Methuen, 1982), he comments briefly on the difference between irony so understood and the "uncertain" irony that Barthes extols in *S/Z*, pointing out, rightfully, that there is little place for the term *irony*, used in the classical sense, in contemporary Continental criticism (30, 100–101).

2. See, for instance, Muecke, *The Compass of Irony*, 47; Norman Knox, *The Word "Irony" and Its Context, 1500–1755* (Durham, N.C.: Duke University Press, 1961), 3–5; for Aristotle's comments on ironic behavior, see his *Rhetoric*, 1379b; 1382b; 1408b; 1419b.

3. Wayne C. Booth, *A Rhetoric of Irony* (Chicago: University of Chicago Press, 1974), 138–39. Hereafter cited in the text as *RI*.

4. Quintilian, *Institutio Oratoria*, 9: i, 4–5. The translation is by H. E. Butler, the Loeb Classical Library (New York: Putnam's, 1922).

5. It is not clear how Booth manages to "leave Plato aside" in his evaluation of Socrates, since he is relying on Plato's presentation of him. See *RI*, 217, for a homily on the "genuine value" of ironic communication.

6. Quoted by Knox, *The Word "Irony,"* 41.

7. David Worcester, *Art of Satire*, quoted by Knox, 18.

8. Quoted by Marcel Gutwirth in "Réflexions sur le comique," *Revue d'Esthétique*, 17 (1964), 12.

9. The remark is attributed to a "great moralist" by Oliver Wendell Holmes, in *The Autocrat of the Breakfast Table* (Boston: Houghton, Mifflin, 1886), 12–13. In *Les Genres du risible: Ridicule, comique, esprit, humour* (Marseille: C.N.R.S., 1948), Elie Aubouin identifies the moralist as Addison.

10. The "bad" Socrates is, of course, the "good" Socrates (infinite absolute negativity) of the first part of *The Concept of Irony*. The economic metaphor is certainly not new. In his *De Sophisticis Elenchis* (1646), Aristotle asserts that genuine reasoning and refutation are as silver and gold, while sophistic reasoning (primarily that which depends upon language) is gold in appearance only.

11. The same is true of Muecke's and Knox's examples of irony. I have developed this point in greater detail in an article, "Irony/Humor: Assessing French and American Critical Trends," *Boundary 2* 10, no. 3 (1982), 271–302.

12. This despite Booth's assertion that his reconstruction metaphor "makes it impossible to think of irony as something that can be fully paraphrased in non-ironic statement" (*RI*, 39). Every statement is a speech act, he declares, which must be performed. But a content/form (intention/expression) notion of language pervades Booth's book, and with it, a nostalgia for im-mediate communication; it is clear that for him no statement, whether an "original" ironic utterance or a reconstructed paraphrase, is an adequate expression of an idea. "All literal statements mislead," he affirms in his conclusion; even metaphorical statements are "still misleading" (275). Thus any linguistic utterance is always already a paraphrase. Furthermore, it can be argued that speech act theory fails to elude the traditional model of communication; see Derrida's "Signature Event Context," *Glyph 1: Johns Hopkins Textual Studies* (Baltimore: Johns Hopkins University Press, 1977), 172–97.

13. This theme runs throughout Booth's *Critical Understanding: The Powers and Limits of Pluralism* (Chicago: University of Chicago Press, 1979); moreover,

Booth himself explicitly acknowledges the theological foundations of his critical enterprise (see, for instance, page 347).

14. Alan Wilde, *Horizons of Assent: Modernism, Postmodernism, and the Ironic Imagination* (Baltimore: Johns Hopkins University Press, 1981), 3. Hereafter cited in the text as *HA.*

15. With the advent of a twentieth-century mentality, Wilde claims, "we witness . . . a rejection of modernism's dualisms" (*HA,* 16). I would not presume to criticize Wilde's reading of the English and American authors he deals with in his book; they may well cling to a dualistic world view; but if so, they essentially remain modernists.

16. Wilde quotes the phrase from Wylie Sypher, *Literature and Technology* (New York: Random House, 1968), 239.

17. Wilde explicitly equates Derridean "playfulness" and irony: "But in the light of White's strictures and de Man's own linguistic emphasis, it is hard to avoid once again the sense, which emanates from so much deconstructive criticism, that writers are being relegated or indeed forced to smother in the folds of language, while their words are scanned and undermined by the ironic—in Derrida's case playful—surveillance of a relentlessly hygienic philosophical intelligence" (*HA, 7*).

18. Gary J. Handwerk, *Irony and Ethics in Narrative: From Schlegel to Lacan* (New Haven: Yale University Press, 1985), 14. Hereafter cited in the text as *IEN.*

19. "Whereas the symbol postulates the possibility of an identity or identification, allegory designates primarily a distance in relation to its own origin, and, renouncing the nostalgia and the desire to coincide, it establishes its language in the void of this temporal difference. In so doing, it prevents the self from an illusory identification with the non-self, which is fully, though painfully, recognized as a non-self." Paul de Man, "The Rhetoric of Temporality," in *Interpretation: Theory and Practice,* ed. Charles S. Singleton (Baltimore: Johns Hopkins University Press, 1969), 191. Hereafter cited in the text as RT. The article has been republished in de Man's *Blindness and Insight: Essays in the Rhetoric of Contemporary Criticism* (Minneapolis: University of Minnesota Press, 1983). Wilde mentions this article, but does not discuss it.

20. Charles Baudelaire, *Oeuvres Complètes,* ed. Y.-G. le Dantec and Claude Pichois (Paris: Pléiade, 1961), 982. Hereafter cited in the text as *OC.*

21. De Man does however mention Kierkegaard in passing, and refers frequently to Schlegel, who is one of the principal targets of Kierkegaard's polemic against romantic irony.

22. Many of the recent attacks on Continental criticism are directed primarily at the type of metaphorical, analogical, or "homeopathic" reasoning that it applies to literary texts. I have discussed this in "Aberrance in Criticism?" *Substance* 41 (1983), 3–16.

23. Roland Barthes, "Ecrivains, Intellectuels, Professeurs," *Tel Quel* 47 (1971), 9. I have quoted the translation by Stephen Heath in *Image, Music, Text* (New York: Hill and Wang, 1977), 201. Barthes's use of the term *écriture* in his later works should not be confused with the sense given it in *Le Degré zéro de l'écriture,* as one term of the opposition *style/écriture.* This couple was later superseded by *écriture/écrivance,* in which *écriture* is closer, though not identical,

to the earlier *style*. See Barthes's own comments on this in the interview "Réponses," also in *Tel Quel* 47 (1971), 103.

24. "Irony divides the flow of temporal experience into a past that is pure mystification and a future that remains harassed forever by a relapse within the inauthentic. It can know this inauthenticity but can never overcome it. It can only restate and repeat it on an increasingly conscious level, but it remains endlessly caught in the impossibility of making this knowledge applicable to the empirical world" (RT, 203).

25. Baudelaire is far from unambiguous on the status of the *comique absolu* versus the *comique significatif*. However, on pages 985–86 of "De l'essence du rire," he claims that the laughter provoked by the grotesque "is the expression of the idea of superiority, not of man over man, but of man over nature," and goes on to develop this idea as follows:

> Le rire causé par le grotesque a en soi quelque chose de profond, d'axiomatique et de primitif qui se rapproche beaucoup plus de la vie innocente et de la joie absolue que le rire causé par le comique de moeurs. Il y a entre ces deux rires, abstraction faite de la question d'utilité, la même différence qu'entre l'école littéraire intéressée et l'école de l'art pour l'art. . . .
>
> J'appellerai désormais le grotesque comique absolu, comme antithèse au comique ordinaire, que j'appellerai comique significatif. Le comique significatif est un langage plus clair, plus facile à comprendre pour le vulgaire, et surtout plus facile à analyser, son élément étant visiblement double: l'art et l'idée morale; mais le comique absolu, se rapprochant beaucoup plus de la nature, se présente sous une espèce *une*, et qui veut être saisie par intuition.

> Laughter caused by the grotesque has in it something profound, axiomatic, and primitive, which is much closer to innocence and absolute joy than is the laughter caused by the comedy of manners. There is between these two forms of laughter, setting aside the question of utility, the same difference that is to be found between literature with a social purpose and art for art's sake. . . .
>
> From now on I shall refer to the grotesque as the "absolute comic," as opposed to the ordinary comic, which I shall call the meaningful comic. The meaningful comic is a clearer language, easier for the vulgar to understand, and above all, easier to analyze, its prime element being obviously double: art and a moral idea; but the absolute comic, being much closer to nature, appears as a unity, which must be grasped by intuition.

The passage is particularly striking in that it opposes the concept of a moralistic, didactic art in which form is in the service of an anterior content (and which gives the spectator a feeling of superiority over his fellow man) to the notion of an art in which form and content are indissociable, so that it is much more difficult to extract or abstract (or "reconstruct") an idea from it.

26. Paul de Man, *Allegories of Reading: Figural Language in Rousseau, Nietzsche, Rilke, and Proust* (New Haven: Yale University Press, 1979), 301.

27. Ultimately, of course, any discourse is subject to stereotyping, particularly when it is assumed (usually in a caricatural form) by disciples and reduced to a Method.

28. Roland Barthes, *S/Z* (Paris: Seuil, 1970), 52/44. Hereafter cited in the text

as *SZ.* I quote, with slight modifications, Richard Miller's English translation of *S/Z* (New York: Hill and Wang, 1977).

29. I am intentionally using terminology that evokes Foucault's observations on the relationship between reason and unreason in his *Histoire de la folie à l'âge classique,* in order to emphasize what affinity there is between his work and Derrida's.

It is worth recalling as well, in this context, Kierkegaard's assertion that the Law bore irony within it as the agent of its own destruction (see Chapter One, n. 17).

30. The term *ironie* occurs often enough in Derrida, in a sense closely related to that of *le jeu.* Thus Wilde is right to equate the terms (see n. 17, above), but mistaken in his understanding of them. Irony, like play, partakes of the paradoxical duplicity of the *pharmakon* (see Chapter One, n. 25).

31. Barthes himself uses the term *moderne,* but in much the same sense as I have been using *postmodern.*

32. Michel Foucault, "Qu'est-ce qu'un auteur?" *Bulletin de la Société Française de Philosophie* 63, no. 3 (1969), 78.

33. While it is not possible, within the limits of the present discussion, to deal with recent work on the interpretation of specific ironic utterances from a more strictly linguistic point of view, I should point out that there has been a tendency among some French linguists to redefine irony in nontropological terms (i.e., to avoid the meaning/expression dichotomy). See, for instance, Dan Sperber and Deirdre Wilson, "Les Ironies comme mentions," *Poétique* 36 (1978), 399–412; Jean Cohen, "Théorie de la figure," in *Sémantique de la poésie* (Paris: Seuil, 1979), 84–127. For an argument in favor of treating irony as a trope, see Catherine Kerbrat-Orrechioni, "L'Ironie comme trope," *Poétique* 41 (1980), 108–27.

34. I subscribe to Jean-François Lyotard's definition of the distinction between modernity and postmodernity, as he proposes it in "Réponse à la question: qu'est-ce que le postmodern?" *Critique* 419 (April 1982), 357–67:

> Voici donc le différand: l'esthétique moderne est une esthétique du sublime, mais nostalgique; elle permet que l'imprésentable soit allégué seulement comme un contenu absent, mais la forme continue à offrir au lecteur ou au regardeur, grâce à sa consistance reconnaissable, matière à consolation et à plaisir. . . . Le postmoderne serait ce qui dans le moderne allègue l'imprésentable dans la présentation elle-même; ce qui se refuse à la consolation des bonnes formes, au consensus d'un goût qui permettrait d'éprouver en commun la nostalgie de l'impossible; ce qui s'enquiert de présentations nouvelles, non pas pour en jouir, mais pour mieux faire sentir qu'il y a de l'imprésentable. (366–67/81)

Here, then, lies the difference: modern aesthetics is an aesthetic of the sublime, though a nostalgic one. It allows the unpresentable to be put forward only as the missing contents; but the form, because of its recognizable consistence, continues to offer to the reader or viewer matter for solace or pleasure. . . . The postmodern would be that which, in the modern, puts forward the unpresentable in the presentation itself; that which denies itself the solace of good forms, the consensus of a taste which would make it possible to share collectively the nostalgia for the unattainable; that which searches for new presentations, not in order to enjoy them, but in order to impart a stronger sense of the unpresentable.

The English is quoted from Régis Durand's translation of the essay, which appears in an appendix to *The Postmodern Condition: A Report on Knowledge,* trans. Geoff Bennington and Brian Massumi (Minneapolis: University of Minnesota Press, 1984).

35. See Gilles Deleuze and Félix Guattari in *Kafka: Pour une littérature mineure* (Paris: Minuit, 1969), 76n: "Nous appelons interprétation basse, ou névrotique, toute lecture qui tourne le génie en angoisse, en tragique, en affaire individuelle. Par exemple Nietzsche, Kafka, n'importe: ceux qui ne les lisent pas avec beaucoup de rires involontaires, et frémissements politiques, déforment tout." ("We call a petty, or neurotic interpretation, any reading that turns genius into anguish, into tragedy, or into a 'personal matter.' For example, Nietzsche, Kafka, whoever: those who do not read them with involuntary laughter, and political quivers, distort everything.")

36. Jean-François Lyotard, "Le Non et la position de l'objet," in *Discours, figure* (Paris: Klincksieck, 1971), 120. Hereafter cited in the text as "Le Non."

37. Jacques Lacan, "Le Stade du miroir comme formateur de la fonction du Je telle qu'elle nous est révélée dans l'expérience psychanalytique," in *Ecrits* (Paris: Seuil, 1966), 94/2. The English is from Alan Sheridan's translation of "The Mirror Stage," in *Ecrits: A Selection* (New York: Norton, 1977).

38. See, for example, his remarks on Lacan in a 1970 interview, "Sur la théorie," in *Dérive à partir de Marx et Freud* (Paris: U.G.E., 1973), 228.

39. The translation of the essay "Jewish Oedipus," by Susan Hanson, appears in *Driftworks,* ed. Roger McKeon (New York: Semiotexte, 1984).

40. The term *sovereignty* is not intended here in the sense in which Georges Bataille used it.

41. See Lyotard's article "Apathie dans la théorie": "Le moment est venu d'interrompre la terreur théorique. . . . Le désir du vrai, qui alimente chez nous le terrorisme, est inscrit dans notre usage le plus incontrôlé du langage, au point que tout discours paraît déployer naturellement sa prétention à dire le vrai, par une sorte de vulgarité irrémédiable." ("The time has come to stop theoretical terror. . . . The desire for truth, which feeds our terrorist tendencies, is inscribed in our most spontaneous use of language, to the point that every discourse seems to exhibit naturally its pretensions to speak the truth, by a kind of irremediable vulgarity.") *Rudiments païens: Genre dissertatif* (Paris: U.G.E., 1977), 9.

42. *L'Arc* 64 (1976), 12. (Issue devoted to Lyotard.)

43. See also 25–26: "La débauche en matière de savoir est de poursuivre l'idée *soweit er führt,* aussi loin qu'il mène. . . . La scientificité est ainsi parodiée: le discours qu'on tient . . . continue d'avoir une référence . . . les énoncés paraissent toujours obéir aux préceptes de la fonction dénotative; mais la référence . . . n'est plus opposable à aucun énoncé pour la 'raison' qu'elle ne peut être exhibée dans des observations ni donner lieu à contre-énoncés." ("Debauchery, where knowledge is concerned, consists of pursuing an idea *soweit er führt* [as

does Freud in *Beyond the Pleasure Principle*], as far as it may lead. . . . Scientificity is thus parodied: our discourse . . . continues to have a reference . . . the statements still seem to obey the precepts of the denotative function; but the reference . . . can no longer be opposed to any statement, for the 'reason' that it cannot be presented in observations nor give rise to any counter-statements.")

44. Deleuze, *Présentation de Sacher-Masoch: Le froid et le cruel* (Paris: Minuit, 1967), 77. Hereafter cited in the text as *SM*.

45. Deleuze, *Logique du sens* (Paris: Minuit, 1969), 18. Hereafter cited in the text as *LS*.

46. "Le pseudo-sens du tragique rend bête; combien d'auteurs déformons-nous, à force de substituer un sentiment tragique puéril à la puissance agressive comique de la pensée qui les anime." ("The pseudo-sense of the tragic makes us stupid; how many authors we distort, by substituting a puerile tragic sentiment for the aggressive comic power of the thought that animates them.") Deleuze, *SM*, 75.

Chapter Three   Stendhal: Nostalgia

1. Stendhal, *Vie de Henry Brulard* (Paris: Garnier, 1961), 6–8. Hereafter cited in the text as *HB*.

2. See Rousseau's fourth *Promenade* for his own remarks on the subject of autobiographical veracity, in which he distinguishes between falsehood and fiction, claiming that, while there may be fiction in the *Confessions*, there are no lies:

> Je les écrivais de mémoire; cette mémoire me manquait souvent ou ne me fournissait que des souvenirs imparfaits et j'en remplissais les lacunes par des détails que j'imaginais en supplément de ces souvenirs, mais qui ne leur étaient jamais contraires. J'aimais à m'étendre sur les moments heureux de ma vie, et je les embellissais quelquefois des ornements que de tendres regrets venaient me fournir. Je disais les choses que j'avais oubliées comme il me semblait qu'elles avaient dû être, comme elles avaient été peut-être en effet, jamais au contraire de ce que je me rappelais qu'elles avaient été. Je prêtais quelquefois à la vérité des charmes étrangers, mais jamais je n'ai mis le mensonge à la place pour pallier mes vices, ou pour m'arroger des vertus. (*Les Rêveries du promeneur solitaire* [Paris: Garnier, 1960], 55)

> I wrote them from memory; this memory often failed me or only furnished me with incomplete recollections and I filled in the gaps with details that I imagined in addition to these recollections, but which were never contrary to them. I enjoyed elaborating on the happy moments of my life, and I embellished them at times with ornaments that tender regrets furnished me. I told the things I had forgotten as it seemed to me that they must have been—as they had perhaps been in fact—never contrary to what I recalled that they had been. I sometimes lent the truth charms foreign to it, but I never replaced it with a lie to palliate my vices or to ascribe virtues to myself.

3. See editor Henri Martineau's comments on this, *HB*, v. In this context, the reference to J.-J. Rousseau cited above deserves to be quoted at greater

length: "I may have to read and correct this passage, contrary to my intention, for fear of lying with artifice like J.-J. Rousseau" (*HB*, 391).

4. Deleuze defines the three principal historical manifestations of irony as follows: *l'ironie socratique* is intended to "wrest the individual from his immediate existence, to go beyond the sensible particular toward the Idea and to institute laws of language in conformity with the model," but the coincidence of the individual and the universal is achieved only with *l'ironie classique*, which "acts as the instance that assures the coextensivity of being and the individual in the world of representation." Finally, *l'ironie romantique* "determines he who speaks as the person, and no longer as the individual. It is founded on the finite synthetic unity of the person, and not on the analytic identity of the individual. It is defined as the coextensivity of the I and of representation itself" (*LS*, 163).

5. See Michael Sprinker's comments on the emergence of the author in his article "The End of Autobiography," in *Autobiography: Essays Theoretical and Critical*, ed. James Olney (Princeton: Princeton University Press, 1980), 323–25. See also Michel Foucault's article, to which Sprinker refers, "Qu'est-ce qu'un auteur?" (See Chapter Two, n. 32, above.)

6. Rousseau, *Les Confessions*, vol. 1 of *Oeuvres complètes* (Paris: Pléiade, 1959), 5. In *Le Poëme du haschish*, Baudelaire suggests that Rousseau's self-knowledge is a delusion of the kind experienced by the hashish user who has attained the state of exacerbated self-consciousness that Baudelaire elsewhere calls irony. His description of this condition is highly reminiscent of Kierkegaard:

> Il confond le rêve avec l'action, et son imagination s'échauffant de plus en plus devant le spectacle enchanteur de sa propre nature corrigée et idéalisée, substituant cette image fascinatrice de lui-même à son réel individu, si pauvre en volonté, si riche en vanité, il finit par décréter son apothéose en ces termes nets et simples, qui contiennent pour lui tout un monde d'abominables jouissances: "je suis le plus vertueux de tous les hommes!"
> Cela ne vous fait-il pas souvenir de Jean-Jacques, qui, lui aussi, après s'être confessé à l'univers, non sans une certaine volupté, a osé pousser le même cri de triomphe ... avec la même sincérité et la même conviction? ... Jean-Jacques s'était enivré sans haschish. (*OC*, 381–82)

> He confuses dream with action and, his imagination becoming more and more excited before the enchanting spectacle of his own nature corrected and idealized, substituting this fascinating image of himself for his real individual—so poor in will-power and so rich in vanity—he ends up by decreeing his own apotheosis in these clear and simple terms, which contain for him a world of abominable pleasures: "I am the most virtuous of all men!"
> Doesn't this remind you of Jean-Jacques, who, he too, after having confessed himself to the universe, not without a certain voluptuous pleasure, dared utter the same triumphant cry ... with the same sincerity and the same conviction? ... Jean-Jacques had gotten intoxicated without hashish.

7. "*I* refers to the individual act of discourse in which it is pronounced, and it designates the speaker. It is a term that can only be identified in what we have elsewhere called an instance of discourse, and which has no reference but

the present utterance [*n'a de référence qu'actuelle*]. The reality to which it refers is the reality of discourse." Emile Benveniste, *Problèmes de linguistique générale* (Paris: Gallimard, 1966), 261–62. See also page 254. For Louis Marin's analysis of *Brulard* in terms of Benveniste's linguistic categories, see *La Voix excommuniée: Essais de mémoire* (Paris: Galilée, 1981), 23–24. Readers interested in the problematic treated here might wish to consult a related article by Marin, "Remarques critiques sur l'énonciation: La question du présent dans le discours," *MLN* 91, no. 5 (1976), 939–51.

8. In *Le Pacte autobiographique* (Paris: Seuil, 1975), Lejeune defines autobiography as follows: "Retrospective narration in prose that a real person gives of his own existence, when it emphasizes his personal life, particularly the history of his personality." He critiques certain of his assumptions and procedures in a more recent article, "Le Pacte autobiographique (bis)," *Poétique* 56 (1983), 416–34.

9. See Michel Beaujour, *Miroirs d'encre: Rhétorique de l'autoportrait* (Paris: Seuil, 1980), 21. Beaujour asserts that the *autoportrait,* of which he considers as early a work as Montaigne's *Essais* to constitute an example, is "always absolutely modern" (21) in the sense that it is the product of the culture, the language, the commonplaces of its time. He does not discuss the *Vie de Henry Brulard,* although he alludes to it briefly in a footnote (9).

10. The expression *faire du roman* recurs numerous times in *Brulard,* particularly near the end of the text. For a few examples, see 360, 381, 399, 406, 407, 408.

11. Such is the paradox of Beaujour's *autoportraitiste:* "[He] never clearly knows where he is going, what he is doing. But his cultural tradition knows for him: it furnishes him with the ready-made categories that permit him to sort out the fragments of his discourse, of memories, and of phantasms," all the while classifying them as best he can "according to the imperatives of a taxonomy whose configuration and whose reasons escape a subject as blind as Oedipus, and who ascribes everything to his freedom, to his ego [*moi*] and to his enunciation" (10).

12. I take Henri Martineau's word for this. See his introduction to *Brulard,* ii–iii, and 418, n. 4. Martineau admits that the passage could have been written earlier and recopied in 1835, but not on October 16. Marin comments at length on this apparent subterfuge in *La Voix excommuniée.*

13. "The drawing . . . extends the writing by a natural movement that confirms how much Stendhal, even in haste and improvisation, and even if he occasionally dictated certain of his pages, remains very far from any declaimed, murmured, or confessed 'oral' literature. His very acts of negligence are bound up with the act of writing: ellipses, gaps, breaks. It is a style of notes, abbreviations, impatiences, and boldnesses proper to writing. *Oratio soluta.*" Gérard Genette, "'Stendhal,'" in *Figures II* (Paris: Seuil, 1969), 168/158–59. English translations of passages from this article are quoted, with occasional modifications, from *Figures of Literary Discourse,* trans. Alan Sheridan (New York: Columbia University Press, 1982).

14. "A vrai dire, je ne suis rien moins que sûr d'avoir quelque talent pour me faire lire. Je trouve quelquefois beaucoup de plaisir à écrire, voilà tout" (*HB,* 8).

("To tell the truth, I am not the least bit sure of having enough talent to be read. I sometimes get a great deal of pleasure out of writing, that's all.") "Mes Confessions n'existeront donc plus trente ans après avoir été imprimées, si les *Je* et les *Moi* assomment trop les lecteurs; et toutefois j'aurai eu le plaisir de les écrire" (*HB*, 10). ("Thus my confessions will no longer exist thirty years after having been printed, if the *I*'s and *Me*'s overwhelm the readers too much; nevertheless, I will have had the pleasure of writing them.")

On the importance of writing in the Stendhalian universe, see Genette's "'Stendhal,'" 163–66 in particular.

15. In speaking of Rousseau's essentialist conception of autobiography, I am referring to his *Confessions*. It should be noted that Beaujour considers his *Rêveries* as an example of the *autoportrait*.

16. See also page 166:

Mais tout cela ne fut-il pas causé par ses amours avec Séraphie, si amour y a? Je ne puis voir la physionomie des choses, je n'ai que ma mémoire d'enfant. Je vois des images, je me souviens des effets sur mon coeur, mais pour les causes et la physionomie néant. C'est toujours comme les fresques du [Campo Santo] de Pise où l'on aperçoit fort bien un bras, et le morceau d'à côté qui représentait la tête est tombé. Je vois une suite d'images *fort nettes* mais sans physionomie autre que celle qu'elles eurent à mon égard. Bien plus, je ne vois cette physionomie que par le souvenir de l'effet qu'elle produisit sur moi.

But wasn't all that caused by his love affair with Seraphie, if there was one? I cannot see the physiognomy of things, I only have my memory as a child. I see images, I remember their effects on my heart, but as for the cause and the physiognomy, nothing. It's always like the frescoes of the Campo Santo in Pisa where you make out an arm very well, and the piece next to it that represented the head has fallen off. I see a series of *very sharp* images, but with no other physiognomy than that which they had for me. What is more, I only see that physiognomy by the memory of the effect it produced on me.

17. The examples are far too numerous to cite here. Even a quick perusal of Martineau's notes will give the reader an idea of the frequency of quotations in *Brulard*.

18. Again a quotation. According to Martineau (*HB*, 436, n. 235), the expression "le sujet surpasse le disant," which Beyle uses at least twice again in *Brulard*, comes from a line of verse by Francis I.

19. The passage deserves to be quoted at greater length:

Je venais de voir distinctement où était le bonheur. Il me semble aujourd'hui que mon grand malheur devait être: je n'ai pas trouvé le bonheur à Paris où je l'ai cru pendant si longtemps, où est-il donc? Ne serait-il point dans nos montagnes du Dauphiné? Alors mes parents auraient raison, et je ferais mieux d'y retourner. (*HB*, 407)

I had just seen clearly where happiness was. It seems to me today that my greatest torment was: I haven't found happiness in Paris where I thought it was for so long; where is it then? Might it not be in our mountains in the Dauphiné? Then my parents would be right, and I would do better to return there.

20. In fact Beyle telescopes his chronology here: although he fell in love with Angela Pietragrua in 1800, he did not become her lover until 1811 (*HB,* 465, n. 634). The point is, of course, that chronology is of no importance for the pattern of mythical associations which unite Italy, mistresses, mother, and so on, in a kind of beatific vision.

21. Genette, "'Stendhal,'" 175.

22. On the *roman familial,* see Marthe Robert, *Roman des origines et origines du roman* (Paris: Grasset, 1972).

23. Marin, *La Voix excommuniée,* 66–94; see also 82–87.

24. Stendhal, "Les Cenci," *Romans et nouvelles* (Paris: Pléiade, 1952), 2: 703. Beatrice Cenci was also the subject of a portrait that Beyle greatly admired, attributing it, perhaps erroneously, to one of his favorite Italian painters, Guido Reni. See Philippe Berthier, *Stendhal et ses peintres italiens* (Geneva: Droz, 1977), 102.

25. Referring to these passages, Genette comments: "For specialists, such a text ought to be something of a scandal: what does it leave to interpret? One imagines Oedipus, as the curtain rises, declaring without preamble to the Theban people: 'Good people, I have killed my father and given my mother Jocasta four children: two boys and two girls. Don't look any further: all the evil comes from this.' Imagine Tiresias' face. (Imagine Sophocles' face)" ("'Stendhal,'" 158/149–50).

26. Marin cites a portion of these passages from Freud in *La Voix excommuniée,* 37. For Freud's text, "Medusa's Head," see *The Standard Edition,* 18: 273.

27. Cf. Beaujour, *Miroirs d'encre,* 22:

> The self-portrait is haunted by the phantasm of a happy city, of a stable cultural community of which no one has better suggested the maternal symbolism than Roland Barthes, by placing at the beginning of his book a hazy, sunny, summery photograph of his own mother, followed by images of the city, the house, the garden of his childhood.... This little book of man which is the self-portrait stands out against the background of the maternal loci [*lieux*] of memory, of the imaginary, as well as against those furnished him by the great book of the City, of culture, with its ethnical loci which evoke the lost harmony of a timeless order.

28. According to Genette ("'Stendhal,'" 159), more than a hundred pseudonyms have been counted in Stendhal's works. For the reader interested in pursuing the problematic of pseudonymity in Stendhal, Jean Starobinski's "Stendhal pseudonyme," in *L'Oeil vivant* (Paris: Gallimard, 1961) is indispensable. *Beyliste* Georges Blin suggests a spiritual affinity between Beyle and Kierkegaard, "himself a great lover of masks, codes, and pseudonyms." *Stendhal et les problèmes de la personnalité* (Paris: José Corti, 1958), 1: 250, n. 3.

29. Doubtless thinking of his own name, Beyle wrote "five letters" in his manuscript. It is probably from *The Vicar of Wakefield* that Beyle borrowed his famous expression "the happy few."

30. Beyle insists that his memoirs are intended for readers who will discover them fifty, a hundred, or even two hundred years later. See, for instance, *HB,* 9 and 10.

Chapter Four   Baudelaire: Lequel Est le Vrai?

1. Jean-Paul Sartre, *Baudelaire* (Paris: Gallimard, 1963), 32. Hereafter cited in the text as S.

2. Dr. René Laforgue formulates the same critique on medical grounds: "The same nostalgic languor is always expressed throughout this poetry, and one senses how the poet, in pursuit of intense pleasure [*sa grande volupté*], is sinking into a horrifying abyss: death. In this connection, we would like to call the reader's attention to the eroticizing of anguish and horror, liable to take the place of normal orgasms." *L'Echec de Baudelaire: Etude psychanalytique sur la névrose de Baudelaire* (Paris: Denoël et Steele, 1931), 99.

3. On the relationship between poetry and evil in Baudelaire—and for a response to Sartre—see Georges Bataille, "Baudelaire," in *La Littérature et le mal* (Paris: Gallimard, 1957), 37–68.

4. "Poets are men who refuse to *utilize* language. Now, since the quest for truth takes place in and by language conceived as a certain kind of instrument, one mustn't imagine that they aim to discern or expound the true." Sartre, *Qu'est-ce que la littérature?* (Paris: Gallimard, 1948), 17/5. I have slightly modified the translation by Bernard Frechtman in *What Is Literature?* (London: Methuen, 1970).

5. Maurice Blanchot, "L'Echec de Baudelaire," in *La Part du feu* (Paris: Gallimard, 1949), 137.

6. The italics are Baudelaire's, as is the English.

7. See Marcel Ruff, *L'Esprit du mal et l'esthétique baudelairienne* (Paris: Armand Colin, 1955), 82.

8. On the Baudelairean theme of the fall from paradise into *time*, see Georges Poulet's essay on Baudelaire in *Etudes sur le temps humain* (Edinburgh: Edinburgh University Press, 1949), 1: 327–49.

9. The third edition of *Les Fleurs du mal* appeared posthumously; hence I am not claiming that this arrangement necessarily reveals Baudelaire's intentions.

10. The allusion is of course to the "Nirvana principle" formulated by Freud in *Beyond the Pleasure Principle*. Freud's formulation remains ambiguous, however, as to whether it designates a tendency to maintain a constant level of excitation or to return to a state of zero tension. See the comments of Jean Laplanche and J.-B. Pontalis in their *Vocabulaire de la psychanalyse* (Paris: P.U.F., 1967), 331–32.

11. Barbara Johnson, *Défigurations du langage poétique: La seconde révolution baudelairienne* (Paris: Flammarion, 1979), 42. Hereafter cited in the text as *DLP.*

12. Jean Prévost argues that the distancing of the object is intended not to arouse but to "evade desire": "Evasions of desire [*les conjurations du désir*] let love subsist with all its beauty—but ward off insofar as possible the idea or image of possession. The Poet is quite willing to be charmed by beauty, but he wishes this beauty to leave his soul in its contemplative serenity." *Baudelaire: Essai sur l'inspiration et la création poétiques* (Paris: Mercure de France, 1953), 245.

13. For another view of irony in "La Beauté," see Francis S. Heck, "'La Beauté': Enigma of Irony," *Nineteenth-Century French Studies* 10, nos. 1–2 (1981–82), 85–95.

14. The allusion occurs in the section of *Réflections sur quelques-uns de mes contemporains* devoted to Victor Hugo: "But it is particularly in recent years that he has been affected by the metaphysical influence that emanates from all these things, with the curiosity of an Oedipus obsessed by innumerable Sphinxes" (*OC,* 709).

15. The archetypal ironist is God Himself, who in his superior wisdom mocks human foibles. Thus Pascal, in the eleventh of the *Lettres provinciales,* justifies his own use of irony against the erroneous doctrines of the Jesuits by invoking this biblical precedent:

> Dans les premières paroles que Dieu a dit à l'homme depuis sa cheute, on trouve un discours de moquerie, et *une ironie piquante,* selon les Peres. Car, aprés qu'Adam eut desobeï dans l'esperance que le demon luy avoit donnée d'estre fait semblable à Dieu, il paroist par l'Ecriture que Dieu en punition le rendit sujet à la mort, et qu'aprés l'avoir reduit à cette miserable condition, qui estoit deuë à son peché, il se moqua de luy en cest estat par ces paroles de risée: "Voilà l'homme qui est devenu comme l'un de nous: *Ecce Adam quasi unus ex nobis."* Ce qui est *une ironie sanglante et sensible* dont Dieu le *piquoit vivement,* selon S. Chrysostome et les interpretes. (*Les Provinciales,* publiées avec notes et variantes et précédées d'une préface par M. S. de Sacy [Paris: Librarie des Bibliophiles, 1877], 180.)

> In God's first words to man after the Fall we find mockery and "biting irony," according to the Fathers. For after Adam had been disobedient, hoping, as the devil had said, to be made like unto God, Scripture shows that as a punishment God made him subject to death, and after reducing him to this miserable condition, due wages of his sin, mocked his plight in these derisive words: "Behold the man is become as one of us," which, according to St. Chrysostom and the exegetes, is "a bitter and sounding irony" with which God "sorely stung him." (*The Provincial Letters,* trans. A. J. Kraitsheimer [New York: Penguin Books, 1982], 165.)

16. In the same vein, see "La Muse Malade": "Je voudrais qu'exhalant l'odeur de la santé / Ton sein de pensers forts fût toujours fréquenté / Et que ton sang chrétien coulât à flots rhythmiques / Comme les sons nombreux des syllabes antiques" ("I would that, fragrant with health, your breast knew only strong and noble thoughts, and your Christian blood flowed in rhythmic waves, like the measured sounds of ancient verse" [*OC,* 14]).

The consequences of the Fall included not only death, but the experience of desire and of painful childbirth (see Genesis 1:16).

17. "—Certes, je sortirai, quant à moi, satisfait / D'un monde où l'action n'est pas la soeur du rêve" ("As for me, I will certainly be content to leave a world where action is not the sister of dreams" ["Le Reniement de Saint Pierre," *OC,* 115]). See also Baudelaire's review of *La Double vie,* by Charles Asselineau, which opens upon a characterization of *homo duplex,* the quintessential romantic ironist, "dont l'esprit a été dès l'enfance *touched with pensiveness;* toujours double, action et intention, rêve et réalité. . . . L'intention laissée en route,

le rêve oublié dans une auberge, le projet barré par l'obstacle, le malheur et l'infirmité jaillissant du succès comme les plantes vénineuses d'une terre grasse et négligée, le regret mêlé d'ironie" ("whose mind from childhood has been *touched with pensiveness;* always dual, torn between action and intention, dream and reality. . . . Intentions left by the wayside, dreams forgotten in an inn, plans thwarted by obstacles, illness and misfortune springing up from success like poisonous plants from a rich, uncultivated soil, regrets mingled with irony" [*OC,* 658/329]). English translations of this essay, "The Duality of Life," and of "The Pagan School" are quoted, with slight modifications, from *Baudelaire as Literary Critic,* ed. and trans. Lois Boe Hyslop and Francis E. Hyslop, Jr. (University Park: Pennsylvania State University Press, 1964).

18. Baudelairean heaven is a liquid sky: "Va te purifier dans l'air supérieur, / Et bois, comme une pure et divine liqueur, / Le feu clair qui remplit les espaces limpides" ("Go purify yourself in the higher realms, and drink, like a pure and divine liqueur, the clear fire that fills limpid space" ["Elévation," *OC,* 10]). "Je crois boire un vin de Bohème . . . Un ciel liquide qui parsème / D'étoiles mon coeur!" ("I seem to drink a Bohemian wine . . . a liquid sky that scatters stars in my heart" ["Le Serpent qui danse," *OC,* 29]).

19. John Milton, *Paradise Lost,* 1:263.

20. François Mauriac's "Charles Baudelaire the Catholic" is exemplary: "Down to his dying day, [Baudelaire] listened to his poor soul and he confessed it. The flowers of evil are the flowers of sin, of repentence, of remorse and penitence. He suffers, but he knows why." *Baudelaire: A Collection of Critical Essays,* ed. Henri Peyre (Englewood Cliffs, N.J.: Prentice-Hall, 1962), 30.

21. On ironic utterances considered as "(generally implicit) mentions of propositions . . . interpreted as the echo of an utterance or of a thought whose inaccuracy or irrelevance the speaker wishes to emphasize," see Dan Sperber and Deirdre Wilson, "Les Ironies comme mentions," *Poétique* 36 (1978), 399–412.

22. "Eine neue Generation von kleinen Ironien," quoted by Paul de Man in RT, 203.

23. *La Fanfarlo* merits a chapter in itself, which, unfortunately, I cannot accord it in the present context. For two quite different readings of this tale, see Francis S. Heck, "Baudelaire's *La Fanfarlo:* An Example of Romantic Irony," *French Review* 49, no. 3 (1976), 328–36; and Nathanial Wing, "The Poetics of Irony in Baudelaire's *La Fanfarlo,*" *Neophilologus* 59, no. 2 (1975), 165–89. The latter, I think, shows more sensitivity to the ambiguities of the text.

24. In *Le Poëme du haschisch,* Baudelaire cites only "the saddened poet" as the source of his concluding moral (*OC,* 387); in *Un Mangeur d'opium,* he quotes himself: "Everything I said about the weakening of the will in my study on hashish is applicable to opium" (425).

25. Michel Butor, "Les Paradis artificiels," in *Essais sur les modernes* (Paris: Gallimard, 1964), 15.

26. Ironically, Baudelaire seems to suspect De Quincey of being ironic in his conclusion: "What always confirmed me in my idea that this ending was *artificial,* at least in part, is a certain teasing, jesting, even mocking tone that prevails at several points in this appendix" (*OC,* 439).

27. Baudelaire, of course, "borrowed" not infrequently from authors such as

Longfellow, Thomas Gray (see, for instance, "Le Guignon" [*OC,* 16] and "Le Calumet de la paix" [164–67]), and Poe—and himself, republishing some of his own poems with slight revisions.

28. "Vaporization names the very process of writing," argues Arden Reed in "Baudelaire's 'La Pipe': De la vaporisation du *Moi,*" *Romantic Review* 72, no. 3 (1981), 280.

29. "Réponse à la question: Qu'est-ce que le postmoderne?" 366. (See Chapter Two, n. 34, above.)

30. Leo Bersani, *Baudelaire and Freud* (Berkeley and Los Angeles: University of California Press, 1977), 4. Hereafter cited in the text as *BF.*

31. Echoing Baudelaire's expression "*homo duplex,*" Johnson refers to the poet's work as an *opus duplex* (*DLP,* 13). She is, of course, aware that some of the prose poems may have been written before their verse counterparts, but points out, correctly, that the *chronological* priority of one form over the other is irrelevant to her analysis.

32. On the poet's historical situation, and its manifestations in Baudelaire's work, see Walter Benjamin, "On Some Motifs in Baudelaire," *Illuminations* (New York: Schocken Books, 1969), 155–200.

33. If Bersani dismisses it as so much romantic rhetoric, Jean Prévost, on the other hand, claims: "If this poem is enveloped in rhetoric, it is because Baudelaire's feelings for his mother and his wife are too intense for him to dare express them openly; it is an excess of feeling, not a lack of feeling, that obliges him to stylize" (*Baudelaire,* 197). *Dolorisme* is defined in the *Petit Robert* as the doctrine of the usefulness, of the (moral) value of pain [*douleur*].

34. See Ruff, *L'Esprit du mal et l'esthétique baudelairienne.*

35. So warns "un ange furieux" in "Le Rebelle": "Sache qu'il faut aimer, sans faire la grimace, / Le pauvre, le méchant, le tortu, l'hébété, / Pour que tu puisses faire à Jésus, quand il passe, / Un tapis triomphal avec ta charité" ("Know that you must love, without grimacing, the poor, the malicious, the deformed, the dumb, so that you can make for Jesus, when he passes, a triumphal carpet of your charity" [*OC,* 171]).

36. "L'être le plus prostitué, c'est l'être par excellence, c'est Dieu, puisqu'il est l'ami suprême pour chaque individu, puisqu'il est le réservoir commun, inépuisable de l'amour" ("The most prostituted being is the being *par excellence;* it is God, since he is the supreme friend for every individual, since he is the common, inexhaustible reservoir of love" [*OC,* 1286–87]).

37. Susanne Guerlac, "'Monsters of the Sublime'—Hugo, Baudelaire, Lautréamont and the Esthetics of the Sublime" (Ph.D. diss., Johns Hopkins University, 1984), 247–50.

38. In "Le Joueur Généreux," the narrator accepts the loss of his soul as casually as if it had been a "carte de visite" (*OC,* 275)—another form of paper I.D.

For Johnson, the fall into the *mauvais lieu* is emblematic of the passage from verse to prose—a symbolic castration: "The fact that castration is in a sense *constitutive* of the prose poem, is explicitly allegorized in the text of *Perte d'auréole:* the cutting off of the 'insignia' of poetic potency necessarily precedes the poet's entry into the 'place of ill repute' [*mauvais lieu*] of prose" [*DLP,* 154].

39. See Chapter Two, above. It should be recalled that etymologically, irony is defined as "*eirôneia,* act of questioning while feigning ignorance" (*Le Petit Robert*).

40. De Man remarks that the prose poems are ironic (RT, 207), but in fact his definition of allegory suits them better.

41. Furthermore, there is considerable sentimentality to be found in a number of the prose poems (e.g., "Le Désespoir de la vieille," "Le Fou et la Vénus," "Les Veuves," "Le Vieux saltimbanque," "Le Thyrse," "Le Port").

42. Vincent Descombes, *Le Même et l'autre: Quarante-cinq ans de philosophie française (1933–1978)* (Paris: Minuit, 1979), 163. Descombes alludes to Derrida's article on Lévinas, "Violence et métaphysique," in *L'Ecriture et la différence* (Paris: Seuil, 1967), 133.

43. On the dangerously ephemeral sense of superiority experienced by the laughing spectator, see René Girard, "Perilous Balance: A Comic Hypothesis," in *"To Double Business Bound"* (Baltimore: Johns Hopkins University Press, 1978), 127–28: "The man who laughs is just about to be enveloped into the pattern of which his victim is already a part. . . . He falls into the very trap that has already swallowed his victim and becomes laughable in his turn." The philosopher who thinks to occupy a position of exteriority runs the same risk: "Hegel compares philosophy to an owl that begins to fly at dusk. As he contemplates the wreckage left by his predecessors, the philosopher cannot help feeling superior."

Chapter Five   Proust: Forgetting Things Past

1. Gilles Deleuze, *Proust et les signes* (Paris: P.U.F., 1983), 123/166. The English translation is from *Proust and Signs,* trans. Richard Howard (New York: George Braziller, 1972).

2. Marcel Proust, *A la recherche du temps perdu,* texte établi et présenté par Pierre Clarac et André Ferré (Paris: Pléiade, 1954), 3: 880/3: 914. Hereafter referred to in the text only by volume number and page number. For the English, I have quoted, with only a few minor modifications, from *Remembrance of Things Past,* 3 vols., trans. C. K. Scott Moncrieff and Terence Kilmartin (New York: Random House, 1981).

3. Well before Barthes, Proust defined *la bêtise* as the thoughtless repetition of what "they" say; and the Proustian writer, a structuralist *avant la lettre,* is interested, not in the content of such utterances, but only in the general patterns of behavior they exemplify: "The future writer . . . has listened to people only when, stupid [*bêtes*] or absurd though they may have been, they have turned themselves, by repeating like parrots what other people of similar character are in the habit of saying, into birds of augury, mouthpieces of a psychological law. He remembers only things that are general" (5: 900/3: 937).

Furthermore, Proust is as wary as Barthes of the contagion of *bêtise* (i.e., the vicious spiral of irony). To denounce *bêtise* in the other is to become *bête* in turn: "Moreover, those who theorized in this way used hackneyed phrases which had a curious resemblánce to those of the idiots whom they denounced" (3: 881–882/3: 916).

4. His affinity for cinematographic analogies notwithstanding, a Robbe-Grillet, in refusing to simply identify by name a coffee-pot, a tomato, or an eraser, could hardly be further from presenting his readers with "a sort of procession of things upon the screen," at least in the sense specified by Proust, that is, as a series of familiar objects, instantly identifiable because they are wearing their customary name tags. To the objection that Robbe-Grillet was bent on divesting objects of just the sort of humanistic qualities that Proust was bestowing on them, one can only respond that Proust, as is clear from his commentaries on style, was perfectly conscious of the role of intentionality in the artist's appropriation of the world, and suffered not the least delusion as to the inherence of the essences he sought to communicate through style.

Finally, I refer the reader to a passage of Robbe-Grillet's autobiography in which, after evoking the sensations associated in his memory with nightfall in his childhood town, the author comments: "J'ai signalé souvent que je voyais là une des raisons—sinon la principale—qui m'avaient poussé vers le roman. Je comprends très bien ce que signifie: se mettre à écrire à cause de la couleur jaune aperçue sur un vieux mur. Devant la dureté agressive d'un livre comme *La jalousie*, mes lecteurs sont-ils en droit de s'étonner d'un tel aveu? Je ne le crois pas" (*Le Miroir qui revient* [Paris: Minuit, 1984], 55).

5. "In Bergotte's books, which I constantly re-read, his sentences stood out as clearly before my eyes as my own thoughts. . . . All the details were easily visible, not perhaps precisely as one had always seen them, but at any rate as one was accustomed to see them now. But a new writer had recently begun to publish work in which the relations between things were so different from those that connected them for me that I could understand hardly anything of what he wrote" (2: 326/2: 337).

6. Marcel Proust, *Jean Santeuil*, précédé de *Les Plaisirs et les jours*, édition établie par Pierre Clarac avec la collaboration d'Yves Sandre (Paris: Pléiade, 1971), 118/134. All subsequent references are to this edition, and will be cited in the text. Passages from *Les Plaisirs et les jours* will be indicated by the initials *PJ*; passages from *Jean Santeuil*, by *JS*. English translations are quoted, with considerable modifications, from *Pleasures and Regrets*, trans. Louise Varese (New York: Ecco Press, 1984), and *Jean Santeuil*, trans. Gerard Hopkins (New York: Simon and Schuster, 1956).

7. Closer, perhaps, to the language of the *Recherche* is the text entitled "The Shores of Oblivion": "Is it enough to say of the person who, after having made us suffer, is nothing to us any longer, that, in the popular phrase, she is 'dead to us'? . . . She is more than dead to us" (*PJ*, 133/154).

8. "Obscure impressions . . . had solicited my attention in a fashion somewhat similar to these reminiscences, except that they concealed within them not a sensation from an earlier time, but a new truth, a precious image which I had sought to uncover by efforts of the same kind as those that we make to recall something that we have forgotten, as if our finest ideas were like tunes which, as it were, come back to us although we have never heard them before" (3: 878/3: 912).

9. "In Proust, the steeples of Martinville and Vinteuil's little phrase, which cause no memory, no resurrection of the past to intervene, will always prevail over the madeleine and the cobblestones of Venice, which depend on memory and thereby still refer to a 'material explanation'" (Deleuze, *Proust et les signes,* 9–10/3–4).

10. See Gérard Genette, *Figures III* (Paris: Seuil, 1972), 255–56/248. For the English translation of the essay referred to here, "Discours du récit," see *Narrative Discourse: An Essay on Method,* trans. Jane E. Lewin (Ithaca: Cornell University Press, 1980). The diegesis (*diégèse*) is the fictional (hence supposedly real) world, or the series of events (also called *l'histoire*) ostensibly represented or recounted by the *récit,* or narrative. The extradiegetic narrator is "outside" the text in that he is not represented in it as a narrator. The intradiegetic narrator is the teller of a story-within-a-story; Genette gives the example of Scheherazade.

11. The reader will recall the difficulties encountered by Beyle in his attempts to maintain such a distance in autodiegetic narration, in which the narrator is the hero of his own tale.

12. See, for example, George D. Painter, *Marcel Proust: A Biography* (London: Chatto and Windus, 1959). In his *Proust et le roman: Essai sur les formes et techniques du roman dans* A la recherche du temps perdu (Paris: Gallimard, 1971), Jean-Yves Tadié also remarks upon the presence of more undisguised autobiographical elements in *Santeuil* than in the *Recherche* (20–28).

13. "Undoubtedly," writes Genette apropros of *Jean Santeuil,* "to a narrator so eager to accompany his 'story' with that sort of running commentary that is its underlying justification, nothing is more annoying than to have to shift 'voice' incessantly" (*Figures III,* 257/250). The narrator's role as a commentator, or his "fonction idéologique" (263/256), predominates over his other functions in the *Recherche.*

14. Unfortunately, the translator has "corrected" Marcel to read "Jean."

15. The manuscript of *Jean Santeuil* consists of a multitude of uncoordinated and sometimes contradictory fragments, upon which Proust's editors have sought to impose an order for the purposes of publication. In the *Pléiade* edition, Pierre Clarac has placed two versions of an unfinished preface at the head of the text, and, insofar as possible, has ordered the other fragments both chronologically (according to the protagonist's age in the various episodes) and thematically (see Clarac's notes, *JS,* 980–86).

16. In "La Mer," cited earlier, the calm sea is explicitly associated with an idyllic originary state of nature: "For a moment the blending shades are broken up; then all trace is obliterated and the sea becomes calm again as in the first days of creation" (*PJ,* 143/168).

17. Painter also cites evidence from Proust's correspondence that the *Santeuil* account is more factual (*Marcel Proust,* 10–11).

18. As patriarch, "proxy for a family," Jean is reintegrated into the cosmos. Like the narrator of the bedtime scene, Jean the Father surveys his own past from above and beyond:

Et, comparant cette heureuse journée à son enfance prisonnière et qui ne connaissait de la famille que son esclavage, il sentait à la fois la douceur d'en être affranchi et de s'y asservir de nouveau, mais librement, comme à la tendresse d'un frère, aux mérites, aux détails d'un auteur préféré et semblable à nous. (*JS*, 857/709)

Comparing this happy day with the years of his imprisoned childhood, when the parental home had seemed to him a place of slavery, he was conscious both of the sweetness of his freedom from those bonds, and of his delight in occasional acts of obedience, though this time dictated by his own unfettered will, as in response to a brother's tenderness, or to the faults and merits of a favourite author with whom he had much in common.

19. Roland Barthes, *Le Plaisir du texte* (Paris: Seuil, 1973), 75–76/47. English translations are quoted from *The Pleasure of the Text*, trans. Richard Miller (New York: Hill and Wang, 1975). Hereafter cited in the text as *PT*.

20. The exact dates of the composition of *Contre Sainte-Beuve* are uncertain. Indeed, the limits of the work itself are only loosely defined, for it is but a collection of texts belonging neither to *Jean Santeuil* nor to the *Recherche* (yet clearly announcing the latter). Thus editions vary greatly.

21. In Philippe Lejeune's terms, the text of the *Recherche* occupies an "ambiguous space" because it vacillates between a "novelistic pact" and an "autobiographical pact" (*Le Pacte autobiographique*, 29).

22. Marcel Proust, *Contre Sainte-Beuve* (Paris: Gallimard, 1954), 157. Hereafter cited in the text as *CSB*.

23. Serge Gaubert, *Proust ou le roman de la différence: L'individu et le monde social de* Jean Santeuil *à* La Recherche (Lyon: Presses Universitaires de Lyon, 1980), 119.

24. Albertine is of course another incarnation of the lost object. Thus in the account of her sudden departure, she is explicitly associated with the mother—and their absence, with death: "Each of [my 'selves'] in turn had to hear for the first time the words 'Albertine has asked for her boxes' (those coffin-shaped boxes which I had seen loaded onto the train at Balbec with my mother's), 'Albertine has gone'" (3: 430/3: 437).

25. Thus the narrator of the *Recherche*, seeking in vain an informant who knows the truth about Albertine's lesbian affairs, likens such a person to the informed narrator of the traditional novel:

Les romanciers prétendent souvent dans une introduction qu'en voyageant dans un pays ils ont rencontré quelqu'un qui leur a raconté la vie d'une personne. Ils laissent alors la parole à cet ami de rencontre, et le récit qu'il leur fait c'est précisément leur roman. . . . Combien nous voudrions, quand nous aimons, c'est-à-dire quand l'existence d'une autre personne nous semble mystérieuse, trouver un tel narrateur informé! (3: 551/3: 561)

Novelists sometimes pretend in an introduction that while travelling in a foreign country they have met somebody who has told them the story of another person's life. They then withdraw in favour of this chance acquaintance, and the story that he tells them is nothing more or less than their novel. . . . How gladly would we, when we are in love, that is to say when another person's existence seems to us mysterious, find some such well-informed narrator!

Proust takes up the dream motif again in the final pages of *Le Temps retrouvé*. "And it was perhaps also because of the extraordinary effects which they achieve with Time that Dreams had fascinated me" (3: 912/3: 950). Like the dream, writing can effect the juxtaposition or simultaneity of the most disparate points or moments of space and time.

26. In Genette's system of classifications, the iterative belongs to the category of *fréquence narrative;* it is defined by the formula "*narrating one time* (or rather: *at one time*) *what happened n times*" (*Figures III,* 147/116; Genette's italics).

27. On Proustian humor in the narrow sense, see Maya Slater, *Humour in the Works of Proust* (New York: Oxford University Press, 1979).

28. At times the information introduced into the narrative of the *Recherche* exceeds the bounds of what could have feasibly belonged to the narrator's own experience, a problem that Proust does not always solve gracefully. As Genette observes, "the Proustian novel manages only with much difficulty to reconcile two contradictory courses: . . . that of an omnipresent speculative discourse"—which makes the adoption of the first person a near-necessity—and "that of a comprehensive narrative content that widely overflows the hero's inner experience and at times requires a quasi-'omniscient' narrator (whence the embarrassments and pluralities of focalization we have already met)" (*Figures III,* 258/251).

29. "It is doubtless the same poem continuing. If the themes sometimes blur, they only recur somewhat later, all the more clearly, virtually identical. Yet these repetitions, these tiny variations, halts, regressions, can give rise to modifications—though barely perceptible—eventually moving quite far from the point of departure." Alain Robbe-Grillet, *La Jalousie* (Paris: Minuit, 1957), 101. The English translation is from *Two Novels by Robbe-Grillet,* trans. Richard Howard (New York: Grove Press, 1965), 84.

30. "Proust had only to exploit the genre of the childhood narrative in an intelligent manner," according to Anne Henry, in order to develop the real plot of the *Recherche*—the story of the narrator's misadventures with (and thus his changing relationship to) language. *Proust Romancier: Le tombeau égyptien* (Paris: Flammarion, 1983), 97.

31. In fact, Proust assimilates the realm of Parisian high society to the "realms of Thetis" as early as the *drame du coucher* narrative (1: 18/1: 19).

32. "The real subject is the felicitious use of language [*bonheur du langage*]. The passage becomes a kind of celebration of pure verbal artistry." Joan Rosasco, "Aux sources de la Vivonne," in *Recherche de Proust,* ed. Gérard Genette and Tzvetan Todorov (Paris: Seuil, 1980), 154n. It is worth noting that in the Goncourt passage, the narrator cites his inability to notice such things as a pearl necklace as an example of his lack of powers of observation: "I knew neither how to listen nor, once I was not alone, how to look. My eyes were blind to a pearl necklace an old woman might be wearing, and what people said never entered my ears" (3: 717/3: 737).

33. Roland Barthes in *Prétexte: Roland Barthes* [Actes du Colloque de Cérisy] (Paris: U.G.E., 1978), 259–60.

34. "To desire is to believe in the transcendence of the world suggested by the Other. But let it only open up to the desire that besieges it, and that fine totality proves itself illusory." René Girard, "De l'expérience romanesque au mythe oedipien," *Critique* 222 (November 1965), 899. It seems scarcely necessary to direct the reader to Girard's analysis of mimetic desire in Proust, in *Mensonge romantique et vérité romanesque* (Paris: Grasset, 1961). (English translation: *Deceit, Desire, and the Novel: The Self and Other in Literary Structure* [Baltimore: Johns Hopkins University Press, 1965].)

35. If the humor of *A la recherche du temps perdu* is a *humour juif* in the Deleuzean sense, it is so as well in the most vulgar sense of "I don't get no respect."

36. "For I had already realised long ago that it is not the man with the liveliest mind, the most well-informed, the best supplied with friends and acquaintances, but the one who knows how to become a mirror and in this way can reflect his life, commonplace though it may be, who becomes a Bergotte . . . and could one not say as much, and with better reason, of a painter's models?" (3: 722/3: 742).

Chapter Six Barthes: Ecrire le Corps

1. See the fragment devoted to "L'arrogance" (characteristic of "all triumphant discourse"), in which Barthes singles out three particularly offensive arrogances: "that of Science, that of the *Doxa*, that of the Militant" (*RB*, 51/47).

2. "His relation to psychoanalysis is not scrupulous (though without his being able to pride himself on any contestation, any rejection). It is an *undecided* relation" (*RB*, 153/150).

3. Jacques Derrida, *L'Ecriture et la différence*, 133. (See Chapter Four, n. 42, above.)

4. Quoted in Paul Robert, *Dictionnaire alphabétique et analogique de la langue française*.

5. Quoted in Emile Littré, *Dictionnaire de la langue française*.

6. Roland Barthes, *Le Degré zéro de l'écriture, suivi de Nouveaux essais critiques* (Paris: Seuil, 1972), 12. The English is quoted from *Writing Degree Zero*, trans. Annette Lavers and Colin Smith (New York: Hill and Wang, 1968), 10–11.

7. Roland Barthes, *Sade, Fourier, Loyola* (Paris: Seuil, 1971), 162/159. The English is quoted from *Sade, Fourier, Loyola*, trans. Richard Miller (New York: Hill and Wang, 1976).

8. See Tzvetan Todorov, "Le dernier Barthes," *Poétique* 47 (1981), 323–27.

9. Steven Ungar, "RB: The Third Degree," *Diacritics* 7, no. 1 (1977), 68.

10. Barthes himself executes an exercise in dissection in the "Phases" fragment, commenting that "the articulation of a period, of a work, into phases of evolution—though this be a matter of an imaginary operation—permits enter-

ing the interaction of intellectual communication: one makes oneself *intelligible*" (*RB*, 148/145).

11. Roland Barthes, "Barthes puissance trois," *La Quinzaine littéraire* 205 (March 1975), 5. It should be understood that in French, *consistant* retains a meaning its cognate has lost in English, i.e., *hard, solid.*

12. On irony and humor in Deleuze's *Présentation de Sacher-Masoch*, see Chapter Two, above.

13. On the classic "divided subject," see the fragment "La personne divisée?":

> Pour la métaphysique classique, il n'y avait aucun inconvénient à "diviser" la personne . . . ; bien au contraire, pourvue de deux termes opposés, la personne marchait comme un bon paradigme (*haut/bas, chair/esprit, ciel/terre*): les parties en lutte se réconciliaient dans la fondation d'un sens: le sens de l'Homme. C'est pourquoi, lorsque nous parlons aujourd'hui d'un sujet divisé, ce n'est nullement pour reconnaître ses contradictions simples, ses doubles postulations, etc: c'est une *diffraction* qui est visée, un éparpillement dans le jeté duquel il ne reste plus ni noyau principal ni structure de sens: je ne suis pas contradictoire, je suis dispersé. (*RB*, 146/143)

> For classial metaphysics, there was no disadvantage in "dividing" the person . . . ; quite the contrary, decked out in two opposing terms, the person advanced like a good paradigm (*high/low, flesh/spirit, heaven/earth*); the parties to the conflict were reconciled in the establishment of a meaning: the meaning of Man. This is why, when we speak today of a divided subject, it is never to acknowledge his simple contradictions, his double postulations, etc.; it is a *diffraction* which is intended, a dispersion of energy in which there remains neither a central core nor a structure of meaning: I am not contradictory, I am dispersed.

14. See also *RB*, 93/90: "The stereotype is that emplacement of discourse *where the body is missing.*"

15. Hence R.B.'s distaste for adjectives (see "L'adjectif," *RB*, 47/43), and consequently, for description: "*description* strives to render what is strictly mortal in the object by feigning (illusion by reversal) to suppose it, to desire it living: 'as if alive' [*faire vivant*] means 'apparently dead' [*voir mort*]. The adjective is the instrument of this illusion; whatever it says, by its descriptive quality alone, the adjective is funereal" (*RB*, 72/68).

16. The fragment "La coïncidence," quoted in part at the beginning of this chapter, concludes thus: "Freewheeling in language, I have nothing to compare myself to; and in this movement, the pronoun of the imaginary, 'I,' is *impertinent;* the symbolic becomes literally *immediate:* essential danger for the life of the subject: to write on oneself may seem a pretentious idea; but it is also a simple idea: simple as the idea of suicide" (*RB*, 61/56).

17. In another fragment, Barthes speaks of the intellectual's exclusion, due to "a petit-bourgeois view which construes the intellectual, *on account of his language,* as a desexualized, i.e., devirilized, being" (*RB*, 107/103). All these allusions to castration recall Barthes's commentaries on the exclusion of Zambinella in *S/Z* (168/162, for example).

Not coincidentally, Gerald Graff, in *Literature against Itself* (Chicago: University of Chicago Press, 1979), charges that vanguard critics (Derrida, Barthes, etc.) "emasculate the language of morality and politics" (87). It is not too surprising, either, to see an age-old economic metaphor crop up in his attack, as he claims that the application of "strict canons of objectivity and evidence in academic publishing today would be comparable to the American economy's returning to the gold standard: the effect would be the immediate collapse of the system" (97). Gold = phallus.

Because the Father/Law (i.e., the phallus) is associated with the unidirectional logic of the univalent *oeuvre* and the (idealist) monism that underlies them, the call for an *écriture féminine* is often formulated in terms of a return to the (female, nonphallic) body. Hence the echo of Barthes's *écrire le corps* in the title of a recent essay by Ann Rosalind Jones on French feminist critics: "Writing the Body: Toward an Understanding of *l'Ecriture féminine*," in *The New Feminist Criticism,* ed. Elaine Showalter (New York: Pantheon Books, 1985), 361–77.

18. Barthes attributes his lack of aptitude for foreign languages to "his love for the mother tongue (the language of women)" (*RB,* 119/115). On the incestuous connotations of playing with language, I can only re-cite Addison's characterization of a punster as one "who would violate the sanctities of his mother tongue" (see Chapter Two, above).

19. It should be noted that the Law—*Doxa,* Medusa—is always feminine in *Roland Barthes,* and it is always a convention parading as an absolute. Not coincidentally, structuralism's primary transgression against the old order consisted of unmasking the natural to reveal the conventional behind it.

20. It will be recalled that, according to Kierkegaard, the Greek state was undermined by "the arbitrary freedom of finite subjectivity," incarnated primarily in the Sophists. Sophistry, he wrote, "is the troll which haunts the landscape of reflection, and its name is legion" (*CI,* 224–25).

It is not merely fortuitous that in his 1971 manifesto of textuality, "De l'oeuvre au texte," Barthes alluded to the same biblical parable in describing the text's subversion of monist philosophy, for which "plural is Evil": "Against the work, therefore, the text could well take as its motto the words of the man possessed by demons (Mark 5:9): 'My name is legion, for we are many.'" *Revue d'esthétique* 3 (1971), 229. The English translation appears in *Image/Music/Text,* ed. and trans. Stephen Heath (New York: Hill and Wang, 1977), 160.

21. In the fragment "Décomposer/détruire," "*décomposition,*" which presupposes the impossibility of stepping outside (one's language, culture, etc.), is a tactic virtually identical to Derridean deconstruction:

> La *décomposition* s'oppose donc ici à la *destruction:* pour *détruire* la conscience bourgeoise, il faut s'en absenter, et cette extériorité n'est possible que dans une situation révolutionnaire. . . . Pour détruire, en somme, il faut pouvoir *sauter.* Mais sauter où? dans quel langage? Dans quel lieu de la bonne conscience et de la mauvaise foi? Tandis qu'en décomposant, j'accepte d'accompagner cette décomposition, de me décomposer moi-même, au fur et à mesure: je dérape, m'accroche et entraîne. (*RB,* 67–68/63)

> Hence *decomposition* is here contrary to *destruction:* in order to *destroy* bourgeois consciousness we should have to absent ourselves from it, and such exteriority is possible only in a revolutionary situation. . . . In order to destroy, in short, we must be able to *overleap.* But overleap where? into

what language? Into which site of good conscience and bad faith? Whereas by decomposing, I agree to accompany such decomposition, to decompose myself as well, in the process: I skid, catch, and drag.

Irony destroys; humor decomposes.

22. On Barthes's relation to Proust, see his own observation in *Le Plaisir du texte:*

> Je comprends que l'oeuvre de Proust est, du moins pour moi, l'oeuvre de référence, le *mathésis* générale, le *mandala* de toute la cosmogonie littéraire— comme l'étaient les Lettres de Mme de Sévigné pour la grand-mère du narrateur, les romans de chevalerie pour don Quichotte, etc.; cela ne veut pas du tout dire que je sois un 'spécialiste' de Proust: Proust, c'est ce qui me vient, ce n'est pas ce que j'appelle; ce n'est pas une 'autorité'; simplement *un souvenir circulaire.* Et c'est bien cela l'inter-texte: l'impossibilité de vivre hors du texte infini—que ce texte soit Proust, ou le journal quotidien, ou l'écran télévisuel: le livre fait le sens, le sens fait la vie. (*PT,* 59/36)

> I recognize that Proust's work, for myself at least, is *the* reference work, the general *mathesis,* the *mandala* of the entire literary cosmogony—as Mme de Sévigné's letters were for the narrator's grandmother, tales of chivalry for Don Quixote, etc.; this does not mean that I am in any way a Proust "specialist": Proust is what comes to me, not what I summon up; not an "authority," simply a *circular memory.* Which is what the inter-text is: the impossibility of living outside the infinite text—whether this text be Proust or the daily newspaper or the television screen: the book creates the meaning, the meaning creates life.

23. In her book, *Humour in the Works of Proust* (New York: Oxford University Press, 1979), Maya Slater has called attention to this aspect of Proust's metaphors.

24. See *PT,* 20/10:

> . . . le plaisir du strip-tease corporel ou du suspense narratif. . . . un dévoile-ment progressif: toute l'excitation se réfugie dans l'*espoir* de voir le sexe (rêve de collégien) ou de connaître la fin de l'histoire (satisfaction romanesque). . . . plaisir oedipéen (dénuder, savoir, connaître l'origine et la fin), s'il est vrai que tout récit (tout dévoilement de la vérité) est une mise en scène du Père (absent, caché ou hypostasié)—ce qui expliquerait la solidarité des formes narratives, des structures familiales et des interdictions de nudité, toutes ras-semblées, chez nous, dans le mythe de Noé recouvert par ses fils.

> . . . the pleasure of the corporeal striptease or narrative suspense. . . . a gradual unveiling: the entire excitation takes refuge in the *hope* of seeing the sexual organ (schoolboy's dream) or in knowing the end of the story (novel-istic satisfaction). . . . an Oedipal pleasure (to denude, to know, to learn the origin and the end), if it is true that every narrative (every unveiling of the truth) is a staging of the (absent, hidden, or hypostatized) Father—which would explain the solidarity of narrative forms, of family structures, and of prohibitions of nudity, all collected in our culture in the myth of Noah's sons covering his nakedness.

25. "The alphabetical order erases everything, banishes every origin. Perhaps in places, certain fragments seem to follow one another by some affinity; but the important thing is that these little networks not be connected, that they not slide into a single enormous network which would be the structure of the book, its meaning" (*RB*, 151/148).

26. To cite a few examples:

As in prisoner's base [*comme aux barres*], *language upon language*, to infinity, such is the law which governs the logosphere. Whence other images: that of choosing up hand over hand [*la main chaude*] (the third hand returns, it is no longer the first one). (*RB*, 54–55/50)

Fascination . . . grips me (it is intractable, nothing prevails [*rien n'a barre*] over it, it takes you in an endless hand-over-hand race [*jeu de la main chaude*]. (*RB*, 56/51)

In order to thwart Origin, he first acculturates Nature thoroughly: nothing natural anywhere, nothing but the historical; then this culture (convinced as he is, with Benveniste, that all culture is only language) is restored to the infinite movement of various discourses, set up one against the other (and not engendered) as in hand-over-hand choosing [*le jeu de la main chaude*]. (*RB*, 142/139)

Author/Title Index

Subject Index

Allegory, 50–54, 70, 88
Anironic, 46
Arrogance, 168, 223 n. 1
Art: and absence, 152; and desire, 83–84; mediation by, 82–84; mimetic, 148–49, 156, 190; production of reality, 133; Proust's theories of, 132–33, 135, 143; romantic conception of, 132–33. *See also* Writing
Authenticity: and autobiography, 167, 183; in Baudelaire, 122–30; and irony, 29, 52
Author: appearance in text, 136, 184, 191–92; disappearance of, 13, 45, 166; history of concept, 73
Authorial voice: disintegration of, in Baudelaire, 115; in postmodern text, 59; *See also* Intent, authorial
Authority, 73; renunciation of, 64–65
Autobiography: humorous, 10, 13; ironic, 9; rewriting of self, 187; totalizing narrative, 73–77, 167, 178; traditional project, 9, 72–73, 93, 152; versus novel, 10, 88, 95, 135–36, 144, 165, 187, 190–91, 221 n. 21. See also *Autoportrait*
Autoportrait, 74, 79, 93, 212 n. 15

Bad faith, 4, 96, 98, 111, 123, 129, 201 n. 12
"Beautiful soul," 52, 97, 100, 201 n. 12
Bêtise, 58, 67, 133, 180
Blindness: and humor, 55; and self-knowledge, 84, 88, 93, 180; and writing, 53, 88, 181–83
Body: and feminist criticism, 225 n. 17; function in Barthes, 175–78, 183–87, 191–92

Carnavalesque, 186
Castration, 89, 91, 93–94, 167–69, 184–85, 189, 217 n. 38

"Catholic" interpretation of Baudelaire, 111, 216 n. 20
Citation: in Baudelaire, 112–15; and imaginary, 182–83; irony as, 58–61, 207 n. 33, 216 n. 21
Code, irony as, 58–60
Cogito. See Subject
Comique absolu, 54–55, 130, 176, 206 n. 25
Contract: masochistic, 67, 180–81, 185; of prostitution, 180–81, 183
Corps. See Body
Criticism, contemporary: continental, condemned as ironic, 1; humorous, 6–8, 36, 65, 193; Kierkegaard's relevance to, 1, 37
Criticism, ironic, 2, 5–6, 36, 193, 204 n. 13

Dandy, dandyism, 97, 99–100, 112, 181; and art for art's sake, 111; and poetry, 97
Deconstruction, 48, 50, 55–57, 170, 194–96, 225 n. 21
Deconstructive reading of Baudelaire, 116–18, 128–29
Defamiliarization, 133
Desire: and art, 152; in Baudelaire's poetry, 103–11; and narrative, 188
Dialectic: derision of, 186; of irony, 170; nonsynthetic, 170; Platonic, 202 n. 25; Platonic versus Hegelian, 20; Socratic, 22–23, 30; two forms in Plato, 20, 199 n. 2. *See also* Negativity
Dialectical readings of Baudelaire, 112, 115, 116
Dichotomies: in Barthes, 170, 171–72, 174–75, 185; in Stendhal, 9–10. *See also* Dualism; Paradigms
Disjunction, ironic. *See* Self, ironic splitting of
Distance, ironic, 106–9, 145–46
Doubt, 18, 29, 201 n. 15

Irony/Humor

Designed by Chris L. Smith
Composed by A. W. Bennett, Inc., in Garamond Antiqua text and display
Printed by Edward Brothers, Inc., on 50-lb. Glatfelter, B-16 and
bound in Kivar 5 and Holliston's Sturdeflex and stamped in black